Drupal
for Humanists

Coding for Humanists

Laura Mandell and Quinn Dombrowski,
General Editors

Drupal
for Humanists

Quinn Dombrowski

Texas A&M University Press
College Station

This paper meets the requirements of ANSI/NISO Z39.48-1992 (Permanence of Paper).
Binding materials have been chosen for durability.
Manufactured in the United States of America

Library of Congress Cataloging-in-Publication Data

Names: Dombrowski, Quinn, author.
Title: Drupal for humanists / Quinn Dombrowski.
Description: First edition. | College Station: Texas A&M University Press,
    [2016] | Includes index.
Identifiers: LCCN 2016009099 (print) | LCCN 2016010038 (ebook) | ISBN
    9781623494728 (pbk.: alk. paper) | ISBN 9781623494735 (ebook)
Subjects: LCSH: Drupal (Computer file) | Web sites—Authoring programs. |
    Open source software.
Classification: LCC TK5105.8885.D78 .D66 2016 (print) | LCC TK5105.8885.D78
    (ebook) | DDC 006.7/8—dc23
LC record available at http://lccn.loc.gov/2016009099

Dedicated to Kent Hooper.
In memory of Rick Peterson.

Contents

Series Editors' Foreword   xxv

Preface   xxvii

CHAPTER 1: First Things   1

1.1 Overview   1

1.2 Audience and technical approach   2

1.3 Why Drupal?   3

1.4 Drupal's strengths and weaknesses   5

     1.4.1 Flexibility   5

     1.4.2 Developer community and module ecosystem   6

     1.4.3 Modest infrastructure requirements   6

     1.4.4 Strengths and shortcomings of "no-code" Drupal   7

1.5 About the example site   7

1.6 Using the *Drupal for Humanists* site   8

1.7 Summary   8

CHAPTER 2: Introducing Drupal   9

2.1 Overview   9

2.2 The Drupal community   9

2.3 What about Drupal 8?   10

2.4 Understanding Drupal's components: code and database   12

     2.4.1 Drupal core code   13

     2.4.2 Module code   14

     2.4.3 Theme code   14

2.4.4 Database   15

2.4.5 Summary of code and database   16

2.5 Drupal components   16

2.5.1 Content types   16

2.5.2 Nodes   18

2.5.3 Taxonomies   18

2.5.4 File types   19

2.5.5 Views   19

2.5.6 Blocks   20

2.5.7 Menus   21

2.5.8 Users   21

2.6 Overview of site building   22

2.6.1 Deciding on Drupal   22

2.6.2 Basic configuration   23

2.6.3 Data modeling   23

2.6.4 Implementing the data model   23

2.6.5 Improving the display   23

2.6.6 Theming   24

2.6.7 Prelaunch configuration   24

2.7 Summary   24

CHAPTER 3: Installing Drupal   25

3.1 Overview   25

3.2 Options for hosting Drupal   25

3.2.1 On your own computer   26

3.2.2 Your institution   26

3.2.3 Generic shared hosting   27

3.2.4 Cloud hosting   28

3.3 Installing Drupal   28

3.3.1 Choose a profile   28

3.3.2 Choose language   29

3.3.3 Verify requirements   29

3.3.4 Database configuration   29

3.3.5 Install profile   30

3.3.6 Configure site   30

    3.3.6.1 Site information   31

    3.3.6.2 Site maintenance account   32

    3.3.6.3 Server settings   32

    3.3.6.4 Update notifications   33

3.3.7 Your new Drupal site   33

3.4 Summary   34

CHAPTER 4: Modules   35

4.1 Overview   35

4.2 Finding modules   36

4.3 Assessing modules   37

    4.3.1 Modules published on Drupal.org

        vs those published elsewhere   38

    4.3.2 Module versions   39

    4.3.3 Number of users   41

    4.3.4 Maintenance and development status   42

    4.3.5 Release notes   44

4.4 Essential modules   44

    4.4.1 Disabling the core Toolbar module   46

4.5 Installing and enabling modules   46

    4.5.1 Installing modules using the Drupal interface   47

    4.5.2 Installing modules by accessing the file system   49

        4.5.2.1 Why sites/all/modules?   50

        4.5.2.2 Installing modules that use libraries   50

    4.5.3 Enabling modules   51

    4.5.4 Configuring modules   53

4.6 How many modules do you need?   54

4.7 Disabling and uninstalling modules   56

    4.7.1 Disabling   56

    4.7.2 Uninstalling   57

    4.7.3 Removing the code from your site   57

4.8 Summary   58

CHAPTER 5: Content Types and Introduction
to Data Modeling   59

5.1 Overview   59

5.2 Introducing content types   59

5.3 Drupal's default content types: Basic Page and Article   60

5.4 Data modeling for content types   62

    5.4.1 Data vs metadata   62

    5.4.2 Content type vs taxonomy   64

    5.4.3 When to merge similar content types   66

    5.4.4 File types vs content types   67

    5.4.5 User profiles vs content types   68

    5.4.6 Drupal-based considerations for
determining content types   69

    5.4.7 Drupal's "title" field vs real-world titles   70

5.5 Preliminary data modeling for the example site   72

    5.5.1 The data   72

    5.5.2 The goal   73

    5.5.3 Breaking down the data   76

    5.5.4 Enriching the content types   77

        5.5.4.1 Person   77

        5.5.4.2 Event   80

        5.5.4.3 Image   81

5.6 Summary   82

CHAPTER 6: Configuring Content Types and Fields   83

6.1 Overview   83

6.2 Creating new content types   83

    6.2.1 Submission form settings   84

    6.2.2 Publishing options   84

    6.2.3 Display settings   85

    6.2.4 Comment settings   85

    6.2.5 Menu settings   86

6.3 Adding and configuring fields   87

    6.3.1 "Manage fields" interface   87

    6.3.2 Adding fields   89

6.4 Core Drupal fields   90

   6.4.1 Text   90

   6.4.2 Long text   91

   6.4.3 List (text)   91

   6.4.4 Term reference   92

   6.4.5 File and the media browser widget   93

      6.4.5.1 Configuration for uploaded files   93

      6.4.5.2 Configuration for externally hosted files   94

   6.4.6 Image   95

6.5 Fields provided by modules   96

   6.5.1 References   96

   6.5.2 Date   98

   6.5.3 Partial date   101

      6.5.3.1 Partial date formats   101

      6.5.3.2 Base estimate values   102

      6.5.3.3 Minimum components   104

      6.5.3.4 Field configuration   104

   6.5.4 Link   105

   6.5.5 Geofield   106

   6.5.6 Field group   107

6.6 Media   108

   6.6.1 Configuring the file system   108

   6.6.2 Configuring file settings   108

   6.6.3 Configuring media browser settings   109

   6.6.4 Configuring file type profiles   110

6.7 Conditional fields   110

6.8 Configuring Automatic Nodetitles   114

6.9 Improving node URLs with Pathauto   117

6.10 Summary   118

CHAPTER 7: Further Data Modeling and Applied
            Content Type Creation   119

7.1 Overview   119

7.2 Person content type   120

   7.2.1 Content type settings   120

   7.2.2 Fields   120

7.2.2.1 Given name	120
7.2.2.2 Middle name(s)	121
7.2.2.3 Surname	121
7.2.2.4 Biography	121
7.2.2.5 Birth date	121
7.2.2.6 Death date	122
7.2.2.7 Image	122
7.2.2.8 Medical institution attended	123
7.2.2.9 Profession	125
7.2.2.10 Specialization	126
7.2.3 Rearranging fields	129
7.2.4 Automatic node titles	130
7.2.5 Pathauto	130
7.3 Event content type	131
7.3.1 Content type settings	131
7.3.2 Fields	131
7.3.2.1 Person	131
7.3.2.2 Date	131
7.3.2.3 Location	133
7.3.2.4 Description	134
7.3.2.5 Title	134
7.3.2.6 Event type	134
7.3.2.7 Institution	135
7.3.2.8 Main time line	135
7.3.3 Rearranging fields	136
7.3.4 Pathauto	136
7.4 Image	137
7.4.1 Content type settings	137
7.4.2 Fields	137
7.4.2.1 Profession	137
7.4.2.2 Institution	137
7.4.2.3 Person	137
7.4.2.4 Image	138
7.4.2.5 Body	138
7.4.2.6 Source collection	138
7.4.2.7 Source URL	138
7.4.2.8 Title	138

7.4.3 Automatic Nodetitles   139

7.4.4 Pathauto   139

7.5 Summary   140

CHAPTER 8: Configuring Input Forms and Adding Content   141

8.1 Overview   141

8.2 Text formats   141

  8.2.1 Field configuration   141

  8.2.2 Text format configuration   142

  8.2.3 Configuring a text format   143

  8.2.4 Additional filters   144

8.3 WYSIWYG configuration   145

  8.3.1 Installing modules and CKEditor library   146

  8.3.2 Selecting CKEditor in the WYSIWYG module   147

  8.3.3 Configuring CKEditor for the Filtered
         HTML text format   147

  8.3.4 Facilitating internal linking   149

8.4 Adding content   150

  8.4.1 Configuration options   150

  8.4.2 Previewing content   152

8.5 Viewing and editing content   152

8.6 Accessing saved content   153

8.7 Revisions   153

8.8 Summary   154

CHAPTER 9: Node Display   155

9.1 Overview   155

9.2 Configuring node display   155

  9.2.1 Label and field visibility   156

    9.2.1.1 Labels and visibility for
             Person content type   156

    9.2.1.2 Labels and field visibility for
             Event content type   156

    9.2.1.3 Labels and field visibility for
             Image content type   156

  9.2.2 Configuring date fields   157

9.2.2.1 Date fields in the example site 157

9.2.3 Configuring partial date fields 158

9.2.3.1 Partial date field in the example site 159

9.2.4 Configuring geospatial fields 159

9.2.4.1 Geospatial fields in the example site 160

9.2.5 Configuring image fields 160

9.2.5.1 Configuring image styles 161

9.2.5.2 Advanced image style configuration 162

9.2.5.3 Colorbox 162

9.2.5.4 Image fields on the example site 163

9.2.6 Configuring file fields and multimedia 163

9.3 Advanced configuration of node display 165

9.3.1 Display Suite and CCK blocks 165

9.3.2 Blocks created by views 166

9.4 Summary 166

CHAPTER 10: Users and Permissions — 167

10.1 Overview 167

10.2 User configuration settings 167

10.3 Account settings 168

10.3.1 Registration and cancellation 168

10.3.1.1 Account registration 169

10.3.1.2 Account cancellation 169

10.3.2 Personalization (user avatars) 169

10.3.3 System emails 170

10.4 Creating user profiles 170

10.4.1 Real Name 171

10.5 Roles and permissions 172

10.5.1 Content permissions 173

10.5.2 Field permissions 174

10.5.3 Permissions for unpublished nodes 175

10.6 Spam prevention 176

10.6.1 Honeypot 176

10.6.2 CAPTCHA 177

10.7 Summary 178

CHAPTER 11: Blocks and Menus | 179

11.1 Overview | 179

11.2 Blocks | 179

11.2.1 "Demonstrate block regions"
and positioning tricks | 181

11.2.2 Assigning blocks to regions | 181

11.2.3 Block configuration | 181

11.2.4 Region settings | 182

11.2.5 Visibility settings | 182

11.2.6 Custom blocks | 183

11.3 Menus | 183

11.3.1 Default menus | 184

11.3.2 Adding a menu | 184

11.3.3 Adding items to menus | 185

11.3.3.1 Editing a node | 185

11.3.3.2 Add link | 185

11.3.4 Arranging menu items | 186

11.3.5 Displaying menus | 186

11.4 Summary | 187

CHAPTER 12: Views | 188

12.1 Overview | 188

12.2 A very simple view using "Add a new view" | 189

12.2.1 Choosing what to display | 189

12.2.2 Displays | 190

12.2.3 Next steps for new views | 192

12.2.3.1 Sort order | 193

12.2.3.2 Format | 193

12.2.3.3 Editing a view | 193

12.3 Displays | 194

12.3.1 Titles, and overriding and reverting
display settings | 196

12.4 Format | 199

12.4.1 Grouping fields | 200

12.4.2 Show | 202

12.5 Fields | 203

12.5.1 Adding fields   203

12.5.2 Configuring date fields   204

12.5.3 Configuring image fields   205

12.5.4 Rearranging fields   206

12.5.5 Style settings   207

12.5.6 In-line fields and rewriting fields   207

12.5.6.1 Using "Format" to display in-line fields   208

12.5.6.2 Excluding and rewriting fields   209

12.6 Filter criteria   210

12.6.1 And/or options   212

12.7 Sort criteria   212

12.8 Display-specific settings   213

12.8.1 Page settings   214

12.8.1.1 Path   214

12.8.1.2 Menu   214

12.8.1.3 Access   214

12.8.2 Feed settings   214

12.8.3 Block settings   215

12.9 Header and footer   215

12.10 Pager   215

12.11 Caching   216

12.12 Final result   217

12.13 Summary   217

CHAPTER 13: Advanced Views   **219**

13.1 Overview   219

13.2 Troubleshooting Views   219

13.3 Maps   220

13.3.1 Installing modules   220

13.3.2 Basic view creation   221

13.3.3 Adding fields   222

13.3.4 Configuring Leaflet maps   222

13.3.4.1 Troubleshooting Leaflet maps   223

13.3.5 Contextual filters   225

13.3.6 Caching   227

13.3.7 Enabling the block   227

13.4 Site time line   227

    13.4.1 Installing modules   228

    13.4.2 Basic view creation   228

    13.4.3 Adding fields   228

    13.4.4 Adding filters   229

    13.4.5 Configuring the simple time line   229

    13.4.6 Relationships   230

        13.4.6.1 Relationships and duplicate results   232

    13.4.7 Caching   234

13.5 Individual time line   234

    13.5.1 Installing modules   234

    13.5.2 Basic view creation   234

    13.5.3 Adding fields   235

    13.5.4 Configuring TimelineJS   235

    13.5.5 Enabling the block   236

    13.5.6 Contextual filter   236

    13.5.7 Caching   238

13.6 Image gallery with exposed filters   238

    13.6.1 Installing modules   238

    13.6.2 Basic view creation   238

    13.6.3 Adding fields   238

    13.6.4 Exposed filters   239

    13.6.5 Caching   242

13.7 Slide show   242

    13.7.1 Installing modules   242

    13.7.2 Basic view creation   243

    13.7.3 Fields, filters, and sort criteria   243

    13.7.4 Configuring the slide show   244

    13.7.5 Caching   244

13.8 Table with exposed filters   245

    13.8.1 Basic view creation   245

    13.8.2 Adding fields   245

    13.8.3 Configuring the table   246

    13.8.4 Exposed filters   247

    13.8.5 Other configuration   247

    13.8.6 Caching   247

13.9 Other noteworthy Views modules   247

    13.9.1 Editview   248

    13.9.2 Views Conditional   248

    13.9.3 Views Bulk Operations   248

    13.9.4 Views Autocomplete Filters   249

13.10 Summary   249

CHAPTER 14: Importing Data   250

14.1 Overview   250

14.2 Essential modules for data import   250

14.3 Overview of Feeds settings   251

    14.3.1 Basic settings   252

    14.3.2 Fetcher   253

        14.3.2.1 HTTP Fetcher   253

        14.3.2.2 File upload   253

    14.3.3 Parser   253

        14.3.3.1 Common syndication parser   253

        14.3.3.2 CSV parser   254

        14.3.3.3 HTML Xpath parser and XML Xpath parser   254

    14.3.4 Processor   255

        14.3.4.1 Node and taxonomy term processor   255

        14.3.4.2 User processor   256

    14.3.5 Mapping   256

        14.3.5.1 Unique targets   257

        14.3.5.2 Term reference fields   257

        14.3.5.3 Node reference fields   258

        14.3.5.4 Image targets   258

        14.3.5.5 Date targets   259

    14.3.6 Feeds Tamper   259

        14.3.6.1 Adding a plug-in   259

        14.3.6.2 Explode   260

        14.3.6.3 Trim   260

        14.3.6.4 Rewrite   260

        14.3.6.5 Find replace/find replace REGEX   261

        14.3.6.6 HTML entity decode   261

14.3.6.7 Convert case 262

14.3.6.8 Strip tags 262

14.3.6.9 Keyword filter 262

14.3.6.10 Boolean filter 263

14.3.7 Importing data 263

14.3.8 Import page options 263

14.4 Example: Importing People nodes 264

14.4.1 Source data 264

14.4.2 Creating the importer and basic configuration 266

14.4.3 Mapping 267

14.4.4 Feeds tamper 268

14.4.5 Import and cleanup 268

14.5 Example: Importing Event nodes 269

14.5.1 Source data 269

14.5.2 Creating the importer and basic configuration 270

14.5.3 Mapping 270

14.5.4 Feeds tamper 271

14.5.5 Importing 272

14.6 Summary 272

CHAPTER 15: Exporting Data and Settings | 273

15.1 Overview 273

15.2 Exporting data with Views Data Export 274

15.2.1 Configuring a CSV data export display 274

15.2.2 Configuring an XML data export display 276

15.2.3 Output 277

15.3 Exporting configuration using Features 278

15.3.1 Building a feature module 278

15.3.2 Saving a feature module 280

15.3.3 Modules that extend Features 280

15.3.4 Using Features 281

15.4 Other means of exposing data: Services, JSON, RDF 281

15.5 Summary 282

CHAPTER 16: Search   283

16.1 Overview   283

16.2 Search block and search pages   283

16.3 Configuring Drupal's built-in search   284

     16.3.1 Indexing and cron runs   284

     16.3.2 Search modules   285

     16.3.3 Search ranking   285

     16.3.4 Debugging search   285

16.4 Customizing the search result display   286

16.5 Hiding content from the index   286

16.6 Creating a custom advanced search page using Views   286

16.7 Search API   287

16.8 Summary   288

CHAPTER 17: Managing Taxonomies   289

17.1 Overview   289

17.2 Configuring taxonomy term pages   289

     17.2.1 Displaying content and users that both
         use a given term   291

17.3 Tag clouds   292

17.4 Taxonomy manager and term merge   293

17.5 Importing and exporting taxonomies   295

17.6 Summary   296

CHAPTER 18: Themes   297

18.1 Overview   297

18.2 Drupal themes   297

18.3 Approaches to site theming   298

     18.3.1 Using an existing theme   298

         18.3.1.1 Identifying requirements for your theme   298

         18.3.1.2 Researching and testing existing themes   299

     18.3.2 Modifying or configuring an existing theme   300

     18.3.3 Developing a highly customized theme   301

18.4 Installing and enabling themes and subthemes   303

    18.4.1 Installing themes   303

    18.4.2 Enabling themes and administration themes   304

    18.4.3 Configuring global settings   305

    18.4.4 Configuring theme-specific settings   305

18.5 AdaptiveTheme and its subthemes   306

    18.5.1 Layout and general settings   307

    18.5.2 Extensions   307

        18.5.2.1 Custom CSS   308

    18.5.3 Color scheme   309

    18.5.4 Toggle display, logo image, shortcut image   309

    18.5.5 Example site configuration   310

18.6 Summary   311

CHAPTER 19: Finishing and Launching the Example Site   312

19.1 Overview   312

19.2 Front page   312

    19.2.1 Adding a view of news posts   312

    19.2.2 Introducing Panels   313

    19.2.3 Creating a Panel node   314

    19.2.4 Configuring a Panel node   315

    19.2.5 Changing the front page of your site   317

19.3 Review of steps for creating the example site   317

19.4 Writing documentation   320

19.5 Preparing for site launch   322

    19.5.1 Turning off and uninstalling unneeded modules   322

    19.5.2 Updating and testing permissions   322

    19.5.3 Creating 404 pages   323

    19.5.4 Performance tweaks   323

    19.5.5 Error messages   324

    19.5.6 Status report   325

    19.5.7 Link checking   325

    19.5.8 Setting up analytics   326

19.6 Postlaunch monitoring   326

19.7 Summary   327

CHAPTER 20: Running, Maintaining, and
Debugging a Drupal Site   328

20.1 Overview   328

20.2 Maintenance activities   328

20.3 Core, module, and theme updates   330

    20.3.1 Suggested frequency   330

    20.3.2 Method: Drupal UI (modules & themes)   331

    20.3.3 Method: file system (core, and possibly
            modules & themes)   333

        20.3.3.1 Updating modules   333

        20.3.3.2 Updating core   334

    20.3.4 Module and core updates on Drupal
            multisite setups   334

20.4 Database backup   335

    20.4.1 Suggested frequency   335

    20.4.2 Method: quick back up   335

    20.4.3 Method: nightly back ups   336

    20.4.4 Other methods   336

    20.4.5 Restoring your database   336

20.5 File backup   337

    20.5.1 Suggested frequency   337

    20.5.2 Method: Backup and Migrate   337

    20.5.3 Method: SFTP   337

    20.5.4 Other methods   338

20.6 Whole-site backup   338

    20.6.1 Frequency   338

    20.6.2 Method: Backup and Migrate   338

    20.6.3 Other methods   339

20.7 Drush   339

20.8 Major version upgrades   339

20.9 Debugging Drupal   340

    20.9.1 When a module seems to not work correctly   340

        20.9.1.1 Using a -dev version of a module   341

        20.9.1.2 Patching modules   342

        20.9.1.3 Filing a bug report   343

20.9.2 When the site suddenly looks
            strange or behaves oddly   343
20.9.3 Error messages   344
20.9.4 White Screen of Death   344
20.10 Contributing to the Drupal community   345

APPENDIX: Using an SFTP Client   346

Glossary   355
Index   359

Foreword

With the advent of the Internet, the citadel of coding expertise opened its doors, expanding its purview decisively outside of the discipline of computer science. Because so much information comes to us in digital form, everyone, from physicists to psychologists, now needs to perform computational tasks. Unfortunately, how-to books on coding—even those for dummies—typically address people who wish to become coding professionals, not those of us who need no more knowledge of code than is necessary to accomplish specific tasks within our own home disciplines.

Humanists in particular confront a new landscape: our cultural heritage is being digitized on a massive scale—Google Books now contains upwards of 25 million volumes; the Digital Public Library of America, 13 million; Europeana, 54 million items; and HathiTrust, 15 million, 5 million of which are in the public domain. JSTOR and ProjectMuse have digitized over 2,500 journals, many of them from their inception up through current issues, and they have begun digitizing books. University presses are digitizing their out-of-print books. The Internet Archive / Open Library contains over 10 million texts, along with 502 billion archived websites. And the Gutenberg Project and the Text Creation Partnership together have made available 100,000 hand-typed texts.

When humanities scholars sit down at their desks to do their research, the tasks they must perform no longer resemble those in which they were trained. This series is designed so that you do not have to confront those tasks alone.

Each book in the series addresses humanities scholars, presuming no computer science expertise of any sort. The typical book on Python, XSLT, or XQuery—languages that are particularly good at manipulating texts—will often explain a bit of code by referring to other programming languages, offering non-experts no insight whatsoever. The books in this series never do so, offering full explanations to the non-expert, resorting to metaphors rather than math. Moreover, the accompanying websites for each volume, available at http://coding.forhumanists.org, offer supplementary materials such as basic installation instructions, regularly updated, as well as examples to follow and reusable code snippets that can be adapted to your own needs, the books themselves explaining how. Authors can be contacted through the website to provide clarification and make corrections.

The books in this series are designed to get you up-and-running in accomplishing specific tasks, not to turn you into a full-time coding professional. They are designed to give you the information you need to do *humanities* research and publication in the digital environment: creating sophisticated websites and databases, interrogating massive amounts of textual data, creating and understanding visualizations, and building archival-quality digital editions, to name a few of the volumes currently planned. But, in addition to imparting the skills you need to perform these tasks effectively, they also provide a solid understanding of coding languages and thus offer the foundation you need to acquire greater expertise should you wish to do so.

Our goal in publishing these books is to meet you where you are, take your hand, and walk with you into the digital forest so that you can find what you need.

Laura Mandell
Quinn Dombrowski
General Editors

Preface

The collection, organization, and thoughtful presentation of curated research materials is an area where the adoption of new tools and practices can have a transformative impact on humanities scholarship. Rather than gathering data—whatever form "data" may take in a given discipline—in a word processing document that is little more than a direct digital surrogate for paper, scholars are increasingly exploring how digital approaches to collecting and presenting information can offer new ways to draw connections within and between their research materials, to elucidate impressions and interpretations, and to provide opportunities for other scholars to respond and engage with the material in ways that were not previously possible.

The digital humanities projects that become well known outside their own discipline are typically those supported by large grants; however, the potential for digital tools and methodologies to have a transformative impact on individual research agendas and smaller fields of study is far greater than the grant funding available to support expansive and expensive technical undertakings. Luckily, within the last decade, digital humanities project development has begun to shift away from custom, boutique programming for each project towards developing and adopting ecosystems of reusable and extensible tools and platforms.

Today, researchers who wish to use digital methodologies for organizing and presenting their research data and the associated scholarly arguments can, in many cases, do so without hiring a programmer or first learning to write code, by instead learning to use an open source platform such as Drupal. Although all flexible, robust tools involve a learning curve, learning to use Drupal to create digital humanities projects poses a significantly lower barrier than learning a programming language or building a database from scratch. The skills one develops in data modeling and project implementation using Drupal can also pay off in other contexts. A remarkable amount of digital humanities infrastructure continues to be built using Drupal, including tool and project directories, collaborative research and pedagogical environments, journals and peer review systems, and sophisticated web presences for centers, labs, and organizations. For students and others who are considering "alt-ac" or non-academic employment, Drupal site building skills can also open employment options both within and outside the academy.

This book draws on more than a decade of experience supporting the development of digital humanities projects, mostly with little or no funding, and many from disciplines other than English literature or history. While learning Drupal requires an investment of time and energy, it is not beyond the reasonable reach of even those students, staff, and faculty in the humanities who see themselves as "non-technical." This book aims to empower that audience in particular, namely scholars who are willing to follow along, step by step, and learn by working through an example project from start to finish. Technical jargon is minimized, and is thoroughly explained where its inclusion is unavoidable. While those with previous experience working with digital tools will be able to work through the book more quickly, such experience is by no means a prerequisite.

I would like to thank Ray Siemens for the invitation to teach Drupal at the Digital Humanities Summer Institute (DHSI) at the University of Victoria in 2014, which spurred the development of the course pack that directly evolved into this book, although its earliest origins date to 2012. For the availability of this book as a structured, organized, and complete publication rather than as a rambling set of half-written, web-based tutorials, I have Laura Mandell of Texas A&M University to thank, as well as Jay Dew, my editor at Texas A&M University Press who worked miracles with timely peer review. Rafael Alvarado and SHANTI (the Sciences, Humanities & Arts Network of Technological Initiatives) at the University of Virginia have generously allowed me to use one of their projects as the inspiration for the example site described in the book. I would also like to thank all my students at DHSI 2014 and 2015, the Digital Humanities at Berkeley Summer Institute 2015, and workshops at UC Berkeley's D-Lab, as well as the over 120 scholars and research staff who "beta tested" drafts of the book. Finally, I would like to thank my husband, Andy, for his unwavering support and flexibility, as well as Sam, for his sound sleep while I wrote this book, and Paul, for his excellent timing.

Drupal
for Humanists

First Things

1.1 Overview

The collection, organization, and presentation of curated research collections form a frequently used approach to digital humanities project development, particularly for scholars new to digital tools and methodologies. These kinds of projects hold great promise for opening up new areas of inquiry, but particularly in smaller disciplines, they may be impeded by a lack of funding for the development and/or ongoing maintenance of the necessary technical infrastructure.

Drupal, a free, open-source software package that scholars themselves can use to develop sophisticated environments for gathering, annotating, arranging, and presenting their research and supporting materials, can put certain digital humanities methodologies in the hands of scholars who might not otherwise be able to use them, due to lack of project funding. For funded projects, Drupal can enable those funds to be used for the development of new tools or further data entry, rather than basic technical infrastructure. The cost of developing a scholarly project using Drupal is significantly lower than building the same project from scratch. Instead of dedicating funding to a team of programmers who will have to spend some of their time implementing generic things like user logins and integration with geospatial services, in addition to the project-specific work, Drupal provides you with the equivalent of hundreds of thousands of hours of "cost share" through the work of the international Drupal developer community. The work necessary to customize Drupal to your specific project can be undertaken by individual scholars at any level, even with very little prior technical experience.

This book walks through the steps involved in setting up a Drupal site, using a single example site throughout. If you want to develop experience with Drupal before starting on your own project, you can follow the instructions closely to create your own copy of the example site from start to finish. If you want to immediately begin with your own project, you can read through the general description and example site instructions, and undertake a similar but modified process to create your project site.

In practice, creating a Drupal site is not a linear process; you will likely go back and forth between module installation, content type creation, importing or adding content, and creating displays for that content using Views. The ordering of the chapters provides a reasonable linear path through the site creation process, but the "Summary" section of each chapter includes pointers to other ways to traverse the content.

1.2 Audience and technical approach

This book is written for scholars at any level, from advanced undergraduate through professor emeritus, as well as librarians, museum professionals, and other individuals involved with humanistic research or public engagement. It assumes no technical experience beyond general computer and Internet literacy, though some experience using (i.e., adding content to) other content management systems like WordPress or Omeka may be helpful.

The book also takes a "no-code" approach to Drupal. All the functionality that you will use in creating your Drupal-based site has already been written by a large international community of open-source developers who build and maintain Drupal core and *modules*, bundles of code that allow your site to do additional things. Using Drupal, you can combine and configure existing modules in order to build robust websites that can include functionality like mapping, time lines, image galleries and slide shows, custom tables, as well as searching, browsing, and sorting data.

The no-code approach not only makes complex web development accessible to a wider range of users who have expertise in a content area but lack programming skills, it also can benefit your project from a sustainability perspective. Custom code is expensive to build and even more expensive to maintain—a factor worth considering for projects that don't have an ongoing funding stream after an initial grant. Using Drupal without custom code, passionate scholars, librarians, or museum professionals can make a collection accessible in a compelling, highly customized way; build and publish a directory of resources; or create a community hub around concepts or content without first seeking grant funding. Because the developers of modules published on Drupal.org also maintain those modules, site builders can apply these regular updates to ensure their site remains secure.

　　While you don't need custom code to build a Drupal site, there are opportunities to extend your site if you know CSS, JavaScript, and/or PHP. Because of the no-code emphasis of the book itself, pointers for how to make use of those languages are available on the *Drupal for Humanists* website, http://drupal.forhumanists.org.

1.3　Why Drupal?

Drupal has a steeper learning curve than any of the other content management systems that are commonly used for digital humanities projects. This is due to the extremely high level of customization that it provides, allowing users full control over the kinds of data and metadata that the project site stores, the relationships between those kinds of content, and the ways the content is displayed. Most content management systems provide some kind of functionality out of the box that allows users to immediately start adding content. In contrast, a clean installation of Drupal without any additional modules is like a much less functional and less user-friendly version of WordPress. This is by design; because Drupal supports a tremendous range of very different sites—including weather.com, mint.com, and fema.com, in addition to e-commerce sites, many university websites, and digital humanities projects—its core, which all sites share, should only contain modules that most or all sites are likely to use. Your choice of modules and how you configure them will transform Drupal from a very generic platform into an environment that is highly customized to your particular data and goals—but without the cost or sustainability risks of custom programming.

Drupal is not the right technical solution for every project. Other content management systems make it very easy to execute common types of projects without the extensive configuration work that would be necessary to recreate the same functionality in Drupal. The *Drupal for Humanists* website includes more information about commonly used content management systems and approaches, and how they relate to Drupal.

For building simple websites for publishing general information, updates, and outcomes from your project, WordPress[1] is a better choice. There are also WordPress plug-ins developed for scholars that support robust text annotation[2] and development of scholarly networks and communities of practice.[3] WordPress also has the benefit of having a large, international developer community that reaches beyond the academy. Omeka[4] makes it easy to publish standard metadata about objects, and present those objects in curated "exhibits." The Neatline plug-in[5] provides support for maps and related time lines.

For projects that are considering using FileMaker Pro or creating a custom database from scratch, Drupal is often a better option. FileMaker Pro requires an expensive license, and while it is possible to produce a web-based display of a FileMaker Pro database, it is not very attractive or customizable. The situation is similar with other database software like Microsoft Access. Creating a custom MySQL database requires a higher degree of technical skill than using Drupal, and it puts the project in the position of having to write custom code to produce a web-based display, which requires technical expertise and puts the project in a more precarious state from a sustainability perspective.

The relationship between Drupal and TEI (Text Encoding Initiative) markup[6] is more complex. If the project's goal is to annotate the structure and/or content of a text while treating it as a text, a traditional TEI workflow is usually a better choice. For a simple web presentation, there

---

1. https://wordpress.org/
2. http://futureofthebook.org/commentpress/
3. http://commonsinabox.org/
4. http://omeka.org/
5. http://neatline.org/
6. http://www.tei-c.org/

are ways to ingest TEI into Drupal. In situations where text is being treated more like data (e.g., encoding historical financial records), Drupal may provide a much more efficient workflow, and may also make it easier to present the data in interesting and insightful ways. See the *Drupal for Humanists* website for more about the intersection of Drupal and TEI.

1.4 Drupal's strengths and weaknesses

1.4.1 Flexibility

Drupal's greatest strength lies in its flexibility. Because Drupal allows users to create their own content types as well as how their content is displayed, it's possible to create a wide range of vastly different kinds of projects, or work with very diverse data, all using the same basic Drupal skill set and modules.

This flexibility also comes with downsides. Even a simple Drupal site requires more configuration work than the equivalent WordPress site; for that reason, if it's a project that doesn't require Drupal's flexibility, it's often better to build it in WordPress instead.

For users who are new to Drupal and don't know what they're doing, it's possible to create a site that's an unusable mess[7] in ways that simply aren't possible with other content management systems. Following the steps laid out in this book should prevent most or all of these mistakes, but some things—such as mastering the art of crafting good content types and complex displays—only come with hands-on experience and practice.

Finally, Drupal's flexibility can also give users the "freedom" to avoid standards and misdirect their time and resources to creating ad hoc systems when existing vocabularies, metadata profiles, and other approaches would have been perfectly effective, and would have improved the project's sustainability and interoperability. For that reason, it is important to research and assess the suitability of existing standards relevant to your project before embarking on defining your content types.

---

7. See the *Drupal for Humanists* site for examples of Drupal configuration gone horribly astray.

1.4.2   Developer community and module ecosystem

Drupal has one of the largest open-source developer communities, when counting the number of individuals who have committed code to the project, as part of Drupal core, or modules and themes. The large number of developers has led to the creation of multiple modules that are relevant for scholarly projects, including an extensive bibliography module;[8] additional sustainability benefits of using such widely-supported, open-source software are discussed in section 2.2. While WordPress and Omeka have tended to be the platforms chosen for developing modules specific to digital humanities use cases, the increasing adoption of Drupal has already breathed new life into modules that are important for scholarly projects, but where development had stalled, such as the Partial Date[9] module. See the *Drupal for Humanists* site for further examples.

1.4.3   Modest infrastructure requirements

While there is no free or super-low-cost hosted Drupal service similar to what Omeka.net offers for Omeka, Drupal has modest infrastructure requirements and can easily be hosted on inexpensive shared hosting services, or on a server or virtual machine that you already run for other purposes. Using a Drupal multisite setup (see the *Drupal for Humanists* site for instructions) allows you to run multiple Drupal sites using the same code base, which reduces the amount of work required to keep the sites updated.

The infrastructure requirements for Drupal become more onerous if you have a very large collection of materials. If you anticipate that your site will have upwards of 50,000 pieces of content, your database may grow large enough that inexpensive shared hosting providers will require you to upgrade to a higher-tier plan. Very large sites, and sites that expect very heavy traffic, will benefit from some of the modules and technical approaches that address Drupal scalability needs, but many of those are not possible if the site is hosted on inexpensive shared hosting.

---

8. https://www.drupal.org/project/biblio
9. https://www.drupal.org/project/partial_date

1.4.4 Strengths and shortcomings of "no-code" Drupal

Building a Drupal site that uses no custom code can significantly reduce the extent to which you need to worry about maintaining the code base of your site. Unless a module has been abandoned, its developer (or their successor) will periodically issue module updates, which you can simply install on the site (see section 20.3). Sometimes one module update can cause a conflict with another module, but in many cases, these problems will be posted to the issue queue for one of the modules (see section 20.9.1), and other users will offer workarounds or patches to the code that resolve the issues. In contrast, any custom code that you develop for your project has to be maintained by your project, unless you release it for other projects to use, and those projects are willing to help with the maintenance if something breaks due to another module's update.

As described in section 1.3.9, no-code Drupal can generally get you to 80 to 90 percent of your ideal vision for the project, but you will likely have to make some small compromises in functionality, user interface, etc. if you don't want to or can't pay for theming or custom module development to close that gap.

1.5 About the example site

The example site that this book uses is inspired by CHAAMP (Consortium on the History of African Americans in the Medical Professions) Resources[10] built by SHANTI[11] at the University of Virginia, and used with their generous permission. It is significantly simplified from the real CHAAMP site, but it shares its topic (the history of African Americans in the medical professions) and many of the same types of content (profiles of individuals, events in their lives, and images related to the overall theme of the site). While the example site does not include some of the pedagogy-oriented capabilities of the real CHAAMP site, such as a content type for posting student essays and projects, the *Drupal for Humanists* site has additional tutorials for how to add that kind of functionality.

---

10. http://chaamp.virginia.edu/
11. http://shanti.virginia.edu/

1.6 Using the *Drupal for Humanists* site

In the section specifically about this book, the *Drupal for Humanists* site (http://drupal.forhumanists.org) has a page for every chapter. This page will include the table of contents for the chapter, along with links to further information, tutorials, and related content referenced in that chapter. In addition to the resources referenced in the book, the website includes a list of recommended modules, case studies of individual sites that use Drupal, and a mailing list you can join to ask questions about using Drupal for humanistic projects.

1.7 Summary

This chapter has highlighted the strengths and weaknesses of Drupal as a content management system, and briefly compared it to other open-source systems and approaches. It has also introduced the example site, as well as the *Drupal for Humanists* website, which can serve as a supplementary resource. Chapter 2 will describe Drupal from a technical perspective, and will provide an overview of the process of building a site with Drupal.

CHAPTER 2

Introducing Drupal

2.1 Overview

This chapter introduces Drupal as a manifestation of an open-source community, and as a software package. It explains the technical components that make up Drupal and how they relate to one another. Lastly, it describes the process of building a site using Drupal using an extended analogy.

2.2 The Drupal community

Drupal is open-source software, supported by one of the largest communities of developers. Over 25,000 people have contributed code to Drupal. These developers include hobbyists who develop or contribute to modules for fun, people who work at companies that build Drupal websites professionally, and people who work for organizations that use Drupal (including universities, businesses, and the governmental and non-profit sectors). While you may think that only the code contributed by people affiliated with a university is likely to be relevant for your project, digital scholarly projects have much more in common with product catalogs and directories of government offices than it may initially seem. All these sites need a way to create user accounts and assign different levels of permissions to different users. They all need to inhibit spammers, display information in menus, and provide intuitive interfaces for data entry and data display. Mapping can be an important feature on a website, whether it's the shipping origin of a package, the reported location of a pothole, or the source of an archaeological artifact.

A vast amount of time has been spent on developing and refining Drupal's code, and the maintenance, support, and development of new and old modules and themes is ongoing. The result of all this work is available to anyone to freely use and modify. All of the modules and themes distributed on the Drupal website are free to download; only a tiny handful of niche modules distributed through other channels require payment. While there is a vibrant marketplace for paid themes (site designs), there are many options available at no cost.

In one sense, it is as if projects that use Drupal have a development staff of thousands of people, even if the project itself includes no programmers. In another sense, because there are no developers dedicated specifically to your project beyond ones you hire yourself, if you encounter obscure bugs or issues with a module (or, worse, a particular combination of modules), they may linger unresolved for a long period of time. Module developers have different levels of personal commitment to maintaining the modules they create. Some modules are widely used by people who have the skills to create "patches" that can fix problems that arise, and these users sometimes offer those solutions to others who are encountering the same problem, even before the module maintainer has addressed it. Choosing widely used modules (see section 4.3) reduces the risk of encountering problems that remain unaddressed indefinitely. Sometimes, though, you may need to hire a developer to fix a bug, or write a module to provide specific functionality for your site. While this may cost a few thousand dollars, by making the fix or the module available to the rest of the community you can give back to the Drupal ecosystem and perhaps save another project some time and money in the future. This approach stands in contrast to the custom development of a project or database from scratch, where little or none of that work is reusable by others.

2.3 What about Drupal 8?

This book covers the steps necessary to build a site using Drupal 7. This choice may seem odd, since Drupal 8 is available. The Drupal philosophy is to provide backward compatibility for data (to make it possible to migrate your site to a new version), but not code,[1] which means that every module has to be rewritten between versions to reflect significant changes to the underlying architecture of Drupal. Because of this, there has historically been a lag time of about a year between when a new major version of Drupal is released and when there's sufficient module support for the new version to truly be usable for new projects.

The architectural changes in Drupal 8 are at a much larger scale than changes between previous versions. Drupal has historically had its own, atypical requirements for how certain programming tasks are implemented. In an effort to attract professional PHP programmers, it was decided that Drupal 8 would adopt conventions and frameworks that are widely used in the broader PHP development community. These conventions are very different from the "Drupal way" of doing things, and some Drupal developers feel like these changes make Drupal less accessible, particularly for small organizations and projects. A group of these developers have started a Drupal 7 "fork" (a new content management system split off from Drupal, but based on the Drupal 7 core and module code at the point of the split) called Backdrop.[2]

As an analogy, imagine a small, vibrant community of philosophers in seventeenth-century Barcelona, where participants only write treatises in Catalan. The use of Catalan within this community is treated as such a given that participants may have never learned Latin, even though Latin is the language of scholarship elsewhere in Europe. In order to increase the influence of this school of philosophy and contribute to conversations happening elsewhere in Europe, a number of influential figures within this group decide that all treatises must henceforth be written in Latin. Other members of the community are disgruntled at the fact that their treatises in progress must be rewritten in Latin. They feel that learning Latin would take too much time and would distract them from their actual work. They see Latin's case system as too difficult to learn fluently, and the philosophers are concerned they won't be able to express themselves with the same nimbleness as they could before. The philosophers with the

1. https://www.drupal.org/node/65922
2. https://groups.drupal.org/node/325403

greatest concerns break away from the original community and continue to develop the same philosophical ideas they worked with before, while maintaining the use of Catalan (perhaps with the adoption of a few more Latinisms as a gesture towards the larger community).

It remains to be seen how many people will adopt Backdrop, and whether the concerns that fueled the origins of the project will in fact be realized once Drupal 8 has been released for some time, and module development does (or does not) flourish for the new version. The fact remains that there are many scholarly sites built on Drupal 7 and Drupal 6, and they all will face migration decisions: to Drupal 8, to Backdrop, or to something else. Drupal 7 will be supported until Drupal 9 is released. This will likely be a few years off; Drupal 8 took more than four years from the time development started until it was released. By building a site in Drupal 7, you can take advantage of the benefits Drupal provides now, while leaving your options open for future migration, depending on how things evolve within the community.

2.4 Understanding Drupal's components: code and database

On a technical level, a Drupal site consists of code, mostly written in the language PHP, with some written in JavaScript, and some CSS (Cascading Stylesheets) to make it look attractive. The code "talks to" a database— usually MySQL—that stores Drupal- and module-specific configuration information, as well as the content you enter into the site (names and birth dates of people, project profiles, transcriptions of documents, etc.).

If you have previous experience with SQL and databases, you may be taken aback if you look directly at Drupal's database. It is not configured in a straightforward, intuitive manner; no one creating a database from scratch would create something that remotely resembles a Drupal database. While this can be frustrating for developers who are trying to build new modules and understand how Drupal stores information, "site builders" who are creating sites by combining and configuring different modules never have to access the database directly. Drupal's code knows how to interact with the database, and it's strongly recommended that you only make changes to the database using Drupal's code (or, for developers, Drupal's APIs) as

a translator and intermediary. Making changes to the database directly
(for instance, by sending SQL commands to the database and/or using an
interface to the database itself like phpMyAdmin) is dangerous, and often
has unpredictable side effects, like data disappearing or getting corrupted.

Most of the work of building a Drupal site involves using the
administrative interface (which is largely determined by the code) to
customize settings for the site and add content, which makes changes to
the database. While Drupal's code can easily remain unseen by the person
creating the site, it is important to have a general understanding of the
different sources of your site's code, so you can make better guesses about
where in the site configuration to go to make different kinds of changes,
and effectively troubleshoot when things go wrong.

At the same time, keep in mind that the code that makes up your
site is *not* what makes the site unique. If all the code for your site were
accidentally deleted, as long as you know what versions of which modules
your site uses, you could regenerate your site exactly as it was within a
couple hours by redownloading Drupal core and modules. If your database
and/or "files" directory vanished, you would be in dire straits without a
backup (see sections 20.4 and 20.5).

2.4.1 Drupal core code

The most basic Drupal site consists of the core Drupal code, plus a
database. The Drupal core is the software available at `http://drupal`
`.org/project/drupal`, and includes all the essential infrastructure
and plumbing for a basic site (menus, user account management, file
uploading capabilities, in addition to the Drupal administrative interface
itself), as well as an extremely limited number of modules that provide
specific site functionality. Modules that are part of Drupal 7 core include
those that enable content types, taxonomies for tagging and classifying
content, comments, a basic discussion forum, and contact forms.

Because Drupal-powered sites can have such diverse needs, but all are
required to use Drupal core, the Drupal development team has deliberately
kept the number of core modules to a minimum. Users are expected to
identify, download, and install the additional modules that meet the needs
of their individual project.

2.4.2   Module code

Modules are code packages that provide some new piece of site functionality. This can range from tweaking the label of some field on the administrative interface to completely overhauling the way content access permissions are handled, to providing a word cloud visualization of tags on your site. There are over 10,000 modules available for Drupal 7, ranging from those that meet nearly ubiquitous needs (like Views, which can display your content in a variety of useful ways, installed on over 800,000 sites), to those that solve specific problems (like Shibboleth User Provisioning, which adds features to a module that enable integration with some university authentication systems, and is used on less than 1,000 sites).

With so many modules, how do you know what to use? Chapter 4 provides recommendations of modules that you should install immediately on almost any site, and subsequent chapters provide recommendations for modules that are useful for different kinds of scholarly projects. In addition, there is a Drupal developer adage that—whatever your site is lacking, or whatever frustration you're encountering—"there's a module for that." While this not always true, particularly when you encounter difficulties related to a discipline-specific problem (such as grappling with different transliteration conventions for ancient alphabets), searching for keywords related to your need or issue, plus "Drupal module" will often surface helpful additions to your site's module list.

2.4.3   Theme code

The design of your site is largely determined by the site theme. Like modules, themes are packages of code that you add to your site to achieve a certain effect (in this case, to give your site a particular look). Unlike with modules, it's okay to modify the theme code that you've downloaded. Theme code consists of PHP files that specify "regions" (i.e., things like how many columns your site can have, whether you can put text in a footer area, etc.). While all themes include one or more CSS files that determine the site's visuals (like color, fonts, and text spacing), some themes provide configuration options you can access through the Drupal interface that allow you to change the site's colors without having to write any CSS yourself.

While it may seem natural to begin the development of a site by
focusing on what the end result will look like, in the big picture, a site's
theme is much less important to a site than its data model, as expressed
through its content types (discussed in chapters 5–7), the data entered
into the site (chapter 8), or the configuration of content display (chapter
9; see also chapters 12 and 13 on the Views module). The theme can be
replaced fairly easily to give a site an updated look, without fundamentally
rebuilding the site. In that way, themes are something like paint on a
sculpture: they serve to enhance the visual appeal of the site, but it doesn't
make sense to start with applying paint before you have sculpted the form
you have in mind. For that reason themes, and how to choose one that is a
good fit for your site, are discussed in chapter 18.

2.4.4   Database

The core Drupal code and the code for the modules you have installed
define what is possible to do on your site. The site's database stores the
information about how you've specifically chosen to configure the site,
based on the possibilities and constraints provided by the code. For
example, the Pathauto module gives you the ability to define the path
(URL) that will be used for your content. When you go into the settings
for Pathauto and specify that you want your blog posts to appear at
`yoursite.org/blog/[year]/[month]/[date]/[title]`, that
information is saved into the database.

In addition to storing information about the site configuration,
the database stores your site content. This lack of separation between
content and configuration can be problematic. For example, if you have
a development version of your site and a live version, and you've made
configuration changes on the development site that you want to move to
the live site, you can't just import the development site's database if there
have been any content changes to the live site (new pages, new comments
on blog posts, new users, etc.) since the last time the two were synced.
Section 15.3 addresses how to move configuration changes between
different versions of a site, or between different sites.

If you have only used HTML to develop websites, switching to a
database-powered content management system like Drupal opens up a

wide range of new options for managing and displaying your data, but it also makes the storage of that data less intuitively accessible. Where you could previously point to a specific HTML file that contained the data displayed on a single webpage, the content that appears on an equivalent webpage in a Drupal site is actually stored in many different places throughout the database. But whether you want to back up your data, share it with someone else, or export it for use with other software, there are many options for getting your data out of the Drupal database in a variety of formats, including PDF, Excel-compatible CSV files, and XML. Section 15.2 covers data export.

2.4.5   Summary of code and database

The *Drupal core* code provides the essential plumbing for your site, and a small group of *modules* provide basic website functionality. The additional modules you install provide much of the functionality of your site, and the choice of which modules to install largely depends on what your site needs to do. Your site's *theme* and its associated configuration options determine what the site looks like. All the information about your site's configuration, as well as your site's content, are stored in the *database*.

2.5 Drupal components

The Drupal core code provides an administrative interface where you will be doing most of the work involved in configuring your site. The following major components of Drupal can be configured using this interface. Collectively, they make up the structure of the site.

2.5.1   Content types

One of Drupal's defining features as a content management system is the ability to create content types—essentially, templates for storing different kinds of data. In contrast to WordPress, where a user can choose between creating a blog post and a page—both of which are by default limited to a title, text area, and some tags—Drupal allows you to create any number of content types, each of which can have as many fields as you need for storing different kinds of content (URLs, structured dates, pointers to other pieces of content or users, videos from external hosting providers like YouTube, in addition to multiple types of fields for text and images). This makes Drupal well adapted for storing and organizing data beyond simple webpage content.

As an example, consider a departmental website. Such a site could make use of Drupal's default "Basic page" content type—which contains a title field and a body field—for general informational pages about the department and its programs. Departmental news items could be added to the site using the "Article" content type. This content type contains a title and body, but also includes an image field, tags, and has comments enabled by default.

The department could also use the "Basic page" content type to publish course descriptions, but Drupal content types enable the site builder to store that information in individual fields—rather than a large blob of text—and then display the information in a variety of useful ways.

Imagine the site builder creates a content type called "Course." By default, Drupal includes a title field and a body field with every new content type, though the body field can be renamed or removed entirely. The developer might then add the following fields:

> A "topic" field, for selecting from a standardized list of course topics (e.g., nineteenth century, sexuality).
>
> An "instructor" field, for selecting one or more faculty members or graduate students affiliated with the department.
>
> A "semester" field, for choosing which semester the course has been and/or will be taught.
>
> A "prerequisites" field, for typing in the names of prerequisite courses, where Drupal will autocomplete based on the courses that have already been entered.
>
> A "syllabus" field, for uploading a PDF of the course syllabus.

When the site webmaster goes in to add information about a departmental course, they will be presented with an easy-to-use form containing these fields.

While this is a fairly simple content type, using only Drupal core modules and the References module,[3] there are modules that enable

---

3. https://www.drupal.org/project/references

fields tailored for data ranging from email addresses, links, and dates to geographic coordinates and temperature data. Content types can be made even more elaborate using Field groups (see section 6.5.6)—for instance, you might want to group the time a class is scheduled with the room number the class is held.

2.5.2 Nodes

In Drupal jargon, a "node" refers to an instantiation of a content type. Whenever you add new content to your site using any content type, you have created a node. For most sites, almost all the data on the site is stored as nodes; an exception might be if your site is primarily a directory of people, in which case your content would be mostly stored in user profiles (see section 10.4).

2.5.3 Taxonomies

Drupal's "taxonomy" system provides an easy way of associating categories, tags, or other controlled or uncontrolled vocabularies with your content and users. You can create multiple *vocabularies*, which each contain *terms*. To continue with the departmental website example, the site builder would need to create a vocabulary for course topics, and populate it with the list of terms that the department uses to topically categorize its courses. When adding terms, there are options for adding a description for the term, as well as specifying its parent terms within that vocabulary in order to form hierarchies of terms (e.g., putting "Folklore" and "Children's literature" under a parent term "Genre studies").

Furthermore, within a particular vocabulary, site builders can configure fields that will be available when creating or editing any term within that vocabulary. For example, a site builder might create a vocabulary called "Universities," where users can specify the university they are affiliated with as part of their user profile. A site builder could add a field, "Address," to the "University" vocabulary. Every university entered by a user would be stored as a taxonomy term, and users with the right set of administrative privileges could edit those terms to add the address for the university. This would make it possible for the site to display a map showing the universities that its users are affiliated with, using the Views module.

When a node or user is tagged with a term from a vocabulary, that term appears by default on the node or user page as a link to a term page that displays all other nodes or users tagged with that same term making it easy to browse related content. Section 6.4.4 describes how to set up a vocabulary and an associated term reference field; chapter 17 describes modules for importing, exporting, and managing taxonomies.

2.5.4 File types

The Media module allows site builders to create "File types," profiles that are associated with one or more kinds of uploaded files, and/or files pulled in from a third-party hosting provider like YouTube. By default, Drupal provides file types for audio, documents, images, and video. You can add fields to any of these file types, just like you would with a content type, so that users who upload a file need to fill in some metadata. You can also create multiple file types for the same kind of file, and give them different fields—for instance, in order to differentiate painting and photography. See section 5.4.4 for more on the choice between using file types and using content types.

2.5.5 Views

By default, Drupal provides two options for displaying content: 1) viewing a full node, and 2) seeing the default "content feed" (much like the WordPress "posts" page) that displays the shortened "teaser" version of the most recent nodes you've created. This may be suitable for a simple blog, but any site that has custom content types will need the Views module to make the best use of those content types. Chapters 12 and 13 cover Views in depth, but at its essence, Views allows you to query your database in simple or complex ways without writing any code. A very small subset of the possible displays you can generate with Views (often with the help of additional modules) includes:

A table of all site users and their university affiliation, with drop-down criteria (drawn from fields in the user profile, such as discipline) that can be used to filter the list.

Rotating slide shows.

A gallery of image thumbnails.

A list of blog posts written by the person whose profile you're currently viewing.

A map displaying all the locations stored as part of nodes, where clicking on a location pushpin pulls up the title and a link to the node where those coordinates can be found.

A CSV export of some or all the content on the site.

An RSS feed.

A list of the most active site users.

Information stored in the user profile of a user referenced in the node you're currently viewing—in the departmental website example, Views could display on a course page whether the instructor is a professor, lecturer, or grad student, without the webmaster having to enter that information as part of the course profile.

The results of these queries can be displayed on your site in many ways, including as a stand-alone page with its own URL, as a feed, as a plain-text file for exporting data as a spreadsheet, or as a block (see below).

2.5.6 Blocks

Blocks are generally small containers of content or site functionality (such as a user login box or a menu) that can appear in different places on the site (e.g., footer, right sidebar on blog post pages, top right corner of the front page). Blocks can be created by modules or views, or you can manually create a custom block, which is convenient for things like a copyright notice for a site's footer.

On the block administration page, you can drag and drop blocks into the different regions (header, footer, sidebar, etc.) that have been defined by your site's theme. In addition to determining where on a page the block appears, you can configure the block to appear only on pages that meet certain criteria. For example, if you have a block that's only relevant within a particular area of the site, like "Related blog posts," you can specify that it should only appear on pages from the "Blog" content type. Section 11.2 describes the configuration of blocks in depth.

2.5.7 Menus

Drupal has a fairly straightforward menu system. You can create any number of menus, and pages within a menu can be nested arbitrarily deep. When you create a node or a view, you can easily add it to a menu. Module-generated pages (e.g., site contact forms) can be added to a menu manually.

Every menu is automatically available as a block. While some themes automatically display the "Primary links" menu, in most cases you need to go to the block administration page and place the block corresponding to the primary menu in the appropriate "menu" region for your theme. How the menu block is displayed varies by theme, but modules like Superfish can provide a drop-down display for menus in order to easily handle nested menu items. Section 11.3 describes menu configuration.

2.5.8 Users

Even small sites that do not accept user-contributed material will likely have multiple users. For security reasons, users should have their own accounts, even short-term research assistants.

By default, Drupal creates a page for each user that includes their username and how long their account has existed. By default, users can upload an avatar (small picture) that will display along with their username on content they've created using the default "Article" content type, though this is entirely configurable and removable if desired. As with nodes and taxonomy terms, you can add any number of fields to user profiles, including fields that only users with administrative privileges—and perhaps not even the user himself—can see and edit.

In a university context, users may expect to be able to log in using their preexisting campus username and password. This also provides better security than using Drupal's own authentication. Modules like LDAP[4] and Shibboleth Authentication[5] (which requires additional configuration at the server level) make this possible, and they can also be configured to pull in data from your campus directory, such as a person's full name (good for populating a "Full name" field, if you've added that to your user profiles)

---

4. https://www.drupal.org/project/ldap
5. https://www.drupal.org/project/shib_auth

and information about whether the person is faculty, student, or staff, which may be useful for managing their level of access to the site using roles (see section 10.5).

2.6 Overview of site building

The process of developing a project using Drupal can be broken down into a set of phases, generally executed sequentially, but usually with some degree of revisiting previous stages as the project progresses. An analogy with creating a face may be helpful here.

2.6.1 Deciding on Drupal

In the analogy, make a decision as to whether you want to create a face.

Decide if Drupal is a good candidate platform (see chapter 1). Create a list of all the things you want your site to be able to do (e.g., search content; filter search results by X, Y, and Z; display maps of all locations; allow users to sign up for accounts without project staff intervention; restrict access to data types A and B). Nothing is too small or obvious to exclude from this list. It may be helpful to organize these by priority. What are the features your site absolutely must have? Which would be good to have, and which are optional, depending on time and resources?

Do some research on modules and techniques (e.g., Views configuration) that can help you accomplish each feature on your checklist. You don't have to have the details of a solution worked out for each feature, but you should get a sense for whether the different features are doable given the modules that currently exist, or whether you may need to budget for some custom development. Alternately, your investigation may reveal that Drupal is not the right platform for the project, and you should explore other options.

Finally, decide whether or not to move ahead with Drupal. Can Drupal do most or all of what you want on your list of site features? How does it compare to other platforms? How do the costs (of time, if not money) of building the project in Drupal compare to alternatives? If you've decided to move ahead with Drupal, continue.

2.6.2 Basic configuration

This phase involves the creation of blood vessels, skin, bones, muscle. Even though some of them will not be visible in the end result, these structures are necessary though not unique to faces.

Install Drupal (see section 3.4) and the modules essential for any site (see section 4.4 and 4.5). Move on to the next step.

2.6.3 Data modeling

In this phase, you decide on what facial structures your face will include. Will it be a human face, or that of a cat? Or will you combine a dragon's snout with a koala's eyes and a chinchilla's fur? Depending on your choices, you will probably need to create some additional fur, eye lenses, skin, bones, or muscle.

Develop a data model for the content you want to store on the site (chapter 5). Depending on your data model, you will probably need to install more modules (e.g., to be able to store URLs, pointers to other content, etc.). Move on to the next step.

2.6.4 Implementing the data model

Create the constituent parts of the face: eyes, nose, mouth, fur, etc. Refine the sculptural details on each as needed. At this point, you have all the components of the face, but they're just jumbled on the underlying skull—not arranged in any particular order.

Create the content types (section 6.2), vocabularies (section 6.4.4), user profiles (chapter 10), and file types (section 6.6.4) for your site. Configure the data input form (sections 8.2–8.4) and add content (section 8.5).

2.6.5 Improving the display

Arrange the parts of the face in their correct positions relative to one another.

Configure the display of your content types, user profiles, and file types (chapter 9). Create the necessary views for your site (chapters 12 and 13). Create menus (chapter 11).

2.6.6 Theming

Apply color to the structurally complete but gray face you have created.

Install and configure a theme (chapter 18) for your site. Arrange the blocks you have created within that theme.

2.6.7 Prelaunch configuration

Make sure that all the moving parts of the face (eyes, mouth, etc.) move smoothly and correctly.

Configure site search (chapter 16). Install anti-spam modules (section 10.6). Double-check permissions for anonymous users and each of the roles on the site. Write documentation.

2.7 Summary

This chapter has described the technical underpinnings of Drupal, as well as the major components that you will need to install and/or configure in order to successfully build a Drupal site. It has also provided an overview of the entire site building process, by use of an extended analogy. Chapter 3 covers options for hosting a Drupal site, as well as the installation process. If you already have Drupal installed, you can move ahead to chapter 4.

CHAPTER 3

Installing Drupal

3.1 Overview

This chapter will cover the most common hosting environments for Drupal sites, along with an explanation of each step in the Drupal installation process. The simplest way to get started using Drupal while minimizing the amount of configuration needed, is to take advantage of free, cloud-based hosting for sites under development, as described in section 3.2.4. If you simply want to get a Drupal site up and running, consult 3.2.4 section and then proceed to section 3.4.

3.2 Options for hosting Drupal

There are many options for hosting Drupal, each with its own advantages and disadvantages. Free, cloud-based development hosting is the fastest way to set up a site, but launching a site using the service can be prohibitively expensive for a digital humanities project. If you need offline access to your site as you build it, you should set up Drupal on your own computer. In the long term, institutional hosting or generic shared hosting are likely to be the best options for hosting your site. The details of how to configure Drupal in each of these environments can change, so please refer to the *Drupal for Humanists* site for pointers to current documentation.

3.2.1 On your own computer

Installing Drupal on your own computer will allow you to work on your site while you're not connected to the Internet. This can be useful if you don't have reliable, constant Internet access, but it inhibits collaboration and limits the reach of your site. This may not always be a problem; you may develop a Drupal site simply for your own research purposes. However, to make your site publicly available, it needs to be hosted on a server. If you do create a Drupal site on your own computer, you should consider using the Backup and Migrate module along with the Backup and Migrate Dropbox module, or other similar modules, to periodically copy your entire site (code, files, and database) to a cloud storage service, in case something happens to your computer.

To install Drupal on your computer, you'll need to install an AMP (Apache, MySQL, PHP) stack. The easiest way to do this is WampServer[1] on Windows, or MAMP[2] on Macs. XAMPP[3] is available for Windows, Mac, and Linux. Once you have some variant of this software installed, you can create a database, upload your Drupal files to a folder inside the htdocs directory on MAMP or XAMPP, or in the `www` directory on `WampServer`, and install Drupal. For detailed instructions for installing Drupal on Windows and Mac, see the *Drupal for Humanists* website.

3.2.2 Your institution

Your institution may provide free or inexpensive web hosting; inquire with your central, divisional, and/or departmental IT staff about campus hosting options. Tell them that you want to install Drupal 7; if they aren't familiar with it, you can point them to Drupal's technical requirements page.[4] Not all services that advertise themselves as "web hosting" will work; they have to support PHP (the language Drupal is written in), as well as allow you to create a MySQL database. The only option available might be a VM (virtual machine); if so, make sure it is a managed machine (i.e., that IT staff will take care of updates to the server infrastructure); updating Drupal itself will be a responsibility that will likely fall to you regardless

---

1. http://www.wampserver.com/en/
2. https://www.mamp.info/en/
3. https://www.apachefriends.org/index.html
4. https://www.drupal.org/requirements

(see section 20.2), but system-level updates should be handled by a system administrator. If your institution offers some kind of hosting for Drupal, you should specifically confirm that you will have the freedom to fully configure your site, as well as to add any module that you need (with the understanding that you will be responsible for updating those modules). Some Drupal hosting services limit your ability to configure your site, or add modules; while these services may be suitable for creating some kinds of websites, they are not a good fit for scholarly projects built on Drupal, which can have specific and somewhat unusual module requirements.

One upside of hosting the project with your institution is that it will probably be easier to get a domain name that includes your institution (e.g., `http://myproject.myinstitution.edu`), if you want such a URL. This may be undesirable if you are a graduate student or postdoc who will likely move institutions in the near future; in such cases, it may be better to purchase a ".org" domain name and potentially host it outside the institution. Institutions vary in the extent to which they are willing to host websites on their servers that don't use the institutional domain name.

The process of setting up a Drupal site hosted by your institution will vary considerably. On one extreme, you may have to set up everything from scratch, including creating a database and uploading the core Drupal code; on the other, you may be provided with the admin username and password for a Drupal site that has already been installed. See the *Drupal for Humanists* website for more about how to talk to your campus IT staff about Drupal.

3.2.3 Generic shared hosting

Most generic shared hosting services cost between $50 to $120 per year, and some allow you to host more than one site on the same account. The *Drupal for Humanists* website has a list of recommended hosting providers, along with links to tutorials for how to set up Drupal on each of them. Particularly if your institution doesn't provide free hosting, or if the conditions on the hosting (e.g., requiring you to use your institutional domain name) are not acceptable, generic shared hosting is a fairly easy and relatively affordable option for most projects.

3.2.4 Cloud hosting

Within the last five years, services have emerged that provide cloud hosting specific to Drupal sites. These services are optimized for Drupal, and may include add-ons that would be expensive or inconvenient to set up separately, such as Apache Solr, which can be used with the powerful Search API module (see section 16.7) for better searching. Cloud hosting services mostly target "enterprise" sites that can afford to pay their high rates (starting at $300 a year for the most basic hosting arrangement).

One of these services, Pantheon,[5] allows anyone with an account to create and host up to two development sites for free. In order to launch your site and make it available under your own domain name (rather than the Pantheon domain name for development sites, which looks something like `http://dev-your-site-name.pantheon.io`), you have to start paying, but you can currently host a development site indefinitely, at no cost. You can sign up for a free account on the Pantheon homepage; while the interface for creating new sites is fairly intuitive, the *Drupal for Humanists* site has links to current documentation. Particularly if you want to just get started with Drupal, without worrying for now about the long-term hosting arrangement for your project, the free Pantheon development hosting is the best option.

3.3 Installing Drupal

3.3.1 Choose a profile

When installing Drupal in most environments, there will be two installation profiles: "Standard" and "Minimal."[6] Choose the "Standard" installation profile; it creates a number of useful things, like default content types and an administrator role. Hit the "Save and continue" button.

---

5. http://pantheon.io
6. If you use a Drupal-specific cloud housing environment, there may be a different installation profile available, specific to the hosting platform. This is usually based on the "Standard" profile, but includes modules that tie your site into the hosting infrastructure. You'll need to disable those modules if you move your site to a different hosting platform.

3.3.2   Choose language

Drupal installs with an English-language administrative user interface
by default. If you want the core administrative interface to be in another
language, click on the "Learn how to install Drupal in other languages" link
and follow the instructions there. The completion status for the translation
of the core Drupal interface varies by language; an overview is available
at `http://localize.drupal.org`. If you want the content of your
site (beyond just the administrative interface) to be available in multiple
languages, there are a number of steps you should take fairly early in the
site development process. Drupal has fairly robust support for multilingual
sites, but it's much easier to set this up before you start adding content,
rather than trying to convert a single-language site to a multilingual site
later. Drupal.org includes a detailed resource guide[7] on this topic.

Hit the "Save and continue" button.

3.3.3   Verify requirements

Hopefully, the Drupal installer will skip the "Verify requirements" stage
because everything is set up correctly. If the hosting environment doesn't
have the correct version of PHP installed,[8] or if there is something wrong
with the file permissions, the installer may stop with an error at the "Verify
requirements" screen. Once you correct the problems described on the
"Verify requirements" screen, restart the installer by once again going to
`http://myproject.org/install.php`.

3.3.4   Database configuration

On this screen, you will enter the name of the database you have already
created, as well as the username and password for the account that you
have granted full privileges to the database (figure 3.1). If you are using a
Drupal-specific hosting environment, such as a cloud hosting provider like
Pantheon, the installer might skip this step because the hosting service
itself can take care of the necessary configuration.

---

7. https://www.drupal.org/resource-guides/configuring-multilingual-site
8. PHP 5.2.5 or higher is required for Drupal 7, but PHP 5.4 is suggested. PHP 5.4 was
released in 2012, and is very widely supported.

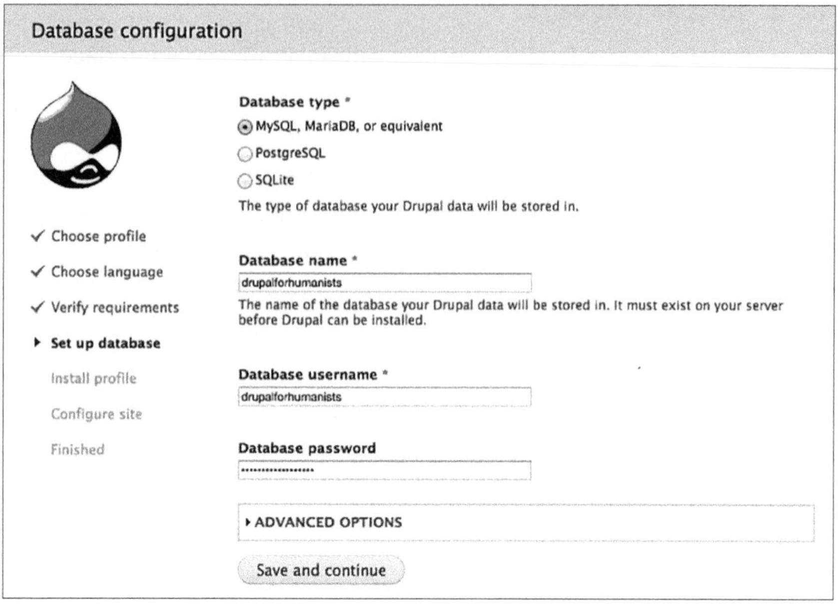

Figure 3.1. Database setup screen.

In almost all cases, the database type will be MySQL. If your database uses a host other than localhost, or requires you to connect through a specific port, you can configure those settings under "Advanced options."

3.3.5 Install profile

A progress bar will move across the screen, listing each module that it enables or configures along the way.

3.3.6 Configure site

The last step in the Drupal configuration process allows you to specify the name of the site, the username and password for the "user1" account (which will always have full permissions to all administrative functionality), the email address from which the site will send mail (e.g., new passwords, notifications, etc.), and how the site will handle update notification. All these things can be changed later through Drupal's administrative interface.

3.3.6.1   Site information

This section includes the site title and the site email address.

Site name

The site name will appear as part of the HTML title for every page on the site. For example, if someone were to bookmark an "About" page on your site, the bookmark would, by default, be saved as "About|Your Site Title," with whatever value you put in for your site title. Most themes (site designs) display the site title in large lettering towards the top of every page, though you can turn this off (for instance, if you want to have a graphic banner image with your site name, instead of just text; see chapter 18 for more on theming).

To change the site name later, go to /admin/config/system/site-information, or *Configuration > System > Site information* using the administration menu module (described in chapter 4).

Site email address

The site email address is the email address that the site uses to send out emails such as password changes, notifications (e.g., of new content), etc. To minimize the risk of those emails being caught in a spam filter, it's best to use an email address that has the same domain name as your site. If you've registered your own domain name (e.g., myproject.org), check the documentation provided by your domain registrar or hosting provider for creating an email address that uses the same domain name (e.g., webmaster@myproject.org). While you could put in an email address that doesn't actually exist (i.e., that doesn't forward to an email address that someone checks, and isn't connected to its own inbox), it's best to use an email address where you'll be able to receive replies from someone who, for instance, responds to a user account creation email with a question about the site.

To change the site email address later, go to /admin/config/system/ site-information, or *Configuration > System > Site information* using the administration menu module.

3.3.6.2 Site maintenance account

This section allows you to create the account often known in Drupal forums as "user 1." This account, the first user account created on a site, has complete, nonrevokable access to all administrative functionality on the site. You should create the "user 1" account with generic information using "admin" (or something similar) as the user name, and an email address affiliated with the site itself rather than any individual person. Each user's email address must be unique, so don't use an email address you'll want to use again for your own account.

For the security of your site, and for better tracking of who is doing what, it's best for every user of your site to have their own individual account. It's much easier to remember to deactivate or remove permissions from a research assistant's own account at the end of their time with the project than to remember to change the password for your "user 1" account.

Create your "user 1" account, and use that username and password to log in just long enough to create an account for yourself with administrative privileges. Record the information about the "user 1" account somewhere safe (and not accessible by anyone other than your most trusted partners on the project), log out, and log in with your own account from then on.

3.3.6.3 Server settings

If your primary audience will be from a specific country, choose that country from the drop-down menu; otherwise, you can leave it as "none." If you choose a default country, Drupal will set the correct first day of the week (i.e., whether weeks should begin on Sunday or Monday when displayed on calendars).

Drupal requires you to set a default time zone, though you can configure the site so that individual users can choose their own time zones.

Both of these settings can be changed later by going to /admin/config/ regional/settings, or *Configuration > Regional and language > Regional settings* using the administration menu module.

3.3.6.4 Update notifications

You should have the "Check for notifications automatically" checkbox
enabled. This will display a notice when a module you've installed (or
Drupal core itself) needs to be updated. It will also add an administrative
option that will allow you to install new modules using the Drupal
administration interface. If you don't enable this checkbox, you can have
the same effect later by enabling the "Update manager" module on the
modules page (/admin/modules).

You might want to have "Receive email notifications" enabled. This
will send a notification to the email address used by the "user 1" account
when there are modules that need updates. If you're working on the
site frequently, you'll catch these updates through the notifications on
the site. Once you're working on the site less frequently, enabling these
email notifications can make it easier to keep up with module and core
updates. You can change this setting, as well as configure the frequency for
checking updates and the list of emails that should receive the notification,
afterwards by going to /admin/reports/updates/settings, or *Reports >
Available updates > Settings*.

3.3.7 Your new Drupal site

If your installation was successful, you should click the "Visit your new
site" link. What you will see should resemble the following (figure 3.2):

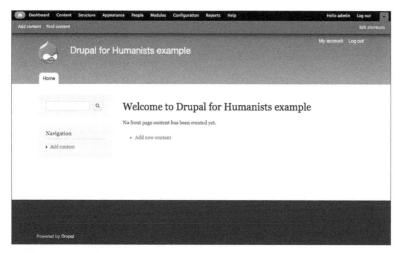

Figure 3.2. Front page of a newly-installed Drupal site.

3.4 Summary

This chapter has covered options for hosting a Drupal site, walking through the Drupal installation interface after you have set up the file system and database.

The front page of a new Drupal site is much less inviting than the WordPress equivalent. There are multiple links for "Add content," which may lead you to think that should be your next step. However, before you add content you need to create and configure *content types*, templates structured to store the data specific to your project (see chapter 6). Before you configure your content types, you need to come up with a plan for your site's *data model*, or how you will break down your data into different content types and fields (see chapter 5). Before you do anything else with the site, however, you should first install and enable a set of essential *modules*, which will add important functionality to your Drupal site; this is discussed next, in chapter 4.

CHAPTER 4

Modules

4.1 Overview

Once you've successfully installed Drupal, you'll be shown a blue screen with a black and gray administration bar at the top of the page. Configuring Drupal will be much easier if you immediately install and enable a number of essential modules (code packages that provide functionality beyond Drupal's core features, similar to WordPress plug-ins) that all or almost all sites need. Once you've installed these modules, you can proceed with developing content types, highly customizable templates for storing your data, as discussed in chapters 5–7.

Sections 4.1 and 4.2 cover how look for modules that fit your project's needs, and how to evaluate whether the module is sufficiently reliable to incorporate into your project. These are important considerations as you develop your own site. Subsequent chapters, which discuss in depth how to build the example site, recommend specific modules; the *Drupal for Humanists* site also includes a list of recommended modules for different purposes. To move directly to the list of essential modules and how to install and enable them, begin with section 4.3. Keep in mind, however, that in some cases there are multiple modules that address a particular need; there are also many modules beyond those listed in this book that can be helpful for your project.

4.2 Finding modules

A visit to the Drupal.org Modules page[1] will show that there are over 15,000 modules that you could download and install. A variety of filters (maintenance and development status, category, core compatibility, and others) offer some options for narrowing down this list. Choosing only core compatibility with Drupal 7.x—thereby limiting the list to only those modules that you can install using the version of Drupal described in this book—still results in a list of nearly 10,000 modules. With so many options, how can you decide which to install?

While Drupal.org should be considered the authoritative place for downloading modules, it's far from the best place to find modules, though simply browsing the modules page can sometimes turn up modules you wouldn't have thought to look for. However, if you have something specific in mind, searching Drupal.org for the name of a module won't always return a link to the module in the first page of results; it is much more efficient to search for *Drupal module Your-Module-Name* on Google or another search engine. The *Drupal for Humanists* website includes a module index with a brief description of all the modules in the book, as well as others that can address common needs. These lists are a good place to start when looking for modules.

If you encounter a situation not addressed in this book, a general-purpose search engine will again be a better resource than Drupal.org for trying to identify useful modules. For instance, a Google search for "drupal module tag cloud" will pull up links to multiple modules on Drupal.org that you can then assess and compare. It will also pull up a few tutorials and forum discussions, for instance, about how to use the Views module to accomplish this task. Even vaguer queries, such as "drupal better taxonomy select," generally turn up useful results.

---

1. https://www.drupal.org/project/project_module

4.3 Assessing modules

Adding a module to your site can be a serious commitment. If you use a module that provides a type of field, the sustainability of data that you store in the corresponding fields is going to depend on the module maintainers. Bugs in the module, or in future updates to the module, may lead to data loss. Also, if a module for a field doesn't provide integration with Views (for displaying the data) and/or Feeds (for importing data in bulk), but the developers promise that integration will be available soon, your project development may have to be put on hold until that integration is ready— and it may never materialize.

Modules that provide additional display options for Views (for data entry, export, or visualizations like maps and slide shows) or data-entry widgets for fields may seem less important than modules that provide field types. If you have to uninstall such a module, you won't lose any data. What you might lose, however, is a good deal of time spent training project assistants in how to do data entry. You would have to figure out an alternative approach to accomplishing the tasks that those modules were supporting, which may not be easily done. You would also have to rewrite your site documentation.

These worst-case scenarios should not deter you from installing modules; Drupal sites are supposed to have modules, and usually, many of them. They do, however, highlight the importance of conducting some assessment of modules, as described below, before you install them, and certainly before you come to depend on them.

Even as a nonprogrammer, you shouldn't see Drupal as software that gets written somewhere else, such that you have to live with the consequences of whatever changes are, or are not, made. Drupal is an open-source project, and many module developers are people with entirely different jobs, who volunteer to write modules in their spare time. If progress isn't being made on an issue as fast as you would like, you can often get in touch with the developer to inquire about it. Maybe the developer would be interested in working with someone at your university as a comaintainer, or perhaps you can write the developer into your next grant proposal to fund some of the work you need done. See section 20.10 for more on getting involved with the Drupal community.

4.3.1   Modules published on Drupal.org
vs those published elsewhere

As a general rule, you should only install modules that you have downloaded from Drupal.org. For a module to be listed on Drupal.org, it has to
meet the Drupal coding standards[2] (which require, among other things,
that the code be well commented upon to make it easier for other programmers to understand—similar to including footnotes in a scholarly
monograph), pass a series of automated tests, and be free of identified
security holes (which could put your site in jeopardy of being hacked).
While the degree to which modules are actively maintained does vary, if a
security hole is found in a module, the module will be removed from
Drupal.org if it is not updated to address the problem in a timely manner.

The Features[3] module allows you to create new modules that reproduce
configuration work you have done on your site, such as creating content
types (as discussed in chapters 5–7) or particular displays of content
(maps, tables, lists, etc.) using Views (as discussed in chapters 12 and
13). Creating this kind of module is a great way to make some of the work
you've done available to colleagues who are working on similar projects.
However, modules created using Features are generally not listed on
Drupal.org, though they may be submodules of module packages that
provide some other functionality. For instance, the Feeds[4] module includes
a feature-based module that provides a sample importer. Stand-alone
modules generated by Features can be shared using a "Features Server,"[5]
but in many cases, people use Github to publish the modules they created
using Features. Installing a module from Github that was created using
Features comes with some risk (there's no easy way to ensure that the code
exported from the source site hasn't been tampered with) but it may not
be as risky as downloading a module from Github that purports to add
some new functionality to the site. See section 15.3 for more on how to use
Features to make your configuration work shareable.

---

2. https://www.drupal.org/coding-standards
3. https://www.drupal.org/project/features
4. https://www.drupal.org/project/feeds
5. See, for instance, from Stanford: https://drupalfeatures.stanford.edu/

There are many modules that are published on Github, or on project websites. In some cases, the developers don't feel like it's worth publishing the module on Drupal.org because it's designed for a niche audience. In other cases, publishing the module on Github is a way to make a module available while it is waiting to be reviewed on Drupal.org. Many well-known Drupal modules that have been developed for digital humanities are not distributed on Drupal.org.[6] For modules that aren't distributed on Drupal.org, it's harder to get information on how many people have the module installed, and it may be more difficult to find out how well the module works, depending on whether the module documentation directs you to a list of problematic issues that developers are currently working on fixing, an active issue queue. There's also no guarantee that the code meets Drupal coding standards. Nonetheless, at least for modules developed within the digital humanities community, you may be able to alleviate your concerns through typical communication channels (e.g., inquiring on Twitter or DH Answers[7]), or even asking the developers directly. You can also send an email to the *Drupal for Humanists* mailing list, linked from the *Drupal for Humanists* site. Particularly since these modules are designed specifically to address digital humanities use cases, they should not be considered off-limits due to the way they are distributed, but a little extra caution is beneficial.

4.3.2 Module versions

Once you've found a module that looks useful, as you're looking at the module's page on Drupal.org, the first thing you should do is check to see if there's a version of the module compatible with your version of Drupal. In this book, we are using Drupal 7, so you need to look for a module version that starts with "7.x." "7.x" is shorthand for "any version of Drupal 7." You should always be running the most recent version of Drupal 7, which will include all the latest security patches (see section 20.3 for how to update Drupal core). For most modules, it doesn't matter exactly what version of

---

6. These include TEICHI for displaying TEI (http://www.teichi.org/downloads), Scripto for crowdsourced transcription (http://scripto.org/download/), and Islandora, which integrates Drupal with Fedora (https://github.com/Islandora).

7. http://digitalhumanities.org/answers/

Drupal 7 you're running, but modules aren't backwards compatible, and there's no way to run a 6.x-version or 8.x-version module on a Drupal 7 site.

To see the versions of the module that are currently available, scroll down to the bottom of the module's page on Drupal.org. The last section in the main column is labeled "Downloads" (figure 4.1). Most modules have at least a green table ("Recommended releases") and a red table ("Development releases").

Downloads

Recommended releases

Version	Download	Date	Links
7.x-1.4	tar.gz (405.94 KB) | zip (618.36 KB)	2014-Feb-12	Notes
6.x-1.11	tar.gz (367.38 KB) | zip (541.09 KB)	2014-Feb-12	Notes

Development releases

Version	Download	Date	Links
7.x-1.x-dev	tar.gz (407.56 KB) | zip (627.5 KB)	2014-Aug-22	Notes
6.x-1.x-dev	tar.gz (367.4 KB) | zip (541.13 KB)	2014-Feb-12	Notes

Figure 4.1. The download section of a module page.

Section 4.5 will cover the steps to take when you actually want to download and install a module; here, it's important just to note that there is a version 7.x-1.4 available as a recommended release. Some modules might only have a development release; others might only have an "other release" (which appears in a yellow table), such as a beta version of the module that is more stable than a development version, but not necessarily ready to be released as a recommended version.

For modules where only a 6.x version is listed under "Downloads," users other than the module's developer may have put together a Drupal 7 version. Look in the issue queue for an issue called something like "D7 port of [module name]," and there may be code in that comment thread that you can use on your site. A word of warning: while such unofficial ports may be usable, they tend to rate poorly on the other sustainability factors described below, especially if they're not taken up by the module's developers and provided as a supported version.

4.3.3   Number of users

With open-source software like Drupal, the number of users of a module is
an important metric. If many sites have a module installed, that indicates
that the module basically does what it claims to do. If a module has a large
user base, more people are keeping an eye on the module and odds are
better that bugs will be reported in a timely manner. Some of those users
may themselves be Drupal developers, and might volunteer to fix bugs
as they arise, if the original module developer can't keep up with the bug
reports. When it comes time for a major version upgrade (e.g., Drupal 7 to
Drupal 8), modules with a lot of users are more likely to be ported to the
new version of Drupal in a timely manner.

The number of sites that report using a module is listed under "Project
information" (directly above the "Downloads" section on the module
page), under the heading "reported installs." If you click "View usage
statistics," you can see a chart for how those numbers have changed over
time, for each release of the module (figure 4.2).

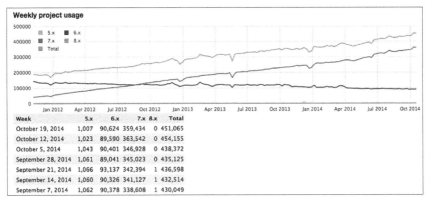

Figure 4.2. Usage statistics for the Date module.

How many users counts as "many" varies by module. Views (which
allows you to display your data in a variety of ways) has over 850,000 sites
reporting its usage. Link (which provides a field for storing URL data)
has over 300,000 sites reporting its usage. Both of these are important
for a wide variety of Drupal sites, in many different industries. The CAS

module,[8] by comparison, is only used by 10,000 sites; this module provides a way for users to log into a Drupal site that's compatible with many institutional and some corporate authentication systems. It's important for university-developed Drupal sites of various kinds (departmental websites, organizational websites, and research websites), but is not generally relevant for small businesses that use Drupal. The Partial Date module[9] provides a field for storing date information with different granularities. For example, if you have a precise date for one document you want to include in your site, and you only know a month and year for another, the Partial Date module can accommodate that better than the Date module. Only around 900 sites report using Partial Date, but since it solves a fairly specialized problem, that counts as a solid number of users.

In general, if a module has fewer than 500 users, you should look carefully at the other factors for module selection before incorporating it into your project. A small user community can be a liability.

4.3.4 Maintenance and development status

The maintenance and development status (directly above the "Downloads" section on the project page; figure 4.3) is self-reported by module developers and may not be current, though the "last modified" date gives you some sense of its currency. Nonetheless, this information can give you some sense of the developers' perception of the module. The full explanation of all the possible taxonomy terms for both maintenance and development status is available on Drupal.org,[10] but "Actively maintained" is the most promising maintenance status for the longevity of a module. As long as there's a recommended, non-beta release available for the module, "minimally maintained" is generally fine. "Seeking new maintainer" indicates that the original developer no longer wishes to be responsible for the module, but a new developer has not stepped into the role of module maintainer—a warning sign for module sustainability.

Drupal project pages include information that allows you to check whether the self-reported information for maintenance and development

---

8. https://www.drupal.org/project/cas
9. https://www.drupal.org/project/partial_date
10. See https://www.drupal.org/node/1066982

Project Information

Maintenance status: Actively maintained
Development status: Under active development
Reported installs: **451,065** sites currently report using this module. View usage statistics.
Downloads: 2,738,075
Automated tests: Enabled
Last modified: October 24, 2014

Figure 4.3. Project information for the Date module.

status is accurate. If a module is said to be under active development, what was the last date a version of the module (including development releases) was released? You can check this by looking at the dates listed next to each version under "Downloads." If a module is said to be actively maintained, how quickly are bug reports and issues addressed? You can check on bug reports and issues in the right sidebar of the module's page, towards the top of the page (figure 4.4). The "statistics" section of this sidebar has some information (including a small graph with the number of open bugs over time), but for modules that aren't particularly active, there may be no data under "statistics" at all. In those cases, it's better to click on "open bugs" and read through the posts yourself, and see whether the issues are being addressed by the developer or others in a timely manner.

As shown in figure 4.4, a very widely used and well supported module like Date can have thousands of issues, including over a thousand open issues. The number of issues by itself shouldn't necessarily lead you to question the sustainability of a module, if other factors are positive. More important than the number of issues is how open issues are handled. Does anyone

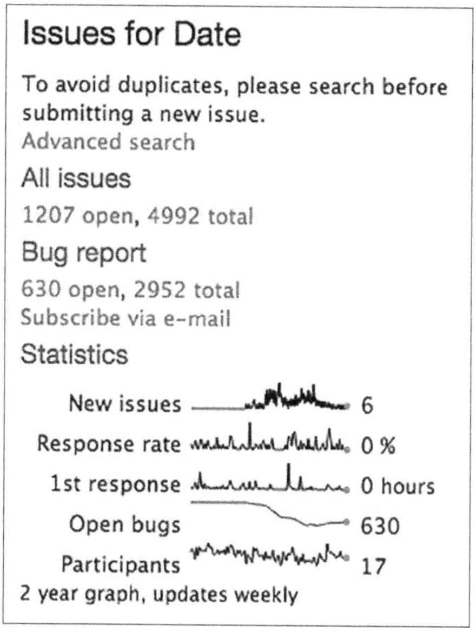

Issues for Date

To avoid duplicates, please search before submitting a new issue.
Advanced search

All issues

1207 open, 4992 total

Bug report

630 open, 2952 total
Subscribe via e-mail

Statistics

New issues	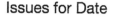	6
Response rate		0 %
1st response		0 hours
Open bugs		630
Participants		17

2 year graph, updates weekly

Figure 4.4. Issues for the Date module.

respond? Are confirmed issues (those that others can re-create) addressed? These are things that require you to read through the issue queue yourself to assess.

In some cases, users who are themselves developers write patches for bugs and post them in the issue thread; it's up to the developers to incorporate those patches into new releases. Seeing threads with a patch that multiple users confirm fixes the problem, but where no developer has stepped in to announce that the patch will be included in a new release, is both a good and a bad sign: good, insofar as there's an active community of users, but bad for the official maintenance of a module.

4.3.5   Release notes

If you click on the "Notes" link next to any release, you'll see some information about it. For non-development releases (as well as many development releases), there'll be a list of bugs that the release fixes, as well as links to the page for each bug. There are cases when it may be best to install a development version of a module (see section 20.9.1.1), and it's important to read the release notes first to make sure there aren't any warnings against using that version of the code.

4.4 Essential modules

The trend in Drupal development is to include more and more universal or near-universal features as part of Drupal core, in order to reduce the number of modules that must be maintained (and updated) separately. Nonetheless, the following modules are worth installing and enabling immediately, on any kind of site, before you move on to other configuration. Section 4.5 covers the process for installing and enabling modules.

Administration Menu:[11] Replaces the default menu bar of administration options with a drop-down version that gives you access to any administration page, from anywhere on the site. Instructions in this book for how to access administrative pages are given with navigating the administration menu in mind,

---

11. https://www.drupal.org/project/admin_menu

though this largely mirrors the internal structure of how administration pages are organized. To enable this module after you've installed it (see section 4.5.3 for more on enabling modules), be sure to enable both "Administration menu" and "Administration menu toolbar style," and *disable* "Toolbar," which is listed under the "Core" section.

Advanced Help:[12] Allows you to see help documents provided by other modules that take advantage of this module's advanced way of handling help files. This module gives developers a way to write more extensive help documents than are normally possible in Drupal, but to use these documents the module has to be enabled. Help documents often make it easier for you to figure out how to configure a module. Just enable the "Advanced help" submodule.

Backup and Migrate:[13] A good module to install, even if you're not facing any impending migrations. This module allows you to easily download your entire database, and restore from a previously downloaded version if your configuration efforts go awry. It also lets you configure automatic, periodic backups. Chapter 20 discusses the use of this module in depth.

Chaos Tool Suite (ctools):[14] Required to install Views. This module includes many submodules, but for now just enable "Chaos tools."

Views:[15] Allows you to create highly custom displays of your data, including lists, galleries, and tables, as well as slide shows, timelines, and maps (with support from additional modules). Be sure to enable both "Views" and "Views UI."

Module Filter:[16] Modifies the Module page interface to make it easy to find modules by searching for module names and filtering them by whether they are enabled, disabled, required, or unavailable. It also replaces the module-enabling checkbox with an on/off toggle. Without this module, there is no way to search for a module by using your browser's search function (e.g., Ctrl-F) since the module name appears everywhere the module is required by another module. This module becomes essential once your list of modules gets beyond a certain size. It also makes it possible to more effectively search and filter permissions on the permissions screen, as described in section 10.5.

---

12. https://www.drupal.org/project/advanced_help
13. https://www.drupal.org/project/backup_migrate
14. https://www.drupal.org/project/ctools
15. https://www.drupal.org/project/views
16. https://www.drupal.org/project/module_filter

> **Token:**[17] Required to install Pathauto; provides access to small bits of text (e.g., the value of a particular field) in other contexts.
>
> **Pathauto:**[18] Lets you define patterns for nicer-looking URLs.

4.4.1   Disabling the core Toolbar module

While you are enabling these modules (using the process described in section 4.5.3), don't forget to *disable* the Toolbar module, which is listed under the "Core" section. If you enable Administration Menu without disabling Toolbar, your site will have two toolbars at the top, one with drop-down menus and one without.

4.5 Installing and enabling modules

Once you've identified a module you'd like to add to your site, you need to *install* it (by adding the code for the module to your Drupal installation) and *enable* it (by checking the box or boxes corresponding to the module on the Drupal Modules page, or toggling the "on" switch if you're using Module Filter, and hitting "Save"). There are two ways to install modules: using the Drupal interface, or by accessing the file system directly. Using the Drupal interface is easiest, but may not be compatible with your hosting environment. Even if you primarily use the Drupal interface to install modules, you should be comfortable accessing the file system because some modules require that you upload additional files, called *libraries*, into a specific directory, which can't be done through the interface. Also, while you can update most modules through the Drupal interface, you have to do Drupal core updates via the file system (see section 20.3.3).

If you're using university hosting for your Drupal site, particularly if you're using some sort of "Drupal hosting service," you may not have permission to install new modules. In this sort of arrangement, the Drupal support team has usually chosen a handful of common modules to make available to users, and they'll do the work of updating those modules for you. Hopefully there is significant overlap between the available modules and at least those listed in section 4.4; if not, the hosting service is probably

---

17. https://www.drupal.org/project/token
18. https://www.drupal.org/project/pathauto

not suitable for developing a digital humanities project site, and you will need to explore other options; see section 3.2 for alternatives.

While you will want to install the modules in section 4.4 right away, installing modules is not a one-time activity when building a Drupal site. It is perfectly normal to install additional modules as part of every step in the site-building process.

4.5.1 Installing modules using the Drupal interface

Click on "Modules" in the black menu bar at the top of the screen (figure 4.5). Right above the list of modules with checkboxes, there should be an option for "Install new module"; click on it. If you don't see this option, scroll down through the "Core" modules, check "Update manager," and save; the "Install new module" option should appear.

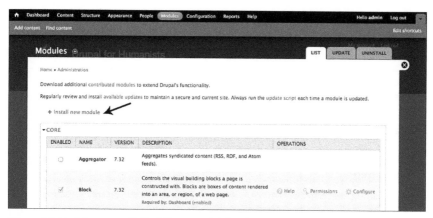

Figure 4.5. Modules page with "Install new module" option.

In another browser tab, go to the page of the module you want to install on Drupal.org, and right-click on one of the download links (either .zip or .tar.gz[19]) to copy the URL. You do *not* need to download the module, just copy the download link.

---

19. If you are installing the module on a server via the Drupal UI as described here, it doesn't matter whether you use the .zip or .tar.gz link. If you are installing the module on a Drupal site running on your own computer (see section 3.2.1), or if you want to open up the module package, to take a look at its contents—such as the README.txt file, which can provide information about how to install and use the module—use the .zip variant because it can be opened on Mac and Windows computers without any additional software.

Back on your site, paste the download link into the "Install from a URL" field (figure 4.6), and click on the "Install" button.

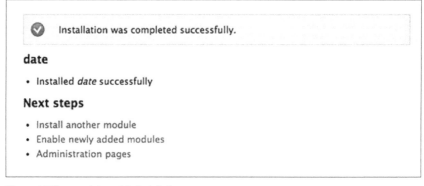

You can find modules and themes on drupal.org. The following file extensions are supported: *zip tar tgz gz bz2*.

Install from a URL

http://ftp.drupal.org/files/projects/date-7.x-2.8.tar.gz

For example: *http://ftp.drupal.org/files/projects/name.tar.gz*

Or

Upload a module or theme archive to install

Choose File   No file chosen

For example: *name.tar.gz* from your local computer

Install

Figure 4.6. Pasting a URL into the "Install from a URL" field.

A progress bar will appear, and once it's complete, you should see a message indicating that the module was installed successfully (figure 4.7).

✓ Installation was completed successfully.

date

- Installed *date* successfully

Next steps

- Install another module
- Enable newly added modules
- Administration pages

Figure 4.7. Successful module installation.

A number of options will appear under this message:

Install another module: This will return you to the screen where you can paste a URL for another module.

Enable newly added modules: This does *not*, in fact, enable the modules. All it does is take you back to the modules page, where you can enable the modules yourself by checking their boxes or switching their on/off toggles, if you're using Module Filter. It may seem counterintuitive, but each module package you install may have multiple submodules, and you might not need to enable all of them. This gives you the choice of which submodules to enable.

Administration pages: This takes you to a page with a list of top-level administrative functions. After you've installed the Administration Menu module, you shouldn't need to access this page, because all administrative functions will always be available through the Administration Menu toolbar.

If you have more modules to install, choose "Install another module"; otherwise, choose "Enable newly added modules."

4.5.2 Installing modules by accessing the file system

Go to the module's page and download the recommended release that corresponds to your version of Drupal (should be highlighted in green, and start with "7.x"). There's no fundamental difference between the .zip and the .tar.gz version, but one might be easier for your computer to unzip than the other. On Windows, choose .zip; on Mac and Linux, either works. (*Note*: sometimes there are good reasons to download versions other than the recommended ones; this will be discussed in section 20.9.1.1.)

Once you've downloaded the module file, unzip it. You'll get a folder with the same name as the file you downloaded, without the version number (e.g., token-7.x-1.5.tar.gz will give you a folder named "token").

Navigate to your Drupal file system; in most cases, this will involve launching an (S)FTP client (see appendix A for instructions on how to install, configure, and use an SFTP client), or if you've installed Drupal on your own computer (as mentioned in section 3.2.1), you simply need to find the right folder on your hard drive. The Drupal file system directory has folders in it including "includes," "misc," and "modules," as well as other files like index.php, install.php, and update.php.

Do not move the module folder into the folder called "modules." This is an easy mistake to make, but it will significantly complicate the process of updating Drupal's core files. Instead, go to the "sites" folder, then go into "all," then go to "modules." Move the module folder into the `sites/all/modules` folder; for instance, if you're installing the token module, it should appear at `sites/all/modules/token`.

Once the module files are in place, load (or reload) the Modules page (click on it in the default toolbar, or using the Administration Menu toolbar) and the module and any submodules should appear on the page.

4.5.2.1   Why sites/all/modules?

Putting "contrib" modules (modules that have been developed by the Drupal community, rather than those that are part of Drupal's core) in `sites/all/modules` is considered best practice. There's also a practical reason: if you later decide to do a multisite setup, where you're running multiple Drupal sites using the same Drupal core code, the modules you've added will automatically be made available to every additional site. Not only does this save you time when building new Drupal sites (since you won't have to redownload every module you want to use), it also saves you time every time you update the modules—you can update the code in `sites/all/modules`, and the latest improvements, security patches, etc. will be present on all sites.

4.5.2.2   Installing modules that use libraries

It's a good idea in general to consult the README.txt file for modules that you're adding to your site. This file is found inside each module's folder. If the module requires you to add a library (an additional package of code that you have to download and install separately) to your site, the README file will tell you where you can get the library, and where in your Drupal site's file system the library should go. Modules that follow Drupal's conventions for external libraries will have you put the library in a specific folder within the **sites/all/libraries directory**. Be sure to follow the instructions precisely; if the README file says the library should be located at **sites/all/libraries/superfish** and you put the library at **sites/all/libraries/Superfishlibrary**, the module won't be able to find the library and it won't work.

There is no way to add a library to your site through the Drupal user interface, so you will need to use (S)FTP software to upload the library to your site (see appendix A), if your site is hosted somewhere other than on your own computer.

Keep in mind that modules with libraries require you to install *two different things*, in two different places: the library code, which usually goes in `sites/all/libraries`, and the module itself that connects the library code to Drupal, which goes in `sites/all/modules`. If you just install the module without the library code, the module won't work. If you just install the library without the module code, it won't appear on the Modules page and you won't be able to enable and use it.

4.5.3 Enabling modules

In the default interface, you can simply enable a module by clicking on "Modules" in either the default toolbar or the Administration Menu, checking the checkbox next to that module, and hitting the "Save configuration" button at the bottom of the screen.

If you've installed and enabled the Module Filter module, the interface is somewhat different. Checkboxes are replaced with on/off toggles. You can also search for a module using the search bar at the top, which is more effective than using the standard browser search. (The standard browser search will pull up *all* references to the module on the page, which may include numerous cases where the module is listed as a dependency for other modules.) You can also use the vertical tabs on the left to filter modules by category, or by whether they have recently been disabled/enabled, or are new.

A word of caution: filters that you set, either through the checkboxes at the top or in the sidebar, stay enabled until you disable them. If you limited the module results to a particular category at some point in the past, and then later search for a module using Module Filter, the only results that will appear are those in the category you previously selected, potentially making it appear as if the module you're searching for doesn't exist. If you're surprised to be not getting any results, make sure that you've selected "All" at the top of the left menu, and all the horizontal checkboxes under the search bar are checked (figure 4.8).

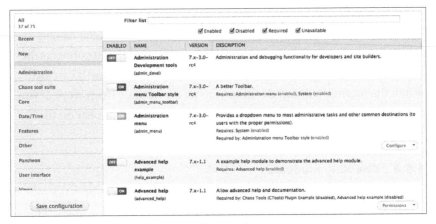

Figure 4.8. Modules page using the Module Filter interface.

The Module Filter module makes the "Save configuration" button "sticky" as part of the left sidebar, so you don't have to scroll to the bottom to use it. With Module Filter, when you enable a module using the toggle, its new status will appear in yellow and the module will be highlighted in green (figure 4.9). This indicates that your changes have not yet been saved. Hitting the "Save configuration" button on the left will finalize the change.

ON	**Simple Timeline** (simple_timeline)	▶ Creates a simple time-line out of posts selected in a view.
ON	**Statistics** (statistics)	▶ Logs access statistics for your site.
OFF	**Stylizer** (stylizer)	▶ Create custom styles for applications such as Panels.
ON	**Superfish** (superfish)	▶ jQuery Superfish plugin for your Drupal menus.

Figure 4.9. Enabling the Statistics module using the Module Filter interface.

A considerable number of modules have dependencies: modules that must be enabled before that particular module can be enabled. If the checkbox (or toggle, using Module Filter) next to the module you want to enable is grayed out, check the list of dependencies (listed in small print under the module description if you're using the standard interface, or accessible via a toggle-down arrow under the module description if you're using Module Filter) for ones that are accompanied by bright red "missing" text in parentheses, and search for and install those modules.

Sometimes, dependencies have maroon "disabled" text in parentheses next to their name. This means that the module has been installed, but not enabled yet. If there are no missing dependencies, but there are one or more dependencies that are listed as disabled, don't worry about enabling the disabled dependencies manually. You should be able to check the checkbox to enable the module that has dependencies, and once you hit the "Save configuration" button, Drupal will offer to enable the dependencies for you.

A note of caution: the dependencies list on the module page is not necessarily a comprehensive list of all the components necessary for the module to work properly. The README.txt file contained in the module directory will provide all the information you need to get the module working. As a rule of thumb, any module that has the Libraries API module[20] as a dependency will require you to upload additional code (libraries) via the file system (see section 4.5.2.2).

4.5.4 Configuring modules

Many modules need to be configured after they are installed, in order to accomplish what you need (figure 4.10). The location of a given module's settings within the Administration Menu is often not intuitive; the fastest way to get to a module's settings the first time is to find the module on the Modules page (click on "Modules" in the Administration Menu), and click the "Configure" link next to its name.

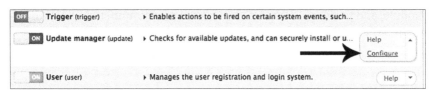

Figure 4.10. Using the Module Filter interface, you can toggle down the list of actions.

---

20. https://www.drupal.org/project/libraries

When you click on the "Configure" link for a module, look at the breadcrumb at the top of the configuration page. This will give you a clue as to where you can find that page again using the Administration Menu. Figure 4.11 shows the configuration page for the Update Manager module. Disregard the first two parts of the breadcrumb path ("Home" and "Administration"); the rest of the components will help you find the page within the Administration Menu (in this case, it's located under *Reports > Available updates > Settings* in the Administration Menu).

Figure 4.11. The Update Manager configuration page.

Most modules have their own set of configuration settings; this book will cover how to configure individual modules as needed for site development in subsequent chapters. The Advanced Help module,[21] which provides a new top-level item in the Administration Menu, may be of use when configuring modules, or figuring out why a module doesn't work as expected (in some cases, you may have to upload an additional library to the file system, as described in section 4.5.2.2). If you're not sure how to configure a module, click on "Advanced Help," click on the name of the module, and you should be able to access, at a minimum, the README.txt file that is included with the code. Some modules, such as Views, provide extensive documentation through the Advanced Help interface.

4.6 How many modules do you need?

Drupal sites vary significantly in the number of modules installed, and which modules those are. Newcomers to Drupal often face the temptation to install and enable any module they come across that they can imagine

---

21. https://www.drupal.org/project/advanced_help

possibly needing, for the convenience of having that functionality available if a situation arises where it would be useful. For the sake of project sustainability (both with regard to the issues described in section 4.2, and with regard to the time necessary to maintain your site), it is important to resist this temptation and be more deliberate in your module selection.

Every time you enable a module, you are responsible for updating it—if not with every release (some releases provide new features rather than important bug or security fixes)—then generally from 1–4 times per year. The more modules you have enabled the more updates you will need to perform on a regular basis. See section 20.3 for more on updating modules.

By default, Drupal checks for module updates periodically, and will notify you (with a yellow or red bar, depending on the importance of the updates) at the top of the module administration page when updates are available. By default, Drupal checks for updates daily, but you can configure this by going to *Reports > Available updates > Settings*[22] using the administration menu. Updating modules isn't hard, but it can be a hassle if you have many modules enabled. The trade-off is worth it if the modules are providing useful functionality for your site, but not if they're enabled "just in case."

Furthermore, modules can sometimes interact with one another in unexpected and problematic ways. If you're trying to figure out why your site isn't working correctly, the fewer modules you have enabled, the easier it may be to troubleshoot. Problems are not always obvious immediately; sometimes a routine module update will cause a conflict with another module, where there hadn't been one before. Many modules create new tables in your database, and if you're using inexpensive commercial hosting for your site (particularly if you have a multisite setup with multiple Drupal sites on the same account), there may be restrictions

---

22. This notation is used throughout the book to describe navigation using the drop-down menu provided by the Administration Menu module. The ">" character is used to indicate that the following word is a submenu item, nested beneath the one before it. In some cases, a path (e.g., /admin/reports/updates/settings) is included in parentheses next to the italicized text. This is the actual URL of the page where the administration menu instructions will take you. You can go to it by typing the base URL of your site (e.g., `http://www.mysite.org`) into the URL bar, and following it with the entire path (e.g., `http://www.mysite.org/admin/reports/updates/settings`).

about the total number of database tables you can have as part of the account. Having many modules installed may also slow down your site's performance.

Don't hesitate to add modules to your site when they might fill a need (especially if you've backed up your database before doing so; occasionally enabling a module can cause catastrophic problems. See section 20.4 for more on backups). However, it's important to be clear about why you've enabled every module on your site. At least twice a year, look through the list of enabled modules and consider disabling—or even uninstalling—modules that you don't need anymore (e.g., modules to support theme development once you're done building your theme, modules that didn't end up doing what you'd hoped they would do, etc.). See section 4.7 for more on disabling and uninstalling modules. Module clutter can build up once a site has been running for some time and has undergone iterative improvements, and it's worth periodically keeping in check.

Finally, every module you install exacts a certain toll on the performance of your site. The precise impact of a module varies, but each module may add to the amount of processing your Drupal site will have to perform every time a page is loaded. There are ways to mitigate this impact, through performance optimization techniques, but the best policy is to run as lean a site as possible to begin with. See the *Drupal for Humanists* site for more on performance optimization.

4.7 Disabling and uninstalling modules

Fully removing a module from your site requires three steps: first, disabling it; then, uninstalling it (which removes any database tables that the module added to your site); and finally, deleting the module from your `sites/all/modules` directory. *Never* simply delete the module without disabling it first; this will cause errors on your site.

4.7.1 Disabling

If there's an enabled module on your site that you're not using and don't plan to use, you should at least disable it, by unchecking the box(es) corresponding to the module on the Modules page. Disabling a module means that you are no longer impacted by security vulnerabilities in its code, and you no longer need to update it. Disabling a module is a prerequisite for uninstalling it.

You can't disable a module if other modules that are still enabled depend on it. Also, if the module provides a field type (e.g., date, link, etc.) you can't disable it if fields of that type exist as part of content types on your site. You must either delete those fields if you aren't using them anymore (this should be the case, if you want to disable a module necessary for their continued existence), or convert the field type to something else (e.g., from a structured date field to text). There is currently no module that allows you to convert field types; if you need to do this, you might be able to find tips and tutorials by Googling for "drupal convert [old field type] field to [new field type]" (e.g., "drupal convert link field to text"). To see an overview of all the fields you have on your site, go to *Reports > Field list* using the Administration Menu; a link to this page is also available as part of the text for any field-providing module: "Required by: Drupal (Field type(s) in use – see *Field list*)."

4.7.2   Uninstalling

Disabling a module makes it no longer active on your site, but changes you've made to the module's default configuration settings are still stored in the database. If you choose to re-enable the module later, those settings will generally return in the state you left them. If you want to completely remove the module and tidy up your database in the process, or if you want to start completely from scratch with the configuration for a particular module, you should uninstall the module after you've disabled it.

Using the Administration Menu, go to *Modules > Uninstall,* and check the box next to the module(s) you want to uninstall.

4.7.3   Removing the code from your site

Uninstalling a module removes all trace of the module from your database, but it does not remove the module code from your `sites/all/modules` directory. As a result, the module will still appear on the list of all modules (albeit disabled), unless you remove the code by accessing the file system directly; there is no way to remove the code through the Drupal user interface (UI).

Removing the module code is not necessary, but if you go through the process of disabling and uninstalling modules, it's generally worth taking the extra step to clean up your `sites/all/modules` directory by deleting the module code. All you need to do is connect to the server, navigate to the `sites/all/modules` directory, click on the module's folder, hit "delete," and confirm that you want to delete it.

Keep in mind that removing the module code should always be the *last* step; *never* remove module code before you have disabled and, ideally, uninstalled the module. When a module is enabled, Drupal will look for the module code and the site will likely display errors if the module isn't where Drupal expects it. If you accidentally remove the code for the wrong module, you can fix the errors by reinstalling the module via the file system (i.e., by downloading the code from Drupal.org, unzipping it, and uploading it to `sites/all/modules`).

4.8 Summary

This chapter has covered essential modules that will be useful on any kind of Drupal site, which should be installed and enabled as a first step after you've installed Drupal. It has also covered the process of installing and enabling modules; you will repeat this process numerous times for every Drupal site you build, throughout the entire site development process. You have also learned how to search for modules that might meet the needs of your site, and what sustainability factors to consider before committing to using a module.

The next step is to plan out what the *content types* should be for your site—what kind of data your site will store, and how it will be structured. Chapter 5 addresses these topics. To implement your content types (chapters 6–7), you will need many more modules, so there will be plenty of additional opportunities to practice installing and enabling them.

CHAPTER 5

Content Types and Introduction to Data Modeling

5.1 Overview

Content types define the structure of your site. Before you dive into creating content types, it's important to carefully think through the data model for your site. While there is no single perfect data model for a given site, some data models are more effective than others in supporting the kinds of browsing, searching, and visualization interfaces that you want to create. This chapter describes content types, the two content types that are configured by default on Drupal sites, and some factors to think about when creating your data model. It concludes by applying these considerations to the example site.

5.2 Introducing content types

On a Drupal site, "content types" are how you store most of the site content, from small pieces of data that will never be shown to the end user in isolation (e.g., the name and geographic coordinates of a location that you want to refer to from another content type), to more complex entities with a lot of different properties (e.g., a project profile, including information about the developers, the funding agency, a description, website URL, links to relevant publications, etc.), to simple content that stands alone for visitors to the site (e.g., basic pages like "about the project," or blog posts). Creating content types in Drupal is a straightforward process; making good choices about how to break down the material you want to present on the site into content types, and how to structure those content types takes some careful deliberation.

One consequence of Drupal's extreme flexibility and customizability is that a Drupal site can easily become a convoluted mess—where it's not clear which modules, blocks, or views are generating any particular snippet of text on the screen, and it's not clear how one would add new data to the site, or why content is showing up in a particular order—in a way that's simply not possible with WordPress or Omeka. The choices made around content types are generally the primary culprit when a Drupal site descends into chaos, as the site developer adds more and more ad hoc fixes to get the data to show up the ways it needs to.

If a project team includes both technically-oriented members and scholarly-oriented members who generally work separately, planning the content types is one occasion that necessitates a high degree of collaboration and communication—in person, if possible. If a developer makes assumptions about whether to make a date field mandatory, or whether a person's profile should have separate fields for given names and surnames, it can impact the kinds of scholarly arguments one can make with the data. Likewise, if a scholar doesn't make explicit their assumptions about what they'll be able to do with the data (e.g., "display all events that happened in the nineteenth century, and filter by person involved"), the content types may get structured in a way that doesn't support it. Restructuring content types can be time-consuming, even more so if data entry has already begun. Content types that are actively used will inevitably evolve to some extent, but investing work in getting the content types reasonably "right" for your project upfront will pay off considerably.

5.3 Drupal's default content types: Basic Page and Article

If you've installed Drupal using the standard installation profile, your site will already have two content types: "Basic Page" and "Article." Both will have a title field and a body field; "Article" additionally has fields for an image and for tags. "Basic Page" and "Article" are essentially equivalent to the WordPress concepts of "Page" and "Post," respectively.

If all the information that you want to capture about the content in your collection could be captured by those two default content types, it is a strong indicator that Drupal is not the right platform for your project. The payoff for the additional configuration work that Drupal requires is its ability to easily capture dates and connections between different types of data, locations, etc. in a structured form that can be leveraged in a variety of ways for display and navigation. If this is not necessary for your project, WordPress is the better platform choice.

There is nothing special about either of the default content types. They're not protected in any way; you can delete the Article content type, for instance, by going to *Structure > Content types > Article > Delete*, and you can add fields to them like any other content type.

For our example project, we could potentially just use the default content types without making any changes. We could use "Basic Page" to store biographies of individual people, putting their name in the title field, and all the other information about them in the body field. "Article" could be used primarily to store images using the image field, with space for a title and description in the title and body fields, respectively, and a few descriptive tags.

Using the default content types in this way might be problematic for your project, even if the title/body field structure is generally a good fit. You might want to have an "about" page that provides an overview of your project, but if you're also using the "Basic Page" to store information about people, you'll encounter some difficulties when using the Views module to generate a display of all people. Informational pages will be mixed in with the biographies (since both use the "Basic Page" content type), and there'll be no way for Drupal to differentiate the two kinds of content, even though you can do so easily as a human. For this reason, it's best to use the default content types as intended—for generally static information ("Basic Page") and blog posts, news, updates and the like ("Article")—and create additional content types tailored specifically to your data, even if some of them look similar to "Basic Page" or "Article," using the title and body fields.

In the case of our example project, storing the data using just a title and body field would drastically limit what we could do with it. There would be no way to connect an image of a person to the biography of that person.

There would be no way to generate a map or time line view of the events in the person's life, because that information would just be stored as part of a big text field. There would be no way to sort people alphabetically by last name (unless we indicated that names must be entered into the title field, last name first). Finding all people affiliated with Howard University would be no easier than if we were working on paper.

Not all data need to be stored in a structured way; for every project, it's important to consider what kinds of visualizations and research questions your site will support, and how much additional data entry work would be required for each new aspect of the data you're considering encoding. Even the small amount of time it takes to put information about a person's birth date into a specific date field can add up over tens or hundreds of individuals. Multiply this by the number of specific fields you wish to include in a content type, and it quickly becomes evident why a project team should carefully identify which fields are truly important for the research questions or displays they intend to support, and which would fail to provide a payoff commensurate with the data entry work required.

5.4 Data modeling for content types

We've concluded that for our example site we need more—and more elaborate—content types than Drupal provides by default. But how can you determine how many content types you actually need, or what fields they should have?

For most projects and data sets, there is no single correct data model: it all depends on what you plan to do with the data, and how you anticipate the project might evolve. Some degree of guesswork is needed, and you'll likely adjust your content types over time, but thinking through the following considerations before deciding on your initial set of content types should reduce the number of changes you'll have to make later.

5.4.1 Data vs metadata

For sites that will be storing data, a rule of thumb is to construct one content type for each kind of data, and use fields within those content types for metadata (information *about* the data). Two projects based on the same data set may have different perspectives of what counts as data, and what counts as metadata, depending on how they want to present the content.

Suppose your data set includes the following:

Full text of an interview, which includes references to important places

Name of the interviewee

Age of the interviewee

Birth place of the interviewee

How many content types should you create for these data? It all depends on the project goals and focus, and how you can see the project expanding.

If the focus is primarily on the text of the interview, perhaps one content type ("Interview") is enough. It can contain some fields to store the information about the interviewee. (Choosing *which kinds of fields* is more complicated and is discussed further below.)

If the people being interviewed are themselves a potential focus—of equal importance to the interview text—you might want two content types: "Interview" and "Person." "Person" would contain the information about the person (name, age, birthplace), and "Interview" would contain the text of the interview, and a node reference field pointing to the person being interviewed.

Technically, not much would change if you included the node reference field as part of the "Person" content type instead, and used it to point to the interview, but doing it that way feels a little less intuitive. There's something incomplete about an "Interview" content type that doesn't store information about who's being interviewed (even though you can use the Drupal Views module to call up that information, if it's stored as part of the "Person" content type), but information about interviews is not an essential part of a stand-alone "Person" content type.

What if the focus of the project has more to do with locations? In addition to "Interview" (and "Person," if you're splitting that into its own content type), you would want to create a "Location" content type. You would then use a node reference field to store the person's birthplace, and you might add a (possibly multivalued) field to "Interview" to capture the important place or places mentioned in the interview text.

5.4.2   Content type vs taxonomy

The taxonomy system in Drupal 7 (but not previous versions) has some characteristics in common with content types. The simplest use of taxonomies involves creating different vocabularies, and either pre-populating them with a set of terms (which you may choose to organize hierarchically) or using them to store user-generated tags. By default, terms in any vocabulary have a name (the term itself) and optionally a description, but you can add fields on a vocabulary-by-vocabulary basis, which will then be available to all terms in that vocabulary (go to *Structure > Taxonomy > Your-taxonomy-name > Manage fields* to see the interface, which is nearly identical to the "manage fields" interface for content types).

The ability to add specialized fields to vocabularies can be useful. A project that invites users to list their institutional affiliation as part of their user profile could use a free-tagging vocabulary for institutions in the user profile, and have a project assistant augment every term added with the geographic coordinates of the institution, in order to generate a user map.

On the other hand, it does blur the line between content type and taxonomy, which complicates the process of data modeling. As a rule of thumb, if you're considering adding more than two fields to a vocabulary, think about why you're not creating a content type for it. If you're still torn between content type and taxonomy, here are a few more factors to consider:

- The content of a node reference field (which you can use to point to content stored in a content type) appears as a link to that single piece of content. For example, if you have a "Location" content type, and use a node reference field in a "Person" content type for the person's birthplace, clicking on the person's birthplace will take you to the corresponding "Location" node.

- The content of a term reference field (which you use to associate a taxonomy term with a piece of content) appears as a link to a page that primarily shows a list of all the content that's been assigned that taxonomy term. The definition, and/or any other fields you've associated with the vocabulary, appears at the top. Drupal also automatically creates an RSS feed for content tagged with each taxonomy term. Therefore, if you use a vocabulary to store locations, clicking on the person's birthplace will give you a list of all people with that birthplace, and any other content that's been tagged with the same location, such as interviews where that location is important.

- Editing taxonomy terms (or adding them, outside the context of adding a new tag when creating content) requires a different set of user permissions than creating/editing content via content types. Drupal doesn't automatically have the fine-grained permission control for taxonomies that it does for content. Where Drupal differentiates "edit own content in Content Type X," "edit any content in Content Type X," "delete own content in Content Type X," and "delete any content in Content Type X," there's an all-purpose "Edit terms in Vocabulary X" and "Delete terms in Vocabulary X." Depending on who's going to be entering the data, you might want the additional control offered by a content type.

- The Views module behaves in surprising, and generally undesirable, ways if you try to display data from a field stored in a taxonomy term as part of a view of node data. For instance, if you have a node reference field in an "Interview" content type pointing to a "Person" node, and you only want to display the person's last name (which exists as a separate field as part of the "Person" content type) as part of a display listing all interviews and interviewees, you can easily substitute the last name field for the person's first name. If you have people stored as taxonomy terms, with separate fields for first and last name as part of the taxonomy term, trying to make that substitution will generate duplicate listings for any interview with more than one person associated with it.

- You can use the Views module to create a taxonomy-like display of all content that refers to certain kinds of nodes, using a node reference field. You can also use Views to create an RSS feed for all content associated with those nodes. Essentially, there's nothing *unique* about the way taxonomy content is presented by default—you just have to do a little more work to get it.

In short, if there are factors that make it preferable to create a content type rather than an elaborate taxonomy vocabulary, but you prefer the way taxonomies display, go with the content type—it's not terribly difficult to re-create a taxonomy-like display using Views.

5.4.3 When to merge similar content types

What if you've looked at your data, broken it down into content types and fields, and discovered that some of the content types will have identical, or nearly-identical, sets of fields? An example might be content types for information about undergraduate students and graduate students: perhaps the "Grad Student" content type has an extra field for dissertation topic, but is otherwise identical in form to the "Undergrad" content type. You could set them up as two different content types, but that means doubling the configuration work, both now and in the future. It's extremely likely that, at some point, you'll need to add another field to the "Grad Student" or "Undergrad" content type, and if it's one that applies to both, you'll have to remember to update it in two places. If these content types are truly so similar, and you anticipate that they'll generally remain so, you might want to consider creating a single "Student" content type, and include a "Text (list)" field for selecting whether the student is a graduate student or undergrad. To accommodate a small amount of variation, you can use the Conditional Fields module[1] to have the dissertation topic field show up only after "graduate student" has been selected.

On the other hand, your site might evolve in a different direction, providing more (and more detailed) information about graduate students than undergraduates. How likely is it that, for example, you might want to provide a "short bio" field for your graduate students (but not undergraduates), or include the courses your graduate students are teaching or assisting with? Is the similarity between the "Grad Student" content type and the "Undergrad" content type more connected to the role that both play within the overall data set of your project, or is it because that aspect of your project (how much data to include, and/or what to do with it) isn't fully worked out yet? Moving data from one content type to another will be a pain regardless of whether you're splitting a content type, or merging two into one. At a certain point, you have to make your best guess about how your project will develop, and move on.

Usability is another factor to keep in mind here. "Undergrad" vs "Grad student" are easy enough to understand as options in a drop-down list as

---

1. https://www.drupal.org/project/conditional_fields

part of a "Student" content type. But what if your site stores the full text of nineteenth century poems, as well as the full text of user-contributed essays about those poems? Maybe in both cases, the only fields you have are the out of the box title and body fields. Should you have one content type (where the user chooses "poem" or "essay" from a text list field), or two? In this case, chances are good that the users of your site think about the poems and essays as very different things, particularly if you're anticipating that scholars with a connection to this material will be contributing to it. Creating a single content type might be easier for you to configure, but at the cost of making the site feel less intuitive to your users. In such a situation, it's often better to create two content types, especially if there's not a lot of field configuration work that would need to be done twice.

5.4.4 File types vs content types

If your site uses images, audio, video, and/or documents in more than an incidental way, the Media module[2] is essential, but it also complicates the data modeling for your site. Without Media to store any sort of information about the file, you'd need to create a content type with fields to capture that information (e.g., a "Photograph" content type to record the photographer, the date the photo was taken, the location, the collection or archive where it comes from, etc.). The Media module provides a new "thing," file types that can store information that will be associated directly with the piece of media, which may appear in multiple places and in multiple ways on the site. Storing that information in a node where the image has been uploaded, as you would have to do without the Media module, does not associate the metadata with the file in such a way that the metadata comes with the file if the file is used in another context (for instance, embedded in a paragraph of text elsewhere on the site).

When should you add fields to a file type? And when should you create a content type to store some of the metadata? It depends on the overall scope and nature of your particular data set. If your data contain photographs of paintings, you may want to add some fields to the file type

---

2. https://www.drupal.org/project/media

in order to document things like the source of the image file (for instance, if you are using images gathered from different museum websites). You might also want to add a field for the person who photographed the painting.

In most cases, you should probably still create a content type for storing information about the painting itself—the date it was painted, the artist, the dimensions, the media, etc.—even though you could add those fields to the "image" file type, or create a new file type for "painting" that has those fields (see section 6.6.4 for how to add fields to a file type). One advantage of using a content type to store this information is that it makes the data entry experience more uniform; creating a blog post and adding a new painting would be done the same way. Due to a constraint in the Views module (which you will use to generate most of the lists and other displays of data on your site), views can only display one kind of data at a time: nodes, users, or files. Storing most of the information about paintings in the same kind of data you might store additional information (e.g., biographies of painters) gives you more flexibility when developing views later on.

5.4.5 User profiles vs content types

If the data on your site are primarily about people, you face a choice between storing that information in user profiles (see section 10.4) and using a content type. The determining factor here is whether the people in question will themselves be logging into the site and editing their information. If people expect to be able to edit their personal information, it's easiest to store those data as part of the user profile. Each user automatically has permission to edit their own profile information; all you have to do is create a user account, and they can edit their information as soon as they log in. If you use a content type in a situation where people expect to be able to edit their own information, you have to create a user account so the person can log in, then create a node for the person, and set the person's user account as the author of the node. Then, you either need to provide the user with the URL of the node you created with their information, or create a block using Views that will display nodes where the user is listed as the author, and put it somewhere visible. (See chapter 11 for more on blocks, and chapters 12 and 13 for more on Views.)

If the data on your site are primarily about historical people, or people who aren't part of the community of site users, using a content type to store information makes the most sense. It becomes more complicated if the people who make up the site's data are a mix of users and nonusers. If a significant number of people are nonusers, it may be better to use a content type, even though it requires more work to set up each user who is also a person in the database. Setting up user accounts that you don't expect will ever be accessed is less than ideal from a security standpoint, and since you have to use a unique email address for every account on the site, generating a large number of unused email addresses that you control can quickly become cumbersome.

5.4.6 Drupal-based considerations for determining content types

There are other Drupal components (both modules and core functionality), the settings of which are based around content types (i.e., different content types can have different setting configurations, but all content of a single type—like undergraduates and graduate students within a "Student" content type—must have the same configuration). Some of these include:

Hiding/displaying author and date information: If you want some content to display "Submitted by [Drupal user name] on [date]" at the top, and other content to not display it, it's a factor in favor of different content types. If you want to customize that text, though, you may need to use the Views module anyway, in which case you can set up more specific conditions than just content type for when that text shows up.

Comments: If you want some content to have comments enabled by default and other content to not have comments by default, that's a factor in favor of different content types. Note that users with the right permissions—"Administer comments and comment settings"—can turn on comments for any new or existing piece of content, regardless of what the defaults are.

Pathauto: If you want the automatically generated URLs for two pieces of content to be radically different (e.g., "mysite.university. edu/2013/07/06/content-title" vs "mysite.university.edu/content-title"), that's one of the strongest factors in favor of different content types. Note that if you have just one example, or a handful of examples, of a piece of content you want to behave differently than the way you've configured Pathauto for its content type, you can always manually change the URL.

Permissions: The Drupal permission system breaks down permissions by content type (e.g., add content type X, edit/delete own content type X, edit/delete all content type X). Using the example above, if you want some users to be able to create "undergrad" content, but not "grad student" content, that's a moderately strong factor in favor of different content types.

5.4.7 Drupal's "title" field vs real-world titles

While content types can vary in the number and nature of their fields, every single content type must have the default "title" field. Every node (an instantiation of a content type) must have a Drupal title. There are ways of hiding it from display, there are ways of automatically generating it, but there is no way to circumvent the fact that *every node must have a title* as Drupal understands it.

By default, the Drupal title is displayed at the top of the page when a user is viewing the node. In addition, if you have a content type that uses a node reference field (a field used for pointing to a different node), you'll have to use the Drupal title of the node you want to reference. There are ways around this by setting up a View that displays some other information from the nodes to be referenced, but using the Drupal title—either via a select list or autocomplete, is by far the simplest. Particularly if your site uses node reference fields, it's important to make good use of the Drupal title, and this might require not thinking of it primarily as a "title."

Depending on the nature of the content type you're creating, the default Drupal title field might be a good fit for capturing real-world titular data. If you have a "Project" content type, you can use the Drupal title field as is to store the project title. Leaving the Drupal title field alone is also a good idea for the default "Basic Page" and "Article" content types (or their equivalents), since web pages and blog posts tend to have titles.

What do you do with a content type that doesn't naturally have a "title" in the same way that a blog post or a project does (e.g., a dictionary word), or where the real-world "title" associated with the content type shouldn't be given the same prominence as some other piece of information (e.g., a content type for a person, where their name should appear most prominently, not their professional title)? Out of the box, Drupal allows you to give the "title" field a different label on the node creation page (part of the "submission form settings" when you're editing a content type or creating a new content type, see section 6.2.1). For these two cases, you could change the label of the Drupal title field to "Word" and "Name," respectively. Somewhat confusingly, in the second case, you might want to add a field that *is* labeled "title" to the person content type, to store the person's professional title.

Even though the Drupal title field will be relabeled "Name," its *machine name* (how it's stored in the database—which is never displayed to the end user and only appears on a few administrative pages) will still be "title." If you add a field to store the person's professional title, that field will be labeled "Title" but its machine name will be "field_title". Keeping an eye on the machine name, and whether it's prefixed by "field_" will be important in a few situations where you'll use the machine name as a placeholder for data stored in that field, such as when configuring Pathauto (see section 6.9).

What if there's no single piece of data in the content type that's a good fit for the Drupal title? As an example, imagine a content type for storing brief weekly updates on a project. Drupal will automatically capture the username of the person creating the update, and the date and time it was created. The default "body" field can be used to store the actual text of the update, but what of the title? Something like "1/1/13 Update (Jane)" might make sense, but if you use the Drupal title field, the people working on the project would have to enter that information manually—in spite of the fact that Drupal is already capturing two of the three bits of information (the date and the username of the person adding the update). You could include instructions about your conventions for the titles of project updates, but that means extra work for your project assistants and is more likely to generate inconsistencies than actually be useful. A better way to generate useful Drupal titles in such cases, without increasing the human work involved, is to use the Automatic Nodetitles module,[3] described in section 6.8.

---

3. https://www.drupal.org/project/auto_nodetitle

5.5 Preliminary data modeling for the example site

The example site described in section 1.5 will provide the context for most of the configuration work in this book. Let's take a closer look at the data and the goals of the site.

5.5.1 The data

The data for this project consist of the following:

> **Biographies** of African Americans in medical professions, and specific events from their lives, including temporal and spatial information about those events. These biographies are stored in a single Word file.
>
> **Images** of African Americans in medical professions, including (but not limited to) photos of people whose biographies will also be stored on the site. The images are sourced from the Flickr Commons (`https://www.flickr.com/commons`) collection of public domain images.

Example 1: Biography

Alexander Thomas Augusta (March 8, 1825 – December 21, 1890) was a surgeon, professor of medicine, and veteran of the American Civil War. After gaining his medical education in Toronto, he set up a practice there. He returned to the United States shortly before the start of the American Civil War. In 1863, he was commissioned as major and the US Army's first African American physician and also the first black hospital administrator in US history. He left the army in 1866 at the rank of Brevet Lieutenant Colonel.

> Alexander Thomas Augusta was born, March 8, 1825, Norfolk, Virginia.
>
> Applied to study medicine at the University of Pennsylvania, was rejected, 1845, University of Pennsylvania, Philadelphia, Pennsylvania.
>
> Moved to California to earn money for medical school, 1846, California, USA.
>
> Married Mary O. Burgoin, January 12, 1847.
>
> Enrolled at Trinity College at the University of Toronto, 1850, University of Toronto, Toronto, Ontario.

Received degree in medicine from the University of Toronto, 1856, University of Toronto, Toronto, Ontario.

Left Canada for the West Indies, 1860, West Indies.

Given a Presidential commission in the Union Army, October 1862, Washington, DC, USA.

Received a major's commission as surgeon for African American troops. This made him the US Army's first African American physician (of a total of eight) and its highest-ranking African American officer at the time., April 4, 1863, Washington, DC, USA.

Assaulted; three people were arrested, May 1863, Baltimore, Maryland.

Commissioned Regimental Surgeon of the Seventh US Colored Troops, October 2, 1863, Washington, DC, USA.

Wrote to Judge Advocate Captain C. W. Clippington about discrimination against African American passengers on the streetcars of Washington, DC:

> Sir: I have the honor to report that I have been obstructed in getting to the court this morning by the conductor of car No. 32, of the Fourteenth Street line of the city railway. I started from my lodgings to go to the hospital I formerly had charge of to get some notes of the case I was to give evidence in, and hailed the car at the corner of Fourteenth and I streets. It was stopped for me and when I attempted to enter the conductor pulled me back, and informed me that I must ride on the front with the driver as it was against the rules for colored persons to ride inside. I told him, I would not ride on the front, and he said I should not ride at all. He then ejected me from the platform, and at the same time gave orders to the driver to go on. I have therefore been compelled to walk the distance in the mud and rain, and have also been delayed in my attendance upon the court. I therefore most respectfully request that the offender may be arrested and brought to punishment.

February 1, 1864, Washington, DC, USA

Awarded a brevet promotion to Lieutenant Colonel, March 1865, Washington, DC, USA.

Accepted an assignment with the Freedmen's Bureau, heading the agency's Lincoln Hospital in Savannah, Georgia, October 1866, Savannah, Georgia.

Left military service at the rank of Lieutenant Colonel, October 13, 1866, Washington, DC, USA.

Began teaching anatomy at Howard University, November 8, 1868, Howard University, Washington, DC.

Returned to private practice in Washington, DC, 1869, Washington, DC, USA.

Received honorary MD from Howard University, 1869, Howard University, Washington, DC.

Attending surgeon to the Smallpox Hospital in Washington, DC., 1870, Washington, DC, USA.

Received honorary AM from Howard University, 1871, Howard University, Washington, DC.

Stopped teaching anatomy at Howard University, July 1877, Howard University, Washington, DC.

Alexander Thomas Augusta died, December 21, 1890, Washington, DC, USA

Example 2: Image

Portrait of Alexander Thomas Augusta.

Example 3: Image

Nurses in training at Lincoln High School in Tallahassee, Florida.

5.5.2 The goal

The goal of the site is to make the data accessible to users, in order to increase their understanding of the topic at hand. This includes incorporating appropriate visualizations (time lines and maps) into the profiles of individual historical figures, as well as creating an image gallery with different parameters for filtering the images.

The Views module (chapters 12 and 13) will be used to actually implement these interfaces, so there's no need to worry about the exact details of how it will work at this point. As you develop more Drupal sites, your familiarity with Views and what it can and can't easily do will inform your data modeling choices, since the decisions made now will have an impact on that later process. With your first Drupal site, you face a chicken-and-egg problem; while understanding Views will help you make better choices about your content types, you need to create some content types and enter some data before you can meaningfully explore Views. For now, keep in mind that any piece of information that you have to point to specifically (for instance, the date of an event in order to place it on a time line, or the location of an event in order to place it on a map) needs to be stored in its own field.

5.5.3   Breaking down the data

The most obvious way to break down the data is into two content types: "Person" and "Image." The "Person" content type will store information about people, and the "Image" content type can store images that are unrelated to the people featured elsewhere on the site. So, we could have content types as simple as the following:

Person

Name (can rename default Drupal title field and use that).

Biography (can rename default "body" field and use that).

Image

Title (can be used to store a brief description of the image).

Description (can rename default "body" field).

Image (a file field; can choose the existing "Image" field that exists as part of the "Article" content type).

Tags

This kind of setup will essentially re-create the sources of your data.

By putting all the information about a person in a single text field, the information is human-readable, but there's not much more you can do with it, because the data are not structured in any way. There's no way to pull out dates for use in a time line, or locations for use in a map, because they're mixed in with many other kinds of data.

The image content type is much like Flickr, where the images come from, with a title, description, and tags. Images that are stored this way can be difficult to find, because everything depends on the tags, an uncontrolled list of terms that may vary in quality. Two different images may use different words that express the same concept in their tags. There's also no way to easily pull out images of a person whose biography is stored on the site.

This simple data model essentially only supports the display of information in the form in which it was entered. If this is sufficient for your project's needs, Drupal is probably not the best choice of platform for your project. WordPress would offer the technical capabilities you need, with less configuration required.

5.5.4   Enriching the content types

The more you structure the data using fields, the more opportunities you'll have to browse, compare, and analyze the data in different ways. The cost of more fields is data entry time—it's much faster to copy and paste a big block of text that contains an undifferentiated mass of biographical description, names, dates, and locations than to put dates into individual fields, names in another set of individual fields, etc. (Note: you can bulk import content into Drupal, as described in chapter 14, but you'd still need to spend time preparing your data for the import, by differentiating the content that will be imported into different fields.) If you know the data set well, you should be able to tell which data should be put into separate fields because of its reasonably high potential for yielding interesting insights, and what data are unlikely to be worth the effort.

Assuming for the moment that we have two content types, "Person" and "Image," here are some possible ways to enrich those content types using more fields.

5.5.4.1   Person

Sometimes, data that start out as prose don't need to be stored or presented as prose. One could create a set of fields as part of the "Person" content type that capture facets of individuals' lives that are likely to be shared across many individuals. For instance:

> Birth date
>
> Birth location
>
> Schools attended
>
> Marriage date
>
> Marriage location
>
> Spouse
>
> Medical program attended
>
> Medical program graduation date
>
> Residency date
>
> Residency location
>
> Employment locations
>
> Death

This kind of spreadsheet-like list of dates and locations may render the data in the biography more accessible to Drupal for reuse in other visualizations, but it makes the data much less accessible to a human audience. In this case, it would be best to maintain at least a short narrative biography as part of the "Person" content type.

Providing narrative prose is not always necessary, as not all content types are meant to be seen directly by users. If the only place a human is going to encounter the data stored in this content type is as part of a table, map, or other presentation form generated by the Views module, there's nothing wrong with replacing prose with fields of data.

Even if you want to maintain the human-readable prose display, with sentences and paragraphs, it is worth considering whether it makes sense to additionally store some of the data in individual fields, so they can be used in other contexts.

Which bits of data do we want to store as fields? It depends on the questions we want to be able to explore with the database. Sometimes it makes sense to pick only the data that seem most likely to yield interesting results, develop the site with those fields, and go back and add more fields later if the site is a success, and you encounter new streams of funding (or sources of inexpensive or volunteer labor). The more fields you include at first, the greater the risk that you'll never get a sufficiently comprehensive set of data entered in order to launch the site.

For our example site, let's include the following fields as part of the "Person" content type:

> **First name:** Separating the person's given name from their surname will allow you to sort the historical figures alphabetically.
>
> **Middle name(s):** See above.
>
> **Surname:** See above.
>
> **Birth date:** Can be used to identify the person's age at the time of any event in his/her life.
>
> **Death date:** Indicates the end of a person's time line.
>
> **Image:** The image that will be used as a general-purpose thumbnail for the person throughout the site.
>
> **Medical institution attended:** A person in the database has affiliations with many institutions, but the institution where the person received

> medical training is a particularly influential affiliation, and we want to capture that information in a way that we can easily use to sort and group individuals.
>
> **Profession:** The person's profession(s) within the medical field (e.g., doctor, nurse, researcher, etc.).
>
> **Specialization:** The person's medical specialty.
>
> **Biography:** A brief prose biography.

Note that there are no fields within the "Person" content type that allow you to store data from the "Biography" in a more granular way, to enable its use in other visualizations, such as maps or time lines. Sometimes, in the process of enriching content types, it becomes clear that what originally seemed like a single content type should in fact be two or more. In the case of our example site, with the "Person" and "Image" content types, the more natural place to capture some of the information surrounding events in a person's life would be part of the "Person" content type. Such an arrangement would be problematic both on a technical level and on an architectural level, as described below.

It's easy to imagine a set of repeating "event" fields as part of the "Person" content type: a date, a location, a description of the event, and perhaps some other metadata. Repeating groups of fields has been a technical stumbling block for Drupal for many years, though the development and stabilization of the Field Collection module[4] has gone a long way towards addressing this need. While storing event information as part of the "Person" content type is now technically possible with Field Collection, it would complicate the work involved in creating views to display time lines, maps, etc.

The possibility of events involving more than one person clarifies the need for a separate "Event" content type. This data set includes events where two people in the database were equal actors, and if we were to store event information as part of the "Person" content type, we'd have to choose between: 1) having to create the event twice, once for each person involved; and 2) having to choose which person to store the event under, possibly with a pointer (such as a node reference) to the other person.

---

4. https://www.drupal.org/project/field_collection

It is much simpler, and more intuitive, to create an "Event" content type, which includes a node reference pointing to the person or people involved in the event. The node reference field should be part of the event, pointing to the person—and not the other way around—because information about the person or people involved is essential to the event. Information about any specific event is less essential to a complete "Person" profile.

The existence of the "Event" content type may cause you to reevaluate the fields you have as part of your "Person" content type. Since birth and death are both events in a person's life, do you need the "birth" and "death" fields in the "Person" content type?

There's no right answer, and it's fundamentally a matter of preference. For our example site, we want the birth and death dates of the person to appear alongside their biography, and the easiest way for that to happen is to have "birth" and "death" fields as part of the "Person" content type. However, one consequence of that approach is that birth and death information would have to be entered twice: once as an event (so it can show up on time lines) and once as part of the creation of a "person" node. To eliminate this duplication in data entry, you could configure a "List (text)" field as part of the "Event" content type where the person doing data entry can indicate whether the event being entered is a "birth" event or a "death" event via a drop-down menu or set of checkboxes. You could then use Views to have information from the "birth" and "death" events for a person appear on their profile page.

For the purposes of constructing our example site, we will accept data entry duplication as preferable to the additional configuration, and will keep the "birth" and "death" fields as part of the "Person" content type.

5.5.4.2 Event

The "Event" content type will store the following information:

Person: The person or people who were involved in the event.

Date: The date of the event.

Location: Where the event took place.

Description: A description of the event.

Event type: What kind of event it is, e.g., marriage, graduation from medical school, children, etc.

Institution: If relevant, what institution the event is connected to (e.g., if the event is graduation, what institution was the person graduating from?).

Main time line: Should this event appear on the main site time line, or just the personal time line for an individual?

5.5.4.3   Image

The image content type might include the following fields:

Description: A description of the image.

Date: When the image was created (the original image, not the digital surrogate).

Person: People with biographies on the site who are depicted in the image.

Profession: A controlled vocabulary indicating different professions within the medical field (e.g., nurse, physician, researcher, surgeon) depicted in the image.

Institution: A standardized way to capture what institution(s) the image depicts or is connected to.

Once you have those fields, you will want to use the "Automatic title generation" setting (on the content type editing page) provided by the Automatic Nodetitles module[5] to take care of the Drupal title field for the image content type, since many images may not have a canonical title. We will also use Automatic Nodetitles to reduce data duplication for the "Person" content type (since we already have separate fields for the person's first name, middle name, and surname, which make sense to use together to form the Drupal title field), and for the "Event" content type.

---

5. https://www.drupal.org/project/auto_nodetitle

5.6 Summary

This chapter has provided a high-level overview of content types, as well as the considerations that should inform how many content types you should create, as well as their structure. Chapter 6 will take a more hands-on approach to content types, providing instructions about how to create them, and how to add and configure commonly used field types. Chapter 7 will return to the data model for the example site and describe how to map the fields described in each section of 5.5.4 onto specific Drupal field types.

CHAPTER 6

Configuring Content Types and Fields

6.1 Overview

This chapter walks through the concrete steps involved in creating new content types and adding fields. Drupal.org includes hundreds of modules that provide field types, and many fields have their own configuration options in addition to those shared by all Drupal fields. This chapter covers the fields we will need for the example site, along with a handful of other commonly used fields. It also provides an introduction to the Media module, conditional fields, automatic node titles, and Pathauto, which allows you to customize the URLs for content you create.

Chapter 6 is a long and detailed chapter; depending on your project and the data that need to be captured, there may be sections that won't apply to you. The best way to understand how to create content types and configure fields is to actually do it, rather than simply reading about the process. For that reason, it may be best to read sections 6.2 and 6.3, and skim the rest of the chapter and/or treat it as a reference as you create your own content types, or work through chapter 7 if you're building your own version of the example site.

6.2 Creating new content types

Go to *Structure > Content types > Add content type* (/admin/structure/ types/add). Give the content type a name (this should be in the singular;

"Entry" rather than "Entries") and, optionally, provide a description. The description will appear on the "Add content" page, which your users may or may not see, depending on how you configure the site (e.g., you might decide to provide a link in the sidebar for authenticated users to "Add a new project," which takes them directly to the form where they can do that, bypassing the "Add content" page entirely). It's still a good idea to include a brief description of your content type, as a form of documenting your work, for subsequent site developers.

The following settings are provided as vertical tabs underneath the title and description. Additional options may be available there, depending on which modules you install.

6.2.1   Submission form settings

Title field label: How the Drupal title field is labeled; see section 5.4.7 for a discussion of Drupal titles.

Preview before submitting: Whether to allow or require users who are creating content to see how it'll look before it's saved.

Explanation or submission guidelines: Additional text that can appear at the top of the content creation/editing interface.

6.2.2   Publishing options

The default settings are generally fine, and two of the options ("Promoted to front page" and "Sticky at top of lists") are only relevant for specific kinds of Drupal sites, and digital projects tend to not be among them. Note, too, that you're configuring the *default* options for content creation—for any given piece of content, users with the correct permission will be able to make different choices.

Published: Enabled by default. One of Drupal's built-in permission options is "view published content." Having a public site means that you want anonymous (non-logged-in) users to be able to view published content. (Note: there are many ways to refine access permissions, such as only allowing anonymous users to view certain content types; see section 10.5 for more information.) You might want to disable this if, for instance, you want to set up a simple review workflow where a data entry assistant creates content, but you review it before you assign it the status of "published."

Create new revision: Drupal can store multiple versions of a piece of content, reflecting different revisions (much like Wikipedia does). Drupal doesn't do it by default, but if you check this box, it will.

6.2.3 Display settings

Display author and date information: Enabled by default, this puts a bit of text that reads "Submitted by [user's login name] on [date, by default a long-format version like "Sat, 09/07/2013 – 07:25]" towards the top of the piece of content. There are ways to configure this information (e.g., replacing the user's login name with their first and last name, pulled from their user profile,[1] or changing the date format), or you may want to remove it altogether. It's disabled on the default "basic page" content type, for instance; for blog-like content, you may want to display a thumbnail of the user's picture and a brief biography in the sidebar instead; this can be done using two advanced Views concepts, relationships and contextual filters, described in chapter 13.

For almost any content type, except perhaps those that feature user-submitted content where you want to ensure the user is credited, you should disable this.

6.2.4 Comment settings

If you used the default Drupal installation profile, comments are enabled and this section will be available.

Default comment setting for new content

By default, comments are open for new content types. If you don't want users to be able to comment on a particular content type's content, change the "Default comment setting for new content" to "Hidden." Even if you only want comments on only one content type out of ten on your site (e.g., your project's blog, but nowhere else), you'll have to change the default comment setting for every content type where you *don't* want comments.

There's another option for comments, "Closed." This shows all existing comments (if they exist, which may be the case if comments were

---

1. See section 10.4.1

previously set to "Open"), and a message that commenting is now closed. It doesn't make much sense to use this as a default comment setting for new content, because unlike "Hidden," it will display a conspicuous message that comments are closed.

Allow comment titles

Enabled by default, this is a setting that may seem odd if you're familiar with comment interfaces on non-Drupal sites. It's a consequence of the fact that Drupal has its own internal "title" requirement, which applies to comments as well as nodes (content created using a content type); see section 5.4.7 for more information. It may be worth disabling this option for the sake of user familiarity—when people leave comments on the internet, they don't often think of the comments as having a title. Drupal will create its own "title" for the comment for internal purposes, consisting of the first few words of the comment text, and the user won't have to deal with this particular quirk.

6.2.5 Menu settings

You can choose which menus are available for the content creator to choose from when creating a menu link, as well as a default parent for new menu items.

Note that these settings *do not* automatically add new content to a menu, they just define the options available when the content creator specifically chooses to do so. The Auto Menu module[2] can automatically add new content to a menu.

Once you're done with these configuration options, choose "Save and add fields" to save your settings and move on to the area where you can define what information you want your content type to store, and how.

---

2. https://www.drupal.org/node/1138946#comment-5200372; there is currently no official Drupal 7 release, but a functioning development version is available in comment #25 of this thread.

6.3 Adding and configuring fields

There are hundreds of modules on Drupal.org that have been written to store particular kinds of data in particular kinds of ways. The content types you configure, and the fields you use to do so, are a significant part of what separates your site from all the other websites that run Drupal. The Drupal developers have included a few very basic field options as part of the Drupal core, but you should fully expect to install modules that provide additional field options.

6.3.1 "Manage fields" interface

You can access the "Manage fields" interface by going to *Structure* > *Content types* > *[Your content type]* > *Manage fields*. If for some reason you can't access this, make sure that the core "Field UI" module is turned on. This administrative screen allows you to add new fields to your content type, and edit fields that you (or Drupal) have already created. It also introduces some new Drupal jargon:

Label: This is the "human-readable" name of the field, which will appear on the content creation/editing form, and may appear as part of how the content is displayed. The label "Body," for instance, would generally not be displayed as part of the content, but it still appears as part of the editing form.

Machine name: This is generally a variant of the "human-readable" name that meets a stricter set of requirements (lowercase, using underscores instead of spaces, etc). It's used by Drupal's database and code, and appears in places like the CSS classes and IDs (information stored in the HTML to facilitate fine-grained web design) that Drupal generates. All fields you add have a machine name starting with "field_," and Drupal automatically generates a machine name based on the label you create; there's generally no need to change this. While it's possible to change the label of a field later, you can't generally change the machine name.

A word of caution: Drupal substitutes an underscore (_) for any spaces and punctuation you use in the label, and you may introduce problems into your site if you have machine names that end in an underscore. Edit the machine name to remove any trailing underscores that appear after you type the label.

Field type: These are defined by modules; the field types that are available before you install any field-specific modules are part of Drupal's core code. See more below.

Widget: Of all the new Drupal terms, this is the most important to remember, because it is most likely to be useful when searching help forums. A field type defines *what* information is stored, whereas a widget defines *how* that data can be entered. Two fields of the same field type will display the same way by default after the content is saved, but choosing different widgets will change what those fields look like on the content entry/editing form. For instance, when adding a date field (as defined by the Date[3] module), you can choose between a calendar-selector widget and a text-entry widget. The choice changes the experience of the person entering the date, but doesn't change the nature of the data that's being stored by Drupal. If, however, you were to instead create a set of integer fields to store your dates, that would change the nature of the data that are being stored.

Both the default fields (e.g., Drupal title) and those fields you add to the content type can be arranged in any order, by clicking and dragging the "+" sign to the left of the field name up or down (figure 6.1). Be sure to save after you've rearranged fields.

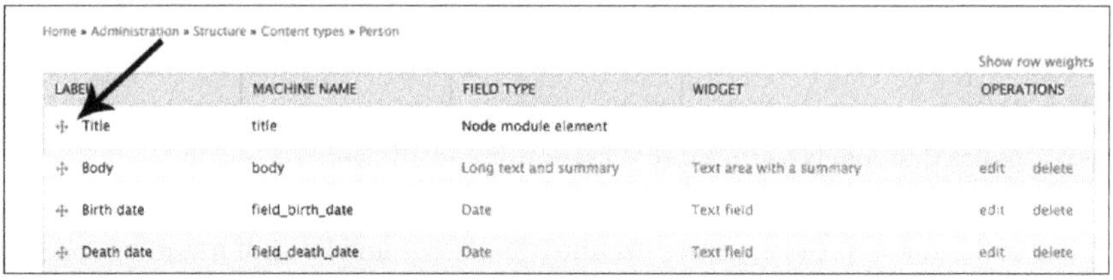

Home » Administration » Structure » Content types » Person

Show row weights

LABEL	MACHINE NAME	FIELD TYPE	WIDGET	OPERATIONS	
Title	title	Node module element			
Body	body	Long text and summary	Text area with a summary	edit	delete
Birth date	field_birth_date	Date	Text field	edit	delete
Death date	field_death_date	Date	Text field	edit	delete

Figure 6.1. Clicking and dragging the "+" sign to rearrange fields.

The order you use for arranging fields here will be reflected in the node creation/editing interface for that content type, but not the display of the nodes you create. A separate order can be created for the display under the "Manage Display" tab (or by going to *Structure > Content types > Your-content-type > Manage display*).

3. https://www.drupal.org/project/date

6.3.2 Adding fields

By default, every new content type comes with two fields: the Title (which you may have labeled something else, but it will retain the machine name "title"), and a Body field. Not every content type will need a "Body" field or a functional equivalent; feel free to delete it if that's the case for your content type.

To add a new field, scroll to the bottom of the list of fields for a given content type, and you'll find an "Add new field" option. Give it a label, select a field type, select a widget (the options available will depend on the field type, and any additional modules you may have installed), and hit "Save." You'll be taken to a series of administrative screens where you can further configure the field. The options available on these pages (particularly the first one, "Field Settings") will vary depending on the field type you've chosen; see below for specific notes on individual field types. Options available for all fields (on the second configuration screen) include the following:

> **Required field:** If a user doesn't enter a value for this field, will they be allowed to save the content, or will they encounter an error saying they need to fill out the field?
>
> **Help text:** Text that appears below the field on the content creation/ editing form.
>
> **Default value:** You don't need to set a default value, but it may be a useful option in some cases.
>
> **Number of values:** Can a user enter multiple values for this field? In some cases this clearly wouldn't make sense: for instance, with a long "description" field—you don't want the user to create two descriptions, and if you want two variants of the description—like one for the general public and one for children—it's better to set those up as separate fields. However, for lists of attributes, or references to other content on the site (e.g., a "similar projects" field), it could make sense to allow the user to enter multiple values.

If you want to add a field that already exists in some other content type (for instance, reusing the basic "Image" field that Drupal configures by default as part of the Article content type), you can select it under "Add existing field." There are some properties you can configure differently for each content type where a field appears, but other properties are defined once for all instances.

6.4 Core Drupal fields

The following default field types are the most commonly useful ones for digital scholarly projects. If you don't see some of these listed, go to the Modules page by clicking on *Modules* in the admin bar and under the list of "Core" modules, make sure that "File," "Image," "List," "Number," "Options," and "Text" are enabled.

6.4.1 Text

This is a field for entering a short amount of text (less than a sentence), like a name, or other information where the user should be able to enter free text—as opposed to selecting from a list—and there's no need to try to standardize people's responses to a common set of terms (e.g., by using an autocomplete interface, though the Autocomplete Widgets[4] module can provide such an interface for text fields). Unless you've installed an extra module like Autocomplete Widgets, the widget will always be "text field." Configuration options include:

Maximum length: By default 255 characters, but you may wish to expand this if your data might be lengthy (e.g., full eighteenth-century book titles).

Text processing: In most cases, you'll want to use the default "Plain text" setting, but if for some reason you need users to be able to enter HTML, you can choose "Filtered text (user selects text format)." See section 8.2 for more about text formats.

Size of textfield: The length the actual text field box on the screen is; this does not impose a limit on how much text the user can put in. The default value, 60, is generally reasonable. Having this box be too long may cause display problems on smaller devices, such as mobile phones and tablets.

4. https://www.drupal.org/project/autocomplete_widgets

6.4.2 Long text

This is a field for entering a larger amount of text—a sentence or more. Unless you specifically need a "summary" version of a text field (e.g,. if you're creating a content type for blog posts, and want to have a "teaser" that's something other than a shortened version of the body), the "Long text" field is the one to choose when you want a large text field.

With long text fields, you may want to make it easier for site contributors to format the text without directly entering HTML. Unlike WordPress, Drupal does not have a WYSIWYG editor (What You See Is What You Get—which provides a set of buttons at the top of the field for things like bold, italics, lists, links, etc.) by default, though this feature will be introduced in Drupal 8. Also unlike WordPress, WYSIWYG editors that you can install in Drupal don't automatically include a button for uploading images or other media that you can embed in the text.

To provide WYSIWYG and media upload options for your long text fields, install and enable the CKEditor[5] and Media[6] modules, and configure them as described in sections 8.2 and 8.3.

Configuration options include:

> **Text processing:** Unlike with text fields, "Filtered text (user selects text format)" is often the right choice for long text fields. Filtered text is necessary if you want to use a WYSIWYG editor for that field.
>
> **Rows:** Defines the actual size of the text box. The default value of 5 is usually fine.

6.4.3 List (text)

This is a field type that lets you define a set of options for users to select. By default, Drupal has two widget options here: 1) check boxes (if more than one value is allowed) or radio buttons (if only one value is allowed), or 2) select list. The select list widget is a little awkward, requiring users to hold down the "Ctrl" key if they want to select multiple options; there are modules like Chosen[7] you can add that provide other widgets that may be easier to use.

---

5. https://www.drupal.org/project/ckeditor
6. https://www.drupal.org/project/media
7. https://www.drupal.org/project/chosen

In many cases, you'll want to use a taxonomy field rather than a text list, particularly if the list of options is long, or will see frequent additions. Also, if the name of individual options might change, a taxonomy is a better choice. For instance, if you begin by listing universities in simple alphabetical order (University of Washington) and later decide to reverse the order (Washington, University of), this will be much easier if that data is stored as taxonomy terms.

As part of the field settings, you have to define an "Allowed values list," one value per line in the format key|label (e.g., `grad_student|Graduate student`). It's best to follow the same conventions as machine names for fields when putting in the key values (lower case, underscores instead of spaces), but the labels can be more "human readable." One downside of these key/label values is that—once users have created content using them—you can no longer change them (in contrast to taxonomy terms, where you can change the name of a term and all existing content using the term will be automatically updated).

On the second configuration page, if you increase the number of values the field can accept to more than one, the widget will change from radio buttons to checkboxes (if you're using the radio buttons/checkboxes widget).

6.4.4   Term reference

This is a field type that allows you to present the user with a set of choices pulled from a Drupal vocabulary. It's similar to the "List (text)" field type, but more flexible (and complex). It has the same widget options as "List (text)," plus "Autocomplete term widget (tagging)," which provides autocomplete suggestions as the user types.

The field settings for the term reference field type allow you to choose which vocabulary to pull terms from. By default, Drupal configures a "tags" vocabulary, but you can add new vocabularies by going to *Structure > Taxonomy > Add vocabulary*. It's best to create the vocabulary before you create the term reference field, so the vocabulary is available for you to reference. If you aren't going to use "Autocomplete term widget (tagging)," you should add some terms to the vocabulary so they appear as options. Additional configuration options for term reference fields are much the same as for the "List (text)" field type.

For details about creating taxonomy terms that use parent-child relationships, and other widgets you can use for term reference fields, see section 7.2.2.10. Chapter 17 addresses taxonomy management.

6.4.5   File and the media browser widget

This is a field for uploading one or more files, including audio and video files. The default "File" widget provides a limited set of self-explanatory options. If you will be uploading files (documents, images, or other media) to your site with any regularity, it's worth installing and configuring the Media module,[8] and using the "Media browser" widget with your "File" fields rather than the default "File" widget. It takes more work upfront, but it makes your files much more usable (by providing a way to store metadata along with files) and reusable (by making it easy for you to insert an image that's been uploaded as part of your site's data into a blog post or announcement, without having to re-upload it to a different node). The "File" field type, combined with the "Media browser" widget, is recommended not only for documents, but also for audio and video uploads, as well as pulling in media from third-party hosting providers (like YouTube or Soundcloud); see section 6.4.5.2.

6.4.5.1   Configuration for uploaded files

Install and enable the Media module. To enable Media, you also have to install the File Entity module.[9] Of the submodules, just enable Media, and if you want to embed media from third-party hosting services, enable Media Internet Sources. Be sure to use the 7.x-2.x version, even though the 7.x-1.x version is currently listed as the recommended release. Go through the configuration settings for the Media module as described in section 6.6.

Add a File field, and choose the "Media browser" widget.

On the next configuration screen, you can choose whether users should have the option of choosing to display the file or not on the node where it's been uploaded; you can check the second checkbox to have them

---

8. https://www.drupal.org/project/media; be sure to install the 7.x-2.x version, rather than the 7.x-1.x version that is listed in green on the module page. There are significant differences between the two, and the 2.x branch is much improved.

9. https://www.drupal.org/project/file_entity

displayed by default. In most cases, you won't need this option. You can also choose an upload destination (private or public files); see section 6.6.1 for a description of these options.

On the following configuration screen, in addition to the usual field configuration options (help text, number of values, etc.), there are a number of Media-specific options.

> **Enabled browser plug-ins:** These determine the user interface of the media browser widget. If users are supposed to upload a file, be sure to enable the "Upload" plug-in. "Library" allows users to choose from files that have already been uploaded, and "My files" shows files that the user has personally uploaded.
>
> **Allowed file types:** The kinds of files the user can upload or select from the library. You can configure the file type options (including what file extensions are associated with which file type) as described in 6.6.2. If you leave these checkboxes unchecked, all options will be available.
>
> **Allowed URI schemes:** Leave this with the default value, which should correspond to the private vs public decision you made in the previous configuration step.
>
> **Allowed file extensions for uploaded files:** Specify the file extensions that users can upload. For file fields, this is limited to TXT (plain-text files) by default, so be sure to change this.
>
> **File directory:** If you want files uploaded in this field to be put in a specific sub-directory of the files directory (e.g., if this is a field for MP3 recordings of lectures, you might want to put them in a "lectures" subdirectory), you can indicate the directory here. If it doesn't already exist, Drupal will create it.
>
> **Maximum upload size:** If you want to restrict the file size (in megabytes, kilobytes, etc.) that users can upload, you can specify that limit here.
>
> **Enable description field:** Leave this unchecked; it is redundant with configuration options provided by the Media module.

6.4.5.2   Configuration for externally hosted files

The "Media browser" widget can be configured for uploading files, pulling in files from third-party hosting sites, or both. If you want to be able to pull in media from third-party sources, be sure to enable the "Media Internet

Sources" module. You should also download, install, and enable the add-on modules for Media that provide integration with the individual media hosting sites you want to use. A full list of these modules[10] is actively maintained on Drupal.org. Options include YouTube,[11] Vimeo,[12] and Soundcloud.[13]

Choose the multimedia browser options you want to enable for the field. If you want to allow people to embed media from third-party providers, be sure to enable the "Web" browser plug-in. This works for YouTube as well as other providers. The "YouTube" browser plug-in is slightly different: it allows users to search YouTube from within your Drupal site and choose a video. If you simply want to be able to paste a YouTube link, the "Web" browser plug-in is sufficient.

Under "Allowed URI schemes," choose the third party providers that you want to enable, along with (or instead of) public or private uploads.

Otherwise, the configuration options are identical to those outlined above.

6.4.6   Image

This is a field for uploading one or more images. While you can use the file field type to upload images, using the image field type provides you with the same configuration options as the file field type (see section 6.4.5.1), plus additional options specific to images.

On the first configuration page, in addition to private/public upload, you can choose a default image for the field, or leave it empty.

On the second configuration page, the "Image" file type is enabled by default (instead of "Document," which happens with "File" fields), and the default file extensions are PNG, GIF, JPG, and JPEG. You can also specify maximum and minimum image resolutions, in pixels.

---

10. https://groups.drupal.org/node/168009
11. https://www.drupal.org/project/media_youtube
12. https://www.drupal.org/project/media_vimeo
13. https://www.drupal.org/project/media_soundcloud

6.5 Fields provided by modules

Many scholarly projects will find at least one of the following field types
(provided by modules) to be useful.

6.5.1 References

The node reference fields provided by the References module[14] are the glue
that holds complex data models together in Drupal. Unless you only need
one content type to store your data, and pieces of data are not connected
to other pieces of data, chances are you'll need a Node Reference field.
Even if not, the References module also includes a User Reference field,
which can be useful on sites with a lot of registered users. For instance,
in order to credit multiple authors on a critical essay, you could have a
multivalued User Reference field, and display that information at the top
while hiding the default "author" information, since Drupal only allows
one "author" per node.

References is one of two Drupal 7 modules that provide this functionality, the other being Entity Reference.[15] Both are widely used, and while
References is only minimally maintained, it works well and integrates well
with other modules like Views. The content type configuration descriptions and the Views configuration in this book are based on the assump-
tion that you will be using References, rather than Entity Reference; the
configuration of the latter is slightly different in both contexts. If in the
future you find it necessary to move to Entity Reference, there is a module
that can help with some of that work,[16] but it would be a painstaking process in any case.

First, install the References module, then enable References, along with
Node Reference and/or User Reference (found under the "Fields" category
on the module page). On the "manage fields" page for your content type
(*Structure > Content types > Your-content-type > Manage fields*), you'll
have an option for creating a "Node reference" or "User reference" field.
Your widget options are "check boxes/radio buttons," "select list," or

---

14. https://www.drupal.org/project/references
15. https://www.drupal.org/project/entityreference
16. https://www.drupal.org/project/entityreference_migration

"autocomplete text field"; in most cases, the number of nodes or users to choose from will be large enough that "autocomplete text field" is your best bet, though "select list" (or one of the modules that provides an improved select list) may be another viable option.

On the field settings page, you can choose what content type can be referenced by this field. If you created a user reference field, you can limit the users by role (by default, "authenticated user" and "administrator" are the only options, but you can create and assign additional roles; see section 10.5), or status (active/blocked). If you have the Views module installed, you'll see a drop-down for "Views – nodes/users that can be referenced." This allows you to use the power of Views to put more complex restrictions on the nodes or users that can be referenced than just content type or role/status, respectively. To use this, you have to first create a view and add the "References" display type; see section 12.3 for more on display types.

If you use the autocomplete widget, on the next page you'll have an option for choosing the type of autocomplete matching. The default value is "Contains" (i.e., it matches based on whether the text you've entered is present anywhere in the node title of candidate nodes), but if the node titles are predictable, changing it to "Starts with" might be more intuitive for people doing data entry.

Depending on your project's data entry workflow, you may want to add the Node Reference Create[17] (noderefcreate) module. Imagine a project where the data consist of letters written between members of a community of 20–30 people, with biographies for each person. Every "Letter" node will have pointers to at least two people: the sender and the recipient. For this to work, those Person entries have to already exist in the system before you can add a Letter that points to them, which has implications for the order in which you enter data. But what if you want to assign one assistant to entering people, and assign another to entering letters, without requiring that they closely coordinate their work? Node Reference Create provides a new widget for node reference fields, which allows you to create pointers to nodes that don't yet exist, creating them in the process.

---

17. https://www.drupal.org/project/noderefcreate

If, for instance, a Person node for Person A has been created, but Person B has not been created yet, the assistant can still enter a letter from Person A to Person B. The autocomplete widget will find a match for Person A in the "author" field. In the "recipient" field, the assistant will enter the name of Person B. No existing Person nodes will appear for them to choose from, but as soon as they save the letter, a Person node will be created for Person B (with no data other than a title) and the Letter node they just created will be linked to it. The only potential issue is that the assistant entering the Person data will need to make sure the Person node they intend to create hasn't already been created by Node Reference Create as a side effect of Letter data entry.

One downside to Node Reference Create is that it doesn't work if the nodes it creates use a content type where all titles are generated using Automatic Nodetitles; see section 6.8 for a work-around.

6.5.2 Date

The Date module[18] provides a field for storing date information. It seems to have been developed with event data in mind—i.e., for current, or near-future dates—and it can easily accommodate information that includes a start date and an end date. The date module is very widely used across many different kinds of Drupal sites, and has been thoroughly tested. Depending on how closely your date information resembles modern event data (with a day, month, year, and optionally, a time), the date module may be sufficient to meet your needs.

If your data includes dates of different granularity (some consisting of year, month, day, and others consisting only of year and month), date ranges (e.g., eighteenth century), or incomplete dates (spring 1642), the Date module can't accurately capture your data. The Partial Date module[19] (see section 6.5.3) is intended to address these situations, but as of version 7.x-1.0-beta1, it has a number of bugs and feature requests that have gone unaddressed for a long time, though individual digital humanities projects have begun to fund further development.

---

18. https://www.drupal.org/project/date
19. https://www.drupal.org/project/partial_date

First, install the Date module, and enable the following submodules (grouped under "Date/Time"):

> Date
>
> Date API
>
> Date Views
>
> Date Popup—optional, if you want to enable a calendar pop-up widget for selecting dates; if you don't enable this, you'll be able to enter the date numerically
>
> Date All Day—optional, if you want to create "all day" events
>
> Date Repeat API and Date Repeat Field—optional, if you want to create repeating dates

Once you've enabled those modules, you'll see a notice about setting up the site time zone and first day of the week (*Configuration > Regional and Language > Regional settings*), as well as the date format settings (*Configuration > Regional and Language > Date and time*). Chances are, you already chose a site time zone when you installed Drupal, and the default first day of the week is Sunday. The default date formats use a 24-hour clock to display the time, and the medium and short formats use year-month-day ordering (e.g., 2013–09–15). If you find these default settings agreeable, you can skip any further configuration here, and head to the content type where you want to add a date field (*Structure > Content types > Your-content-type > Manage fields*).

If you want to change the long, medium, or short format, or if you want to add a new date format, go to *Configuration > Regional and Language > Date and time > Formats > Add format* and enter a format using the PHP conventions, which are linked below the field. For easy reference, here are some examples:

> F j, Y   January 3, 2014
>
> M j, Y   Jan 3, 2014
>
> m/d/y   01/03/14
>
> F j, Y g:i a   January 3, 2014 2:15 pm
>
> M j, Y g:i A   Jan 3, 2014 2:15 PM
>
> m/d/y G:i   01/03/14 14:15

Once you've defined a new format, you can go back to Date and Time (*Configuration > Regional and Language > Date and time*) and change any of the existing Date Types (Long, Medium, or Short) to use that format. Or, you can create a new Date Type that uses the format.

On the fields list for your content type, three new field type options will be available: Date, Date (ISO format), and Date (Unix timestamp). Unless your data are server logs, you should almost certainly choose "Date." You'll have a choice between a text widget and a select widget (unless you enabled the "Date Popup" module, in which case you can also choose that option).

The field settings page lets you specify the granularity of the date data you want to collect. A year is required, but any combination of month, day, hour, minute, and/or second in addition to year is allowed. You can also choose whether to collect an end date, and what time zone to use (for instance, on a site with an international user base that submits events, you might want to select "User's time zone" rather than "Site's time zone," so that when a user adds an event with a time associated with it, it doesn't save the time in the site's time zone, which may be many hours off from the actual time of the event). All data need to match the granularity you specify here, unless you use the Partial Date module.

The second configuration screen looks deceptively generic, but two very important settings are buried under "More settings and values" (beneath the "help text" box): *Date entry* and *Default values*. Date entry is the required order for the text-based inputting of date information: e.g., month first, or day first? There's a list of options, or you can define a custom one. Chances are, most projects using the date field will want to change the default value, which sets the date to "now" (i.e., the current date and time when new content is saved). Even if the date field isn't set to be required—which might leave you to assume that a blank date will simply be left empty, as with most other fields—the Date module will fill in the current date and time unless you change it to "No default value" (figure 6.2).

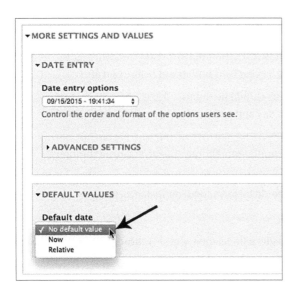

Figure 6.2. Selecting "No default value" for a date field.

6.5.3   Partial date

The Partial Date module is much more flexible than the Date module in how it stores date information. (It is not limited to storing partial dates, despite the name, but it *can* do so, unlike Date.) While it is not very actively maintained, the maintainer accepts patches for new features, and as such it represents an attractive target for digital humanities projects with some funding to contribute to the Drupal module ecosystem. Version 7.x-1.0-beta1 (released in 2012) does not have Feeds integration to support data import, and it isn't compatible with the most flexible time line modules. Some of these issues are already being addressed by digital humanities projects; see the *Drupal for Humanists* site for the latest updates.

6.5.3.1   Partial date formats

The Partial Date module provides two fields: "Partial date and time" and "Partial date and time range." Both draw on module configuration that can be found at *Configuration > Regional and language > Date and time > Partial date formats* (/admin/config/regional/date-time/partial-date-formats). That configuration screen provides four format options you can choose between: Short (default), Medium, Long, and Custom. For each one, you can configure the following:

Uppercase or lowercase for AM/am and PM/pm in times.

Whether to use BC/AD or BCE/CE notation for years, and whether to mark only dates prior to the year 0, or both those before and after.

How different components should be separated (e.g., through the use of "/" to separate month, day and year, and ":" to separate hours and minutes).

The order in which the components should appear, arranged through a drag-and-drop table.

How each component should be formatted; for instance, for "Day" the options are:

Day of the month, 2 digits with leading zeros, 01 through 31.

Day of the month without leading zeros, 1 through 31.

Day of the month, 2 digits with leading zeros with English ordinal suffix.

Day of the month without leading zeros with English ordinal suffix.

A full textual representation of the day of the week.

A textual representation of a day, three letters.

Numeric representation of the day of the week 0 (for Sunday) through 6 (for Saturday).

After you have configured the partial date formats, you can add a "partial date and time" field or a "partial date and time range" field to your content type. The only widget option is "partial date."

On the next configuration screen, there are toggle-down options for "Base estimate values" and "Minimum components."

6.5.3.2 Base estimate values

Base estimate values allow you to define approximate time periods at different levels of granularity (year, month, day, hour, minute, second). These only become relevant if you enable an "estimate year," "estimate day," etc. field on the next configuration page, so if your data don't need approximate dates, you can skip this section. The module provides the following set of default options for year, month, day, and hour. The earliest and the latest time values for the approximate time period are separated by a "pipe" character (|), and a final pipe character separates the time values from the label for the approximate time period:

Year

    -60000|1600|Pre-colonial

    1500|1599|16th century

    1600|1699|17th century

    1700|1799|18th century

    1800|1899|19th century

    1900|1999|20th century

    2000|2099|21st century

Month

    11|1|Winter

    2|4|Spring

    5|7|Summer

    8|10|Autumn

Day

    0|12|The start of the month

    10|20|The middle of the month

    18|31|The end of the month

Hour (note the use of a 24-hour notation for each hour)

    6|18|Day time

    6|12|Morning

    12|13|Noon

    12|18|Afternoon

    18|22|Evening

    0|1|Midnight

    18|6|Night

Any of these options can be changed or deleted, or you can add new ones ("long 18th century," "dawn," etc.).

6.5.3.3 Minimum components

This option allows you to add validation to partial date fields, so that users are required to enter at least as much information as you specify under "Minimum components." If users can leave the partial date field empty, you can leave all the boxes under "Minimum components" unchecked.

If you have chosen a "Partial date and time range" field, the minimum components will all begin with "From" or "To."

6.5.3.4 Field configuration

On the next configuration screen, there is a set of options that only apply to the content type where you've currently added the field. (You can configure these options a different way if you reuse the field as part of a different content type.)

> **Time zone handling:** Addressing time zone handling is mostly a Drupal requirement. Choosing the site time zone for this is generally the best choice.[20]
>
> **Date components/date component estimates:** These are the options that will be available for users to fill in. Uncheck any that are not applicable (e.g., hour, minute, and second are not relevant for many historical dates). By default, the "estimate" options are unchecked. The date components and date component estimates are not mutually exclusive; you could make both available for one or more levels of granularity (e.g., to allow either "April" or "spring"), but if you do include both, be sure to include some guidance in the help text for the field so the people doing data entry know what you're expecting. For instance, if they know the precise month, should they also include the corresponding estimate information, so it says both "April" and "spring," or is the estimate only for when no more precise information is available?
>
> **Increments:** Because partial date fields provide a drop-down menu for entering data other than the year, the second/minute increments configuration allows you to choose between 1, 2, 5, 10, 15, and 30.

---

20. The different options do have some implications: for instance, if you are creating fields for an upcoming event with a specified time, Drupal may list the event along with "past events" even before the event has started if time zone handling is set to UTC but the event takes place in California.

Short/long description: These add a supplemental field for a textual description of the date, which can be used along with or in lieu of storing the date in a numeric way when that is impossible or undesirable. This makes it possible for you to store vague, arguable, or poetic dates (e.g., "the peak of Enlightenment philosophy," "when the nightingales sing") alongside more precise dates.

Approximate checkbox: Including a checkbox to indicate that a date is approximate may be useful when your data include a mix of precise and approximate dates, but you don't want to go all the way to using date estimate fields.

Hide the "remove date" checkbox: The "remove date" checkbox provides an easy way to remove a date, without having to individually clear out each of the dropdown fields. In most cases, it's best to keep it available.

In-line help: This allows you to include additional help information for the short/long description fields, the approximate checkbox, the dropdown menu for specifying dates, or the "Remove date" checkbox.

You can also define a default value for the partial date field, though in most cases that won't be relevant.

As with all fields, you can choose how many values to allow (one, up to 10, or "unlimited").

6.5.4 Link

The Link[21] module allows you to add fields for URLs. There are no widget choices or field settings; all configuration is done on the second page.

The default settings are fairly sensible. By default, the user must enter a URL (and Drupal will make sure it's valid), and they can optionally enter a title. You can make the title required, or set a static title (e.g., if this is a field for a link to a user's personal website, you could just set the title to be "Personal website").

---

21. https://www.drupal.org/project/link

6.5.5 Geofield

There are multiple modules and groups of modules that provide mapping functionality in Drupal.[22] The Geofield[23] field type is compatible with a majority of these approaches. It has multiple prerequisites; you must first install geoPHP,[24] and you also need the Geocoder[25] module to turn the text field indicating a location into coordinates that can be stored in the geofield. Install and enable these three modules, as well as the Geofield Map module (part of the Geofield module, but found under the "Other" section, along with Geocoder, on the Modules page).

In your content type, create a text field where the text indicating the name of the location will be stored. This text can be as specific as an address, or as general as a country, and the Geocoder module will attempt to find reasonable coordinates to correspond to what you've entered.

Next, create a Geofield that will correspond to the text field, and choose the widget "Geocode from another field." While text fields may be the most intuitive source for geocoding, Geofield can also work with geographic information stored in the EXIF data of images stored in an image field (e.g., from a cell phone photo that recorded the phone's GPS data). Configuration options include:

Geocode from field: Select the text field you just created.

Geocoder: Select the service you want to use for geocoding. Selecting Google Geocoder gives you access to advanced configuration settings, such as rejecting results at certain levels of precision (e.g., if you only want precise address coordinates, you can reject the results from Google if they are approximate).

Multivalued input handling: By default, if the text field you're geocoding from has multiple values, it will encode one point for every value of the text field.

Geofield can also be used by itself, without involving the Geocoder. If you know the geographic coordinates of a location, you can choose that

---

22. A comparison of these modules is available on drupal.org: https://www.drupal.org/node/1704948

23. https://www.drupal.org/project/geofield

24. https://www.drupal.org/project/geophp

25. https://www.drupal.org/project/geocoder

Geofield widget. If you have data encoded as Well Known Text (WKT, a markup language for encoding objects on a map), there's a Geofield widget that supports that, too.

6.5.6 Field group

Field group[26] is a module that allows you to display groups of fields together, on the node creation/editing form and on the node display. Field groups have to be set up separately for the node creation/editing form (which is done on the "manage fields" interface where you add new fields), to impact the data entry form, and on the "manage display" interface, to impact how the data stored in the node are displayed. Just because a field appears in a field group under "manage fields" does not mean that field group will carry over to "manage display" or impact how the data are displayed; it's simply a way to organize the data entry form.

It is also important to understand what the field group module does not do. It does not create a new "thing" in the Drupal database with independent, field-like properties. Putting fields inside a field group together doesn't create any real relationship between them. For example, let's say you have two fields—a user reference field ("contributor") and a text list ("activity," with options like "author," "illustrator," "editor," etc). You want your content type to potentially have multiple contributors, with each contributor having a corresponding "activity." You may be tempted to try putting "contributor" and "activity" in a *field group* together, and searching for a way to make that field group have multiple values—the same way Drupal provides you with an "add another" button when you have an autocomplete field that can store multiple values. This won't work—it isn't possible to make a multivalued field group. There have been efforts among Drupal developers to address this "multigroup" problem for many years; the most widely adopted option for Drupal 7 is a separate module called Field Collection,[27] but it has some quirks and shortcomings. See the *Drupal for Humanists* site for more on Field Collection, as well as configuration details for field groups.

---

26. https://www.drupal.org/project/field_group
27. https://www.drupal.org/project/field_collection

6.6 Media

The Media module[28] includes more than just a widget; it also provides a new type of "thing" for storing content, equal in a sense to content types or taxonomy vocabularies. A media file can have metadata that are stored with the file you've uploaded (or pulled in from an online hosting site, like YouTube or Soundcloud), and the metadata profile can vary depending on the type of media (i.e., you can have a one set of fields for describing images, and another for describing documents). These instructions are based on the 2.x version of the Media module, which is listed in yellow as an "other version" on the module page. It is rapidly developing, but significantly improved from the recommended 1.x branch.

Once you've installed and enabled the Media module, you can add media files by going to *Content > Files* (admin/content/file) and clicking the "Add file" link in the upper left. You can also add files by using a field within a content type, where you have enabled the "Media browser" widget for that field. Regardless of which option you choose, any media file that has been uploaded to the site will appear on the files list at *Content > Files*.

6.6.1 Configuring the file system

Go to *Configuration > Media > File system*. The default locations for public, private, and temporary files are fine unless you have a specific reason to change them. You may, however, wish to change the default download method. By default, the "public" method is enabled. This means that if a user who is not logged in gets the URL of a file (for instance, if someone emails it to them), they can download it, even if the link for that file only appears on a page with restricted access. Using the private file method allows you to make use of Drupal's permissions system (see section 10.5) to restrict access to files.

6.6.2 Configuring file settings

Go to *Configuration > Media > File settings* (admin/config/media/file-settings). On this page, you can set a maximum upload size, if you have

---

28. https://www.drupal.org/project/media

concerns about server space. You can also modify the default list of allowed file extensions (.xml, for instance, is not on the list by default). Note that you can override this list by enabling, or restricting, file extensions for each field where you use the "Media browser" widget.

Towards the bottom, under "File upload wizard," you should check the box for "Skip scheme selection" (figure 6.3). This will eliminate a potentially confusing step in the upload process where users are asked to choose between the public and private download method (described in 6.6.1). Decisions about public vs. private download are generally best made at the project level, and users should not be asked to decide this every time they upload a file.

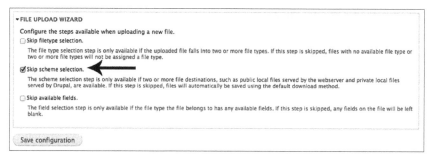

Figure 6.3. Selecting "Skip scheme selection" as part of the Media configuration screen.

6.6.3 Configuring media browser settings

If you go to *Configuration > Media > Media browser settings* (admin/config/media/browser), you can make various changes to the media browser interface. You can choose to restrict some of the options, selecting among "Upload," "Library" (previously uploaded media), and "My files," (files that the current user has uploaded); if you've enabled the Media Internet Sources module, you'll also see "Web" (for putting in a URL to media on a supported site). Some of the modules that provide integration with third-party media hosting providers add further options, such as "YouTube" (which allows users to search YouTube from within Drupal).

You can use the "File directory for uploaded media" field to create potentially elaborate directory structures for your media files, rather than having them in one large directory. You can use tokens (as illustrated in section 6.7) to do things like create directories for each date, and within the directory for a given date, for each user who uploads something on that date. In most cases, though, it's fine to leave this blank.

6.6.4   Configuring file type profiles

Go to *Structure > File types* (admin/structure/file-types). By default, there are four file types: Image, Video, Audio, and Document. Each of them has an associated "name" field (required, just like Drupal's node titles), but the Image file type also has an alt-text field and a title-text field. Including a description in the alt-text will improve the accessibility of your site. The title-text field is for additional information that appears when a user hovers their mouse over the image.

For most cases, these four types and their existing fields are sufficient. For sites with a particular focus on media, however, you may want to consider adding other fields. If many of your images come from archives, you may want to add a "Source" field to the image file type, to store information about the source archive in a way that's directly associated with the image, regardless of where or how you display the image on the site. If you have multiple different kinds of images (for instance, those taken during fieldwork and those from archives) in the same site, you can create additional image file type profiles, each with its own set of fields for capturing important metadata about the file. In such a case, after you upload a new image, the Media upload interface will ask which kind of file type it should belong to, and will then present you with the correct set of metadata fields.

To add fields to an existing profile, simply choose the "manage fields" link for the profile; this will bring you to an interface that looks just like the "manage fields" interface for content type, described above.

6.7 Conditional fields

The Conditional Fields[29] module allows certain fields to remain hidden until "triggered" by a value entered in another field. For instance, if you have a text-list field, and one of the options is "other," you can have a text

---

29. https://www.drupal.org/project/conditional_fields

field that will appear if the user selects "other," to allow them to be more specific.

When you have installed and enabled the Conditional Fields module, a new tab, "Manage dependencies," appears when you're editing a content type, along with "Edit," "Manage Fields," "Manage display," etc.

To set up a dependency relationship, first create all the fields that will be involved: both those that will appear/disappear, as well as those in which values will trigger the behavior. Dependencies can be set up for each content type (by clicking on the "Manage dependencies" tab, alongside "Manage fields") or they can be configured on the screen that shows all dependencies for all content types, taxonomy terms, comments, and user profiles (*Structure > Field dependencies*).

On the dependency configuration screen, the field that will appear and disappear is listed first, and is referred to as the *dependent* field. The field that will trigger that behavior is the *dependee* field, and is listed second. The third column describes the behavior; the default options—that the dependent *is visible* when the dependee "*has value . . .*" (where that value is specified on the next configuration screen)—will generally be the one you'll need to use (figure 6.4). If you explore the other options, you can see that you could use Conditional Fields to trigger other behaviors as well, such as emptying a field (or unchecking a checkbox) when the user enters a value in another field, etc.

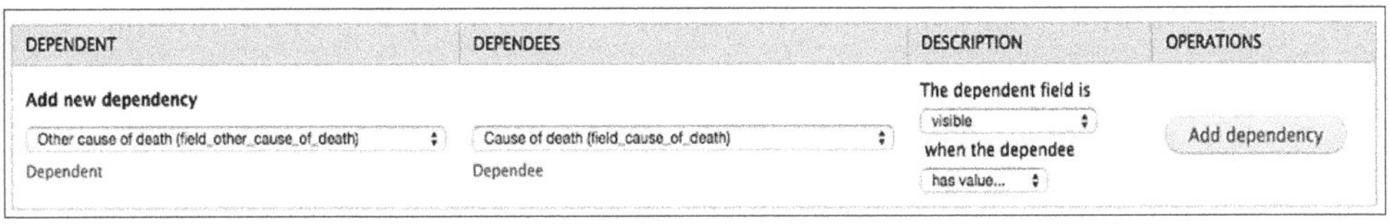

DEPENDENT	DEPENDEES	DESCRIPTION	OPERATIONS
Add new dependency		The dependent field is	
Other cause of death (field_other_cause_of_death) ⇕	Cause of death (field_cause_of_death) ⇕	visible ⇕ when the dependee	Add dependency
Dependent	Dependee	has value... ⇕	

Figure 6.4. The dependency configuration screen.

After you click "Add dependency," the second configuration screen lets you define the conditions (figure 6.5). Because our *dependee* field is a text list, and we only want one value ("other") to trigger this field, we can use the default method "Insert value from widget" and select "other" from the radio buttons.

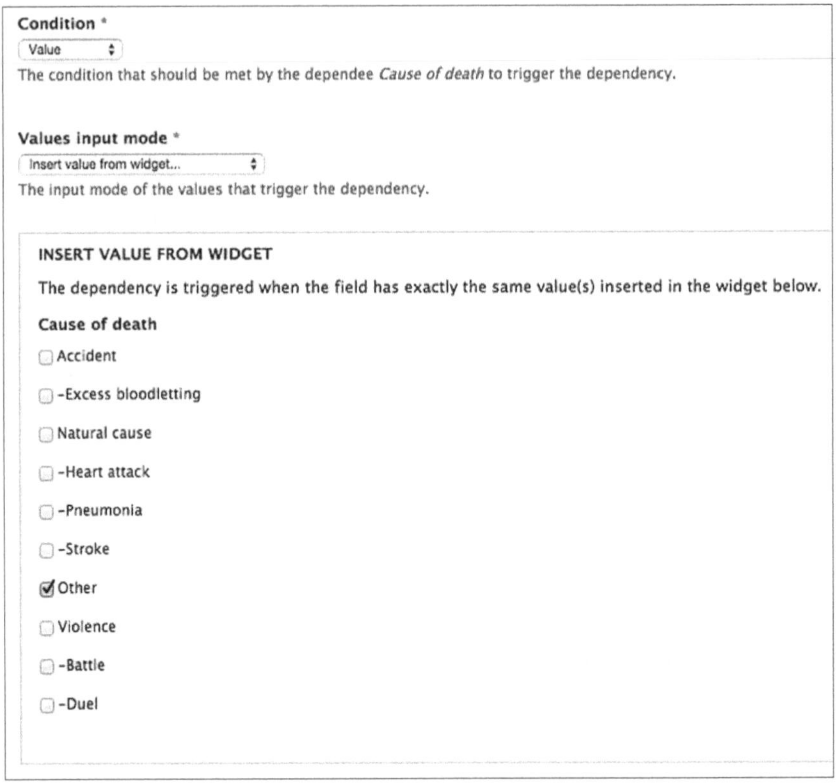

Figure 6.5. Selecting a value from a text list field.

If the dependee field is a term reference field (pointer to a taxonomy), the configuration is slightly more complicated due to a bug in the Conditional Fields module (as of 7.x-3.0-alpha1). In order for Conditional Fields to work with taxonomy fields, for the "Values input mode," choose from one of the options under "Set of values." "Any of these values" is probably the most useful. Unfortunately, you can't enter the name of the taxonomy term(s) you want to use as a trigger, you have to find the term ID.

For the vocabulary you're using for this term reference field, go to *Structure > Taxonomy > Your-taxonomy-name.* You'll see a list of all the terms in the vocabulary. Hover the mouse over the "edit" button for a term you want to use as a trigger. At the bottom of some browsers, you'll see the URL for that link appear; part of that URL is the term ID (figure 6.6). If your browser doesn't support this, click on the edit link and look at the URL bar of that page for the same information.

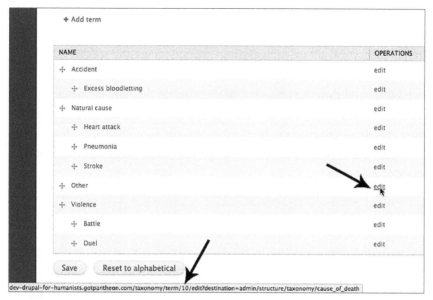

Figure 6.6. The term ID appears as part of the URL path when you hover your mouse over the "edit" link.

In this case, the term "Other" has the term ID "10," so we enter that value in the "Set of values" box (figure 6.7).

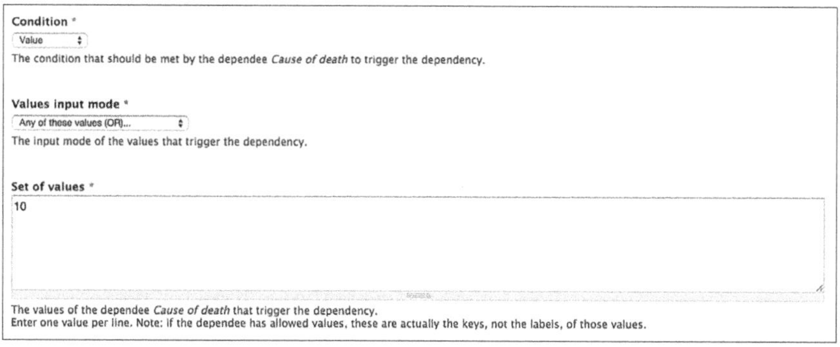

Figure 6.7. Entering a term ID into the "Set of values" box.

A dependent field can have multiple dependees (i.e., it can be triggered by multiple different fields). For instance, you might have a "dissertation topic" field that appears as part of a graduate student's profile if their enrollment date was more than 4 years ago (based on an "enrollment year" date field), or if they've chosen members of their dissertation committee (if there's a value in a user-reference field for "dissertation committee"). In this case, you'd set up each of these dependencies and specify "OR" in the "Interaction with other dependencies" field. "AND" requires that both conditions be met, and "XOR" requires that one be met and other not (if they've specified members of their dissertation committee, their enrollment date has to be *less* than 4 years ago; alternately, if their enrollment date is *more* than 4 years ago, the dissertation committee field should be empty).

6.8 Configuring Automatic Nodetitles

The Automatic Nodetitles module populates Drupal's required "title" field (see section 5.4.7) using other data that already exist as part of a node. This is particularly useful when there is no natural "title" for a particular piece of content, or where the data that would make up the title are already being stored more granularly in other fields.

Install and enable the Automatic Nodetitles[30] module, as well as the Token[31] module, if you haven't already. A new section called "Automatic title generation" will appear on the content type configuration page, above "Display settings," "Comment settings," and the other configuration options described in section 6.2.

Even though Automatic Nodetitles will be available as part of the first step of the content type configuration process (i.e., before you add fields), you should wait to configure Automatic Nodetitles until after you've created the fields you'll want to use as part of the automatic title generation. Once you've added those fields to your content type (see section 6.3), return to the "Edit" area for your content type (*Structure > Content types > Your-content-type*) to access the "Automatic title generation" settings.

---

30. https://www.drupal.org/project/auto_nodetitle
31. https://www.drupal.org/project/token

In most cases where you're using Automatic Nodetitles, it's best to choose the option "Automatically generate the title and hide the title field." That will ensure that your nodes are titled more consistently than if you leave open the possibility for the authors of a node to enter a title on their own. If you are using the noderefcreate module (section 6.5.1), you will need to use the "Automatically generate the title if the title field is left empty" option for any content types that might have nodes created using noderefcreate (e.g., if you are potentially creating Person nodes as part of creating Letter nodes, be sure that the Person content type uses this setting). Once you've selected an option, fill in the pattern you want to use for the automatically generated titles.

If you've installed and enabled the Token module, you'll see a table below the "Pattern for the title" box with arrows that can be toggled to see more options (figure 6.8). To access the fields you've created, click the toggle arrow next to "Nodes."

Figure 6.8. Automatic title generation configuration, with token list.

If you first click in the "Pattern for the title" box, clicking on the blue token link text that corresponds to a field you want to appear as part of the pattern will put that token text into the pattern box. You can also type text directly into that box. Because we want the Person nodes to have titles that include their full name (which we've broken up into individual fields to enable sorting by last name), our pattern for the title might look like:

```
[node:field_first_name]  [node:field_middle_name]
              [node:field_last_name]
```

Things become more complicated if you want to include dates as part of automatically generated titles. Imagine a project where the data consist of quotes by famous people about one another. This project uses a Person content type to capture information about the people, and the Quote content type to capture the quote, pointers to the people involved, and a date.

By default, a date field token includes hours, minutes, and seconds (all "00" if unspecified), and takes the format *year-month-day hours:minutes:seconds*. The result would be: "Emily Dickinson about Louisa May Alcott 1870–06–28 00:00:00." This isn't ideal, but depending on how you want to display the content with automatically generated node titles, it may not be a problem (for instance, if you use Views to display the quotes as part of a Person node). If you do want to use date fields as part of automatically generated titles that users *will* see, some additional configuration is needed.

For the content type where you want to include a date as part of the automatic node titles, go to the "Manage display" page (*Structure > Content types > Your-content-type > Manage display*). Towards the bottom of the screen, toggle down the "Custom display settings" option, check the box for "Tokens," and save. This will create a new subsection for configuring the display of tokens; follow the instructions in section 9.2.2 to select a better-looking date format. The date format you choose will be used for the automatic node titles of any subsequent nodes you create.

If at some point you decide to change the pattern you use for your automatically generated titles, the existing nodes that have had their titles generated automatically won't immediately be updated. However, the next time one of those nodes is saved, its title will be updated. If you want to update all of the old nodes at once, you can use Views and the Views Bulk Operations (VBO) modules to resave all the nodes; for more on how to configure VBO, see the *Drupal for Humanists* site.

Entity Tokens, available as part of the Entity API module,[32] can allow you to create much more complex patterns for your automatic node titles, including pulling in data from separate nodes referenced using a node reference field (section 6.5.1). Using Entity Tokens can cause some unusual bugs; see the *Drupal for Humanists* site for a full description of when to use Entity Tokens, and when to avoid it.

If you decide you no longer need Automatic Nodetitles and disable the module, the Drupal title field will become visible. All the titles that have been automatically generated will be editable, as if they were normal, user-generated titles.

6.9 Improving node URLs with Pathauto

As you create your content types, it might make sense to enter in some dummy data, to see if the content type form is behaving the way you expect. However, before you begin entering the actual data for your project, you should install, enable, and configure the Pathauto module.

Pathauto lets you establish patterns that will be used to generate the visible URLs for the nodes you create. Without Pathauto, nodes you create will have a URL that looks like "yoursite.org/node/123," where the number after "node" reflects the order in which the node was created. Using Pathauto, you can set up URLs that are more meaningful, such as "yoursite.org/people/emily-dickinson" or "yoursite.org/quotes/louisa-may-alcott/emily-dickinson-1870–06–28." Keep in mind that these more user-friendly URLs are actually URL aliases: node/123 will always work as a way to access the node with the node ID of 123, no matter how you configure Pathauto. However, you should resist the temptation to treat the node ID as a long-term, persistent identifier; at some point, you may need to rebuild your site, or upgrade it using a technique that involves exporting

---

32. https://www.drupal.org/project/entity

and reimporting all content, which would change the node ID. See the *Drupal for Humanists* site for more on Drupal and persistent identifiers.

The configuration of Pathauto is much like the configuration of Automatic Nodetitles (see section 6.8); both require the Token module. Once you've enabled Pathauto, go to *Configuration > Search and Metadata > URL aliases > Patterns*. Each content type and taxonomy vocabulary will be listed, and you can set up a pattern for the URL alias for each one. If you toggle down the "Replacement Patterns" link, you'll have the same token navigation interface available on the Automatic Nodetitles configuration screen. If you first click inside the field for any content type, you can then click on blue token links under "Replacement Patterns," and they'll automatically appear in the path field for that content type.

6.10 Summary

This chapter has covered the specific steps needed to create content types, add fields to them, and configure common field types. It has also addressed common modules that enhance content type configuration, such as Conditional Fields, Automatic Nodetitles, and Pathauto. Chapter 7 will return to the example site, refining the earlier data modeling by mapping the information stored in each content type to specific fields, and creating and configuring those fields. If you aren't creating your own copy of the example site, you can use the information covered in chapter 6 to configure your own project site and move on to chapter 8. If you have a difficult time choosing between different field types for storing certain kinds of data on your own site, it may be helpful to skim through chapter 7, which discusses trade-offs between different approaches.

CHAPTER 7

Further Data Modeling and Applied Content Type Creation

7.1 Overview

This chapter builds on the preliminary data model for the example site, established in section 5.5, by discussing how to select a field type for each piece of information that will be stored in each content type. There is not always an obvious choice, and this chapter discusses trade-offs of various approaches. Even if you aren't building the example site, it may be worth looking through this chapter for relevant factors to consider when making choices on your own site.

To walk through this chapter, you will need to install numerous modules. You can install them on an as-needed basis (each is mentioned individually below), or you can begin by installing and enabling the following modules: Automatic Nodetitles,[1] Date,[2] Chosen (including the library),[3] Entity API[4] (and Entity Tokens, which comes with it), File Entity,[5] Geocoder,[6] Geofield,[7] GeoPHP,[8] Link,[9] Media (version 2.x),[10] Partial date,[11] and References[12] (and Node Reference, which comes with it).

---

1. https://www.drupal.org/project/auto_nodetitle
2. https://www.drupal.org/project/date
3. https://www.drupal.org/project/chosen
4. https://www.drupal.org/project/entity
5. https://www.drupal.org/project/file_entity
6. https://www.drupal.org/project/geocoder
7. https://www.drupal.org/project/geofield
8. https://www.drupal.org/project/geophp
9. https://www.drupal.org/project/link
10. https://www.drupal.org/project/media
11. https://www.drupal.org/project/partial_date
12. https://www.drupal.org/project/references

7.2 Person content type

The person content type stores information about individual people in the database. Create a new content type by going to *Structure > Content types > Add content type* (/admin/structure/types/add), and naming it "Person."

7.2.1 Content type settings

Under "Display settings," uncheck "Display author and date information"; it doesn't matter who enters the information about people (figure 7.1). Under "Comment settings," set "Default comment setting for new content" to "hidden." Otherwise, the default settings are fine. Hit "Save and add fields" at the bottom of the page.

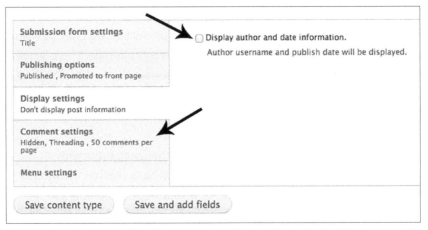

Figure 7.1. Arrows indicate unchecking the box for "Display author and date information" in the "Display settings" section, and the "Comment settings" section where comments have been set to "hidden."

7.2.2 Fields

7.2.2.1 Given name

This should be stored as a text field, with the label "Given name." All the default settings (255 maximum characters, 60 text field length, "plain text" text processing, 1 value) are fine. You should check the "Required field" box towards the top of the second configuration page to ensure that any assistants helping with data entry don't accidentally omit it, since you will use it as part of the automatic node titles. You may also want to put in some help text (which will appear under the field), although this field is easy to understand.

7.2.2.2   Middle name(s)

See configuration for "Given name," above. When you create this field, you should edit the machine name (`field_middle_name_s_`) so it just reads "`field_middle_names`." Having an underscore at the end may cause unexpected errors.

Because not all people in the database have a middle name, this field should *not* be required. However, some people in the database have more than one middle name. You could handle this by increasing the number of values to 2 (if no one has more than two middle names), but doing so may needlessly complicate the data entry screen. If you're not going to use the multiple-middle-name data for anything (e.g., displaying only those people with more than one middle name, or listing all the second middle names), it's simpler to have a single field and include instructions as part of the help text indicating that when a person has multiple middle names, they should be entered together, separated by a space.

7.2.2.3   Surname

See configuration for "Given name," above. This field should be required.

7.2.2.4   Biography

Edit the existing "Body" field and change the label to "Biography." All other settings are fine.

7.2.2.5   Birth date

All of the people in the database have full, known birth and death dates (day, month, year). This consistency allows you to use a "Date" field (just "Date," not one of the other variants) to store this information. If you don't see "Date" as one of the options for field type, make sure you have the modules described in section 6.5.2 enabled. Use the label "Birth date" and the widget "text field." Since some of the people in the database were born and/or died in the nineteenth century, the "select list" widget option would require a lot of scrolling, so it's easier to just type the values in.

Under "Date attributes to collect," choose only "year," "month," and "day" and uncheck the boxes for "hour" and "minute."

On the next configuration screen, you can enter help text if you want, but be sure to toggle down "More settings and values" right under the help text box. Select the date entry format you want to use (see section 6.5.2 for how to configure additional date entry formats), and change the default date from "Now" to "No default value." That way, if the person doing data entry needs to temporarily leave the birth date blank, Drupal won't erroneously fill in the current date as the person's birth date.

7.2.2.6 Death date

Should have the same configuration as the "birth date" field.

7.2.2.7 Image

There are two ways you could handle the storage of an image to be used as a thumbnail for the person throughout the site. The most straightforward would be to create an image field that allows you to upload an image file as part of the Person node. The image would automatically appear alongside the other information in the Person content type. The downside to this approach is that you'd end up with two different groups of images, with different metadata about each. On the Person content type, you could add some extra fields to capture information about the image you've uploaded for the person (description, date, etc.) but that information is not necessarily relevant when the picture appears in the context of the Person node, and in creating those fields, you're significantly duplicating the Image content type.

The other approach would be to create a node reference field for the person's thumbnail image, and point to an Image node. This approach would require you to use Views (and possibly other modules, such as Display Suite) to get the thumbnail image to appear on the person's profile, and pulling in the person's thumbnail image elsewhere would require more complex views.

Using the Media module neutralizes the major disadvantages of including an image field as part of the Person content type, because it allows you to associate metadata about the image with the image file itself, which saves you from having to include those fields as part of a content type. On the example site, we won't take advantage of configuring complex file type profiles (i.e., adding fields to the upload form for different media, as described in section 6.6.4), but if it were important to capture information about the date when the thumbnail images were taken, you could add a date field to the image file type profile, and store that information there instead of as part of the Image content type, which would make the date field available both for images stored in the Image content type, and those stored as thumbnails for individual people.

To simplify the display configuration, we will add an image field to the Person content type. Since Drupal already provides an image field called "Image" by default, we will use it. Under "Add existing field," choose "Image: field_image (Image)," and choose "Media browser" as the widget. If you don't see "Media browser" as an option, follow the instructions in section 6.4.5.1 and section 6.6. Save.

All the default settings related to the Media module (enabled browser plug-ins, allowed file types, allowed URI schemes) are fine. Under "File directory," enter "people." This will put all the images you upload to the Person content type into a "people" subdirectory within your files folder. All other default settings are fine.

7.2.2.8 Medical institution attended

The purpose of having the medical institution the person attended as a field in the "Person" content type is to make it easy to sort and group individuals by where they received medical training. There are a number of possible field choices for capturing these data:

Text (list)

Cons: This is a terrible option; you'd have to prepopulate the options with the name of every single institution that anyone attended for medical training. You'd then have to scroll through all those options when entering a quote (unless you use a module like Autocomplete Widgets).

Text field

Pros: You can populate this field as needed, as opposed to having to prepopulate with a text (list) field.

Cons: It's just text, and other than searching using that text field, it's not actually connected to anything else in the database. This might be less of a problem for some institutions (e.g., if there are institutions that only appear in the database once, connected to one individual), but it limits what you can do with the data. If you wanted to look at all the people who did a medical residency through a hospital associated with the institution where they received medical training, it would be difficult to pull together the data you need. Additionally, a text field provides you with no way to attempt to control for misspellings and variation in the name of an institution, or easily merge entries that use a nonstandard name variant into the correct variant.

Term reference field

Pros: You can populate this field as you enter data, and/or seed the list with commonly referenced institutions. Term reference fields can use an auto-complete widget, to cut down on spelling variation. You can also change the name of the institution (e.g., to use acronyms) after the fact without having to update the nodes that point to that term, since the underlying pointer (to a system-internal identifier for each term) remains the same. It's also fairly easy to merge spelling variants, if they arise, into a single preferred term; see section 17.6. The default display of a term reference field is a link for the term, where clicking on the link takes you to all nodes (People, Images, etc.) that use that term, which is a reasonable and fairly useful way to display the data. You can also easily modify the default display using Views. In addition, if there's a little bit of extra information you need to store as part of each term (for instance, the geographic location of the institution), you can add fields to taxonomy terms.

Cons: Fields in taxonomy terms are not as easy to access when developing Views that use a lot of data stored in nodes. If you want to store a lot of additional information about taxonomy terms (in addition to geographic coordinates, when the institution was founded, an extensive description, images, etc.), you should consider whether this indicates that the information (in this case, information about institutions) is a sufficiently important part of the data to merit being treated as an additional content type, in which case you'd use a node reference field to point to it, rather than a term reference field.

In this case, we don't have so much information about institutions that we need to treat them as content types. Treating institutions as taxonomy terms and using a term reference field to point to them will be sufficient.

To streamline the configuration process, you should first create a vocabulary called "Institutions". Go to *Structure > Taxonomy > Add vocabulary* (admin/structure/taxonomy/add), and name it "Institutions." You can put in an optional description; this will only appear as part of some administration screens, but it's helpful for future maintainers of the site to have that information available. In this case, the description would indicate that these are institutions with which people in the database were affiliated in some way; you *don't* want to be more specific and say that it's for institutions where people received medical training. You'll use this same set of terms for the "Institution" field as part of the "Event" content type, and the relationship between the person and the institution there can vary a great deal.

Once you save your new vocabulary, you could add some terms to help seed it, but since we'll be using the autocomplete widget for this term reference field, the easiest way to populate the vocabulary is to just enter institutions as they arise as part of data entry for the Person content type. As such, let's return to configuring the Person content type *Structure > Content types > Person > Manage fields* (/admin/structure/types/manage/person/fields).

Add a new field, "Medical institution attended," and choose "Term reference field" and "Autocomplete term widget (tagging)." On the next configuration screen, choose "Institutions" as the vocabulary. Provide some help text if desired, and also set the number of values to "Unlimited," in order to accommodate any historical figures who attended more than one institution. Save.

7.2.2.9 Profession

See "Medical institution attended," above—the same discussion generally applies here. In this case, a text list field would not be ridiculous, since the list of types of medical professions is much smaller than the list of relevant institutions. One could potentially imagine going to the other extreme, and having a content type "Profession" that includes long essays on what it meant to be a doctor or nurse, with additional fields for storing bibliographic references to scholarly literature on the topic. In this case, a term reference field pointing to a "Professions" vocabulary (like the "Institutions" one described above) is still probably the best fit, although a text list field would be a reasonable option. It largely depends on whether you want the person's profession to appear, by default, as a clickable link that shows you all other people with that same profession. If so, use a term reference field. If you want it to just be plain text, you can use a text list.

Create the "Professions" vocabulary, but after you save it, click on the "Add term" link corresponding to "Professions." Enter the professions you want to provide as options, one at a time, saving after each one. Section 17.5 addresses how to import taxonomy terms in bulk.

Physician

Surgeon

Nurse

Medical researcher

When you're done, return to managing fields for your Person content type.

Add a term reference field called "Profession," but this time choose the "Check boxes/radio buttons" widget. On the next page, choose the "Professions" vocabulary.

On the next configuration page, enter some help text, and allow unlimited values. Some people in the database have more than one professional role, but you don't necessarily want to guess ahead of time what the maximum potential number of roles is. Making this change will turn the default radio buttons into checkboxes on the node creation/editing form. Save the field.

7.2.2.10   Specialization

Specialization is an intermediate case between "Profession" and "Medical institution attended." There are enough options—including nested options—that the checkboxes used for "Profession" might be cumbersome. Text list fields don't support parent/child term relationships, so that is not a good option in this case. At the same time, there are few enough options that the autocomplete text widget might be overkill. The autocomplete text widget would also allow people to add new terms, which you may not want.

The best way to store these data is going to be as vocabulary and taxonomy terms. Create a new vocabulary, as described above, called "Specializations" and populate it with terms as follows:[13]

Family practice

General surgery

   Cardiothoracic surgery

   Trauma surgery

Internal medicine

   Cardiology

   Endocrinology

   Gastroenterology

   Hematology

   Oncology

   Rheumatology

Obstetrics & gynecology

Pediatrics

Psychiatry

Urology

To create parent/child term relationships (e.g., indicating that Cardiology is a subterm of Internal medicine), first create the parent term (Internal medicine). Then, when creating the child term, click the "Relations" toggle-down menu, and select the parent term from the list of terms under "Parent terms" (figure 7.2).

---

13. This list is adapted and abbreviated from the modern classification used for medical residencies, and was selected primarily for reasons of convenience when developing the example site. A real project focusing on the history of medicine would certainly need to adopt a less problematic taxonomy.

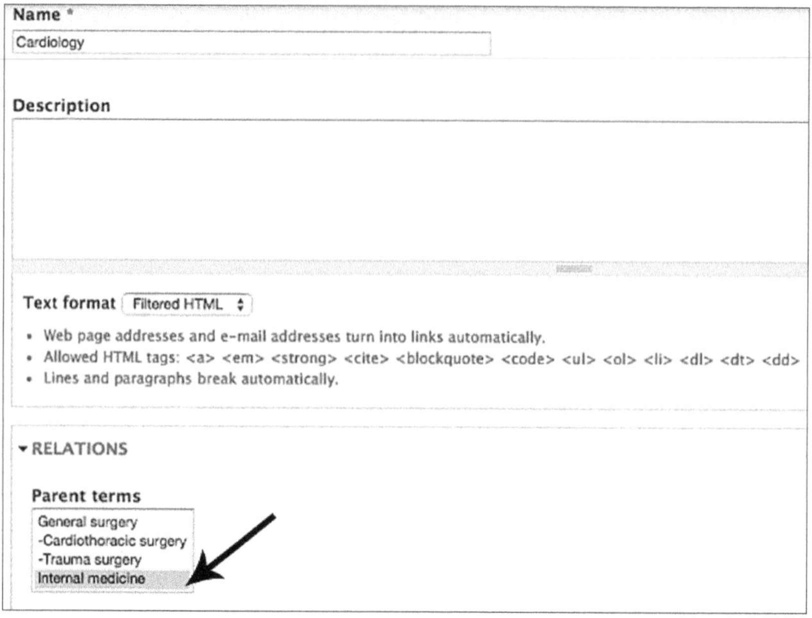

Figure 7.2. Selecting a parent term.

Don't worry about putting a numerical value under "Weight"; by default, terms sort alphabetically. If you want to put them in some other order, it will be far easier to drag and drop them into that order on the vocabulary overview screen (*Structure > Taxonomy > Vocabulary-Name-Here*) than to remember which term you assigned what numerical value.

When creating the term reference field for "Specialization," we don't want to allow users to add new values to this taxonomy, so that rules out the "Autocomplete text widget." Using checkboxes could be awkward, as the list of options would be quite long. The "select list" widget is not particularly intuitive for users selecting multiple options—they have to remember to hold down the "Control" (Windows) or "Command" (Mac) key to choose a second option without deselecting the first.

There are a few modules that provide additional widgets that might be useful in situations like this. If you want to make the most use of the hierarchy you've set up as part of your taxonomy, the Hierarchical Select[14] and Taxonomy Term Reference Tree[15] modules may be useful.

---

14. https://www.drupal.org/project/hierarchical_select
15. https://www.drupal.org/project/term_reference_tree

The former walks users step by step through the levels of a hierarchy, allowing them to choose among the options available at each level. The latter provides sophisticated checkboxes that more clearly show the levels of the hierarchy, can collapse options beyond a certain level so they're not all visible and taking up a lot of screen space, and can do things like automatically selecting the parent term(s) of any term that the user selects. The Simple Hierarchical Select module[16] is a lightweight alternative to Hierarchical Select, which also can be used as a user-configurable filter in Views.

In this case, the hierarchy is convenient, but not essential. It's also fairly limited at only two levels. The autocomplete text widget is close to what we need, other than allowing people to add new terms. As such, the Chosen module[17] is a good substitute. It allows users to type in text, but they can only choose from the options that already exist in the database.

The Chosen module itself is just a wrapper for a Javascript library (i.e., the necessary plumbing to hook up a user interface element that could be used with other platforms or programming languages, with Drupal specifically). To fully install the Chosen module, you'll have to upload the Chosen Javascript library by accessing the Drupal codebase directly; you can't do this part through the Drupal interface. See section 4.5.2.2 for instructions.

After installing and enabling Chosen (including uploading the Chosen library to `sites/all/libraries/chosen`), create the term reference field "Specializations" and choose "Select list" as the widget. Choose the "Specializations" vocabulary. On the next page, under the box for help text, there will be an option for "Apply Chosen to the select fields in this widget"; set it to "Apply." Set the number of values for the field to unlimited.

7.2.3   Rearranging fields

The current arrangement of the fields puts the large text box for the biography at the top of the data input form, which makes it harder to see the rest of the fields. On the "Manage fields" page, click on the "+" sign to the left of the "Biography" label and drag it to the bottom of the list of fields, then hit "Save."

---

16. https://www.drupal.org/project/shs
17. https://www.drupal.org/project/chosen

7.2.4 Automatic node titles

One thing on the field settings list that we have not yet addressed is the "Title" field. One option for this field is to rename it to "Name," but that would mean a lot of repeated data entry, since we already have fields for each name component.

To fulfill Drupal's title field requirement (described in section 5.4.7) without doing additional data entry work, enable the Automatic Nodetitles module and the Token module (see section 6.8), and edit the Person content type (*Structure > Content Types > Person*). Under "Automatic title generation" (most likely the first of the configuration options at the bottom of that screen), select "Automatically generate the title and hide the title field." If you don't see "Automatic title generation," make sure that Automatic Nodetitles is enabled.

To define the pattern for the title, first click in the text field under "Pattern for Title". Then, using the token browser table below that text field, click on *Nodes*, then click on the blue links for each of three fields for the components of the person's name: [`node:field_given_name`] [`node:field_middle_names`] [`node:field_surname`]. Go back up to the text field, and you'll see that each of the fields has appeared in the box. Be sure to put a space between them, otherwise all the names will be squashed together in the generated titles.

7.2.5 Pathauto

Go to *Configuration > Search and metadata > URL aliases > Patterns* (/admin/config/search/path/patterns). If you don't see "Patterns" as an option, make sure that you've installed and enabled the Pathauto module (see section 6.9).

Under "Pattern for all Person paths," first type "people/" then toggle down the replacement patterns, then toggle down "Nodes," and choose the same tokens you did for the Automatic Nodetitles setting: [`node:field_given_name`] [`node:field_middle_names`] [`node:field_surname`]. This time, instead of putting a space between them, put a hyphen, so that the final value of the "Pattern for all Person paths" field is: `people/[node:field_given_name]-[node:field_middle_names]-[node:field_surname]`. Scroll to the bottom of the screen and hit the "Save configuration" button.

7.3 Event content type

The event content type will store information about events in a person's life. An event can be shared by more than one person. Create a new content type named "Event," as you did with "Person."

7.3.1. Content type settings

Under "Display settings," uncheck "Display author and date information"; it doesn't matter who enters the information about people. Under "Comment settings," set "Default comment setting for new content" to "hidden." Otherwise, the default settings are fine; click "Save and add fields."

7.3.2 Fields

7.3.2.1 Person

Create a node reference field called "Person"; this field will point to the person or people involved in the event. If the option for a node reference field is not available, install and enable the References module and the Node Reference submodule, as described in section 6.5.1. Because the site will have a relatively small number of people, choose "Check boxes/radio buttons" as the widget. The only content type it should reference is "Person," and unlimited values should be allowed.

7.3.2.2 Date

The question of how to store information about the date is directly tied to what you want to do with that information. Some options for the types of fields you might choose are listed below.

> **Text field:** If you only want to display the date, and don't want to do anything else with it (e.g., sorting events chronologically), you can use a text field. In most cases, much of the point of including the date is to enable sorting, and using a text field means that dates in April will appear first, followed by ones in August, if you type in names of months. Numeric date entry won't necessarily fare much better. In most cases, a text field is not a good choice for storing dates.

Date field: The best-supported way to store dates in Drupal. Date fields have integration with Views, which means you can use them to generate chronological listings of events. Date fields are also required by the more sophisticated time line modules (Views TimelineJS Integration[18] and Timelinr[19]). Additionally, you can import data in bulk into a Date field. The downside is that all dates in a date field have to have the same granularity (year, month, day, hour, minute, and second are all options, but you have to pick a combination of those traits and use it for all dates). If you choose "year" because that's all the information you have for some of the dates, you won't be able to store month or day information about any of the dates. You can establish project conventions for how to create dummy data for dates where you only know a year (e.g., deciding that people doing data entry should enter "January 1" if the month and day are unknown), and you can set up filters using Views to hide some of the dummy data, but this could lead to confusion if you have any real data that coincides with your dummy data (i.e., events that actually occur on January 1). To address this sort of coincidence, you could add a Boolean (single on/off checkbox) field that indicates that the date/month are unknown, but all these work-arounds are somewhat awkward solutions.

Partial Date field: The need for flexible date granularity motivated the development of this module, which not only allows you to have dates with different granularity, but also allows you to define time periods (spring, nineteenth century, etc.) and make those available as options. Partial Date fields can be used for sorting events chronologically, but the only time line module that Partial Date fields are currently compatible with is Simple Timeline.[20] As its name indicates, this time line is less customizable than the more advanced options. Further development of the Partial Date module has recently been supported by digital humanities projects; see the *Drupal for Humanists* site for updates and details.

To store dates as part of the Event content type, we'll combine two approaches. We'll use a Partial Date field as the primary way to store information, because not all dates will have day/month/year information. However, because this limits the kind of time line modules we can use,

---

18. https://www.drupal.org/project/views_timelinejs
19. https://www.drupal.org/project/timelinr
20. https://www.drupal.org/project/simple_timeline

we'll also use a Date field to store the year. In this case, the ability to use the TimelineJS module is sufficient payoff for the repeated data entry, since the year will have to be entered twice.

Create a Date field as described in "Birth date," above, and call it "Year." For "Date attributes to collect," just check "Year." Be sure to go into "More settings and values" to set the default value to "None."

Then, create a "Partial date and time" field, and call it "Date." If this option is not available, be sure to install the Partial Date module (see section 6.5.3). On the next configuration screen, toggle down "Minimum components" and choose "Year." This indicates which fields must be filled in. If you want to use any of the "Estimate" options, you can toggle down "Base estimate values" to define ranges for centuries, seasons, etc.

On the next page, under "Time zone handling," choose "Site timezone." Enter help text if you'd like (perhaps something about entering as much date information as is available), and at the bottom, choose "Year," "Month," and "Day" as the date components. This determines what granularity options are made available on the data entry page.

There should only be one value allowed for this field.

7.3.2.3   Location

Location is another piece of data where we'll need to add two different fields: in this case, a text field for entering the location information, and a geofield for converting that text to geographic coordinates.

Create a text field called "Location." You can increase the character limit above 255 characters if you expect to include long addresses, but 255 is enough for the example data. This field should have a single value.

Create a Geofield called "Location coordinates," with the widget "Geocode from another field." If you don't see this option, make sure the Geofield module and its dependencies are installed (see section 6.5.5).

For "Storage Backend," go with "Default" and move on to the next configuration page.

No help text is needed for this field, because it will be invisible to users. All users will see is the "Location" text field that you created above, and the "Location coordinates" field will do its work behind the scenes.

Under "Geocode from field," choose "Location" (the text field that you just created).

For Geocoder, choose "Google Geocoder." There are other geocoder options available as well, but the configuration for the Google Geocoder is described below.

With the Google Geocoder, you can reject results that don't meet a certain level of precision—for instance, if you want to only store precise street addresses, you can reject everything other than "Rooftop." Often, issues of precision have more to do with what you put into the "Location" field than what Google's geocoder can find. If your data just says "Philadelphia, PA," the geocoder will necessarily identify approximate coordinates (often around the city center). In most cases, it's best to leave all the "Reject results" checkboxes unchecked.

"Multi-value input handling" doesn't apply here because the "Location" field is set to take one value, but the default setting (Match Multiples) is probably the most sensible, generating one set of coordinates for each value.

The "Location coordinates" field should also only take one value.

7.3.2.4   Description

A description of the event. Rename the default body field "Description."

7.3.2.5   Title

There is no natural "title" for events, but it will be useful to have a succinct but informative text snippet for each event, for use on time lines. The fuller description of the event can go in the "Description" field. On the content type editing screen (*Structure > Content Types > Event*), under "Submission form settings," change "Title" to "Brief description" and save. Keep in mind that the Drupal title field (where the brief description will be stored) is limited to 255 characters.

7.3.2.6   Event type

There are certain kinds of events shared by most or all people in the database (education, marriage, events in their medical career, etc.), and it may be useful to be able to pull together these common kinds of events across multiple different people. As such, this information is best captured through a term reference field. Create a new vocabulary, "Event types," and populate it with the following terms:

Activism

Birth

Death

Divorce

Education

Marriage

Medical career

Then, create an "Event type" term reference field that points to that vocabulary, and use the "Select list" widget. If you enrich the taxonomy with a more elaborate way of classifying events, you may want to consider some of the widget options described under "Specialization." If you're just using the terms listed above, this field should have one value, but that might change if your taxonomy is more elaborate.

7.3.2.7 Institution

Some events are associated with a particular institution. Create a new term reference field and call it "Institution," and associate it with the "Institutions" vocabulary you already created. It only needs to accept one value.

7.3.2.8 Main time line

All events associated with a person will appear on that person's time line, but some events should also appear on an overall site time line. A Boolean field with a single on/off checkbox will allow us to differentiate between those events that belong on the overall site time line and those that don't.

Create a Boolean field called "Main time line," with the widget "Single on/off checkbox." Leave the on/off values empty and move on to the next configuration page. Put in some help text indicating the guidelines for what kind of events should appear on the main site time line.

Underneath the help text box and above the "Default value" box, there's a small checkbox that's easily overlooked entitled "Use field label instead of the 'On value' as label" (figure 7.3). Check that box.

This field should only have one value.

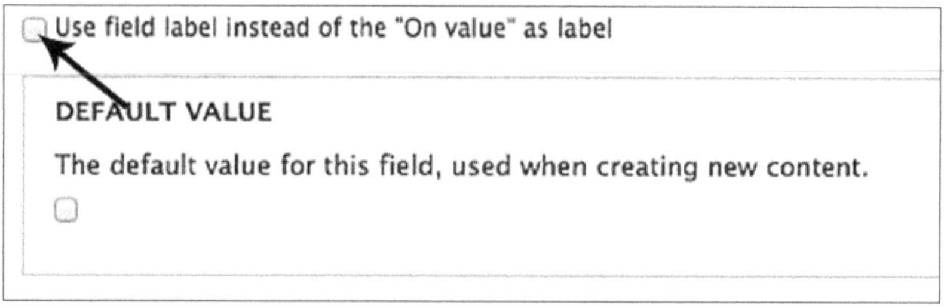

Figure 7.3. Check the "Use field label instead of the "On value" as label" box.

7.3.3   Rearranging fields

As with the Person content type, rearrange the fields so that the large "Description" box appears at the bottom of the list of fields.

7.3.4   Pathauto

Go to *Configuration > Search and metadata > URL aliases > Patterns* (/admin/config/search/path/patterns).

Scroll down to the "Content Paths" section, and under "Pattern for all Event paths," first type "events/" then use the "Replacement Patterns" box to toggle open "Node," then select [node:title], so the final value for the "Pattern for all Event" paths field is `events/[node:title]`.

It may be tempting to make the title more complicated, perhaps including some form of the date, and/or the name of the person associated with the event. There's not a lot to be gained from doing that, in this case. While including more information in URL aliases can be helpful for determining when, for instance, certain information should appear in a sidebar (when configuring block visibility; see section 11.2.5 for more), users will never be looking at an event node by itself, as a stand-alone page; they'll only encounter the information in the context of a time line. In fact, you may ultimately want to configure the Event content type so it can't be viewed on its own by nonadministrators (see the *Drupal for Humanists* site for more on the Rabbit Hole module[21]). Recall, too, that an event can be associated with more than one person, and if you include [node:field_person] in the pattern, you can end up with multiple names

---

21. https://www.drupal.org/project/rabbit_hole

separated by hyphens (e.g., events/john-smith-jane-smith/event-title), which wouldn't even be helpful for block visibility.

7.4 Image

The Image content type will store information about images depicting African Americans involved in medical professions. Go to *Structure > Content types > Add content type* in the administration menu (or /admin/ structure/types/add), and name the new content type "Image."

7.4.1 Content type settings

Under "Display settings," uncheck "Display author and date information"; it doesn't matter who enters the information about people. Under "Comment settings," set "Default comment setting for new content" to "hidden." Otherwise, the default settings are fine; click "Save and add fields."

7.4.2 Fields

To a large extent, you'll be reusing fields you've already created in other content types, as you did in section 7.2.2.7 with the "Image" field.

7.4.2.1 Profession

Under "Add existing field," select "Term reference: field_profession (Profession)." Include the help text "Select the profession(s) depicted in the image." All other settings are the same.

7.4.2.2 Institution

Under "Add existing field," select "Term reference: field_institution (Institution)." Include the help text "Enter the institution depicted in the image, if relevant."

7.4.2.3 Person

Under "Add existing field," select "Node reference: field_person (Person)." Include the help text "Select the people in the database depicted in the image, if applicable."

7.4.2.4 Image

Under "Add existing field," select "Image: field_image (Image)."

Include the help text "Click the 'Browse' button below to access the image uploading screen. After you've uploaded the image, put the title of the image in the 'Name' field. For better accessibility, include the title in the 'alt' field as well."

Under "File directory," enter `images`.

You can leave the rest of the fields (for maximum/minimum resolution and size, etc.) blank.

7.4.2.5 Body

Rename the "body" field to "description" and include help text about entering an extended description of the image.

7.4.2.6 Source collection

The images for this section of the example site are drawn from Flickr Commons, an aggregation of public domain material. For each image, we should capture the name of the original source collection. Go to *Structure > Taxonomy > Add vocabulary* and add a vocabulary called "Sources." Then, in your Image content type, add a term reference field called "Source collection" using the "Autocomplete term widget (tagging)" since you may not know what all the sources will be in advance. Select the "Sources" vocabulary. All other default settings are fine.

7.4.2.7 Source URL

Make sure you have the Link module installed and enabled. Create a field called "Source URL," using the "Link" field type and widget. Under "Link title," choose "No title." The rest of the default values are fine.

7.4.2.8 Title

Because you've already entered the title of the image in the image name field as part of the upload process, we'll use Automatic Nodetitles to pull in that information so you don't have to enter it again.

7.4.3 Automatic Nodetitles

To be able to pull in the information about the file you uploaded, you'll need to enable the Entity API[22] and Entity Tokens modules (the latter is part of the set of modules available once you install Entity API), which provides more flexible options for token configuration. If you don't have Entity Tokens installed and instead try the default [node:field_image] token, nothing will happen, and titles will just appear problematically blank. The [node:field_image] token is only useful for making the image itself appear, whereas what we need is some text-based metadata about the image.

On the content type configuration page, under "Automatic title generation," select "Automatically generate the title and hide the title field." Click in the "Pattern for the title" box, and use the token browser to find [node:field-image:?]. (Field names that use hyphens are provided by Entity Tokens; field names with underscores are provided by the usual Token module.) Click on it so it appears in the "Pattern for the title" box, and replace the "?" with "file," so it reads [node:field-image:file]. A bit counterintuitively, in this case specifying "file" won't get you the file itself, but will get you the file name, which is what we want.

There are currently a number of bugs with Entity Tokens, including having the token placeholder appear if a field is left blank (e.g., "Jane [node:field-middle-names] Smith" for someone with no middle name), and putting in ugly HTML entities instead of certain common punctuation marks (e.g., "Jack & Jill"). See the *Drupal for Humanists* website for more on the use of Entity Tokens.

7.4.4 Pathauto

Go to *Configuration > Search and metadata > URL aliases > Patterns* (/admin/config/search/path/patterns).

Scroll down to the "Content Paths" section, and under "Pattern for all Image paths," first type `images/` then use the "Replacement Patterns" box to select `[node:title]`, so the final value for the "Pattern for all Event" paths field is `images/[node:title]`.

---

22. https://www.drupal.org/project/entity

7.5 Summary

In this chapter, we have walked through a complete example of configuring content types and fields, weighing the pros and cons of different
approaches in certain contexts. Now that the scaffolding is in place for
adding content (through the creation of content types and fields), we need
to improve Drupal's content entry form to make it more user friendly and
then commence adding content. Chapter 8 will address those topics.

CHAPTER 8

Configuring Input Forms and Adding Content

8.1 Overview

Entering data is the best way to validate the content types you have created for your site. Even if you ultimately plan to do a bulk import of your data (see chapter 14), it may be worthwhile to spend some time manually entering a few nodes of each content type to make sure that your data align well with the fields you have created. This process also exposes you to the layout and configuration options in the interface for adding and editing content, allowing you to tweak them before making them available to data entry assistants or other contributors to the site.

This chapter will cover Drupal's text input formats, configuring a WYSIWYG editor (which provides a word-processor-like interface for text fields), adding inline images, and linking to other nodes on your site. It will also address how to edit content you have already created, and how to make use of Drupal's revisions feature.

8.2 Text formats

8.2.1 Field configuration

Every text field (including both short and long text fields) has two text processing options. When you create or edit a text field, you'll see radio buttons with the label "Text Processing" (under the box for help text) with two options: *Plain text* and *Filtered text (user selects text format)*.

For short text fields—such as the "Given name," "Middle name(s)," and "Surname" fields in the example Person content type—it usually makes sense to stick with the default "Plain text." In the case of those fields, there's no reason to include any formatting. We may want to apply various kinds of formatting when the names appear on the site in different places (perhaps in bold on a time line, or as header text at the top of the node that contains the person's profile), but there's no formatting that's *inherently* part of those data.

The likelihood of formatting being an inherent part of the data that must be captured increases when the text field is larger. If you are using the default Article content type to maintain a blog for your project, chances are that the "body" field of many of the Article nodes might include italics (e.g., for titles of books or films mentioned in the prose), URLs, or even inline images (e.g., a screenshot illustrating progress in the site's development). For that reason, long text fields such as the "body" field, or other long text fields you create from scratch, have "Filtered text (user selects text format)" as the default text processing setting. If you want to offer users a WYSIWYG interface (similar to word processing software, with buttons that allow them to turn various formatting options on and off), you must select "Filtered text" as the text processing setting.

Once you have fields as part of your content types that use the "Filtered text" settings (i.e., any long text field, including the body field), you should check on text formats available for your site and ensure that users have permission to use them.

8.2.2 Text format configuration

Go to *Configuration > Content authoring > Text formats* (/admin/config/content/formats). By default, there are three formats:

Filtered HTML: Provides a limited subset of HTML elements that can be used within the text. By default, anonymous, authenticated, and administrator users can use this.

Full HTML: Does not limit the HTML elements that can be used, but does provide some checks such as correcting some faulty HTML.

> Allowing unauthenticated users, or untrusted authenticated users (e.g., if you allow anyone to create an account on your site) to use this poses a security risk.
>
> **Plain text:** Displays any HTML entered into the field as plain text (e.g., if someone enters "<em>Moby Dick</em>," it will display as "<em>Moby Dick</em>" rather than "*Moby Dick*").

You should make sure that anyone who needs to edit a text field that uses the "Filtered text" text processing format has permission to access at least one text format in addition to "Plain text," otherwise they'll see an error message in the field stating "This field has been disabled because you do not have sufficient permissions to edit it." The default configuration, which gives all three default roles on the site (anonymous, authenticated, and administrator) access to "Filtered HTML," is correct, but keep this in mind if you make changes.

8.2.3   Configuring a text format

Click the "configure" link next to "Filtered HTML" to see the available options. On this screen, you can change the name of the text format, as well as select which user role(s) can use the text format. Note that you can also change the permissions settings for each of your text formats using the giant Permissions table (*People > Permissions*), discussed in depth in chapter 10.

You can also select which filters are enabled and, below that, the order in which those filters process the text, via a drag-and-drop table. At the bottom of the screen, there's another table where you can configure settings for individual enabled filters. For the "Filtered HTML" text format, "Limit allowed HTML tags" and "Convert URLs into links" are enabled by default. The settings for "Limit allowed HTML tags" let you specify which tags you want to allow people to use, and the settings for "Convert URLs into links" lets you specify a cutoff point for the display of very long URLs.

The default settings for allowed HTML tags for "Filtered HTML" are very limited, permitting the creation of links (<a>), italics (<em>), bold (<strong>), citing titles (<cite>), block quotes (<blockquote>), code (<code>), bulleted and numbered lists (<ul>, <ol>, <li>), and lists with descriptions (<dl>, <dt>, <dd>). It does not permit tables, the inclusion of images, using various levels of headers, superscript/subscript, or many other things.

Nonetheless, "Filtered HTML" may be a good text format to use in cases where what you fundamentally want is for users to input a number of sentences of plain text, with minimal formatting or markup. If you can expect that your users will be comfortable using a little bit of HTML to handle things like italics and lists as needed, simply using "Filtered HTML" as the text format for a text field will ensure that your site is minimally affected by bizarre formatting cruft that inevitably results from copying and pasting text written in word processing software (be it Microsoft Word, or Google Docs, or Open Office) into a text area that attempts to maintain existing formatting. Text pasted into a simple "Filtered HTML" field will have any existing formatting stripped out, and users will be quite constrained in terms of what formatting they can put back in using HTML.

However, if your users are not comfortable entering any HTML, if they expect that formatting from the source document will appear along with their text when they copy and paste, or if they would prefer a more word-processor-like interface, you will need to install and configure a module that provides a WYSIWYG (What You See Is What You Get) interface, as well as some supporting modules that address things like image upload and text format; see section 8.3.

8.2.4   Additional filters

While they may only be relevant for certain circumstances, these modules provide additional filters that you can enable and configure (if applicable) for individual text formats:

> **Footnotes:**[1] Allows you to insert footnotes on the page that appear at the bottom. The superscript numeral (or other, user-defined characters) of the footnote links to the footnote text, and the corresponding numeral or characters in the footnote links back to the place in the main text.
>
> **BeautyTips:**[2] Allows you to create definitions, explanations, etc. that appear in a bubble overlaid next to specified words.

---

1. https://www.drupal.org/project/footnotes
2. https://www.drupal.org/project/beautytips

Table of Contents:[3] Makes it possible to insert a table of contents anywhere within a text field, which makes use of header (<h1>, <h2>, etc.) tags to define the structure of the table of contents.

Video Filter:[4] Allows you to easily embed videos from YouTube and many other providers into pages. The default embed code from those sites often uses an <iframe> tag which Drupal will filter out, preventing the video from displaying. This is a lighter-weight alternative to using the Media module for this.

SpamSpan Filter:[5] Obfuscates email addresses using Javascript to reduce the likelihood of them being picked up by spammers. This could be useful if, for instance, you have a page of project staff that includes their email addresses.

Collapse Text:[6] Allows you to have sections of text that are hidden, and must be expanded to be visible. This could be useful for a pedagogically oriented site with homework or quiz questions where students can check their own work.

Code Filter:[7] If your site includes snippets of code, this filter allows you to use PHP and <code> tags without having to change all "<" characters to "<" for them to display correctly.

Caption Filter:[8] Allows you to easily add captions to images, similar to how captions are done in WordPress.

Paging:[9] Makes it possible to break up a very long text into multiple "pages" without having to create multiple nodes.

8.3 WYSIWYG configuration

There are numerous modules that provide a WYSIWYG interface for editing text. If you just want an interface that provides familiar buttons for different kinds of formatting, linking, etc., it will likely be easiest to install and configure one such module by itself. CKEditor[10] is the

---

3. https://www.drupal.org/project/tableofcontents
4. https://www.drupal.org/project/video_filter
5. https://www.drupal.org/project/spamspan
6. https://www.drupal.org/project/collapse_text
7. https://www.drupal.org/project/codefilter
8. https://www.drupal.org/project/caption_filter
9. https://www.drupal.org/project/paging
10. https://www.drupal.org/project/ckeditor

WYSIWYG module that will be included by default in Drupal 8. The default configuration for CKEditor doesn't require you to install a library; instead, it points directly to the code on the CKEditor server. This conveniently saves some configuration, but it only works for sites that are connected to the internet (i.e., not for a site that you've set up to run on your own laptop, with the goal of being able to work on it on airplanes, etc.). You can find detailed instructions for installing and configuring CKEditor on its own on the CKSource website.[11] (Their website also talks about the enterprise version of CKEditor that you can purchase, but you don't need it.)

For our example site, we want a WYSIWYG interface that integrates with the Media module, to make it easier for us to upload new images to display inline (e.g., to illustrate a blog post or an essay), and to reuse images that have been uploaded to the site. This is considerably more difficult with the stand-alone CKEditor module. Instead, we will be using the WYSIWYG module,[12] which provides a framework for installing different WYSIWYG libraries. The WYSIWYG module can provide the same type of integration "plumbing" for the CKEditor library that the CKEditor module does, but it's more flexible.

8.3.1   Installing modules and CKEditor library

Download, install, and enable a version of the WYSIWYG module released after October 2014; currently, this means using the developer (dev) version of the module. A major bug was fixed in October 2014 that addresses a problem with the module being incompatible with the latest release of the CKEditor library, but the fix has not yet been incorporated into a nondeveloper (non-dev) release.[13]

Also enable the WYSIWYG Media module, which is part of the Media package of modules.

Download the "Full Package" CKEditor library, from `http://ckeditor.com/download`. When you unzip it, you should get a folder called "ckeditor." Place that folder into the libraries directory in your Drupal code base (/sites/all/libraries), so that it's available as `sites/all/`

---

11. http://docs.cksource.com/CKEditor_for_Drupal/Open_Source
12. https://www.drupal.org/project/wysiwyg
13. https://www.drupal.org/node/1853550

`libraries/ckeditor`. For instructions on how to add a library to your code base, see section 4.5.2.2.

8.3.2   Selecting CKEditor in the WYSIWYG module

Go to *Configuration > Content authoring > Wysiwyg profiles* (/admin/ config/content/wysiwyg); clear the Drupal cache, by hovering over the house icon in the upper left and selecting "Flush all caches," if you don't see this option.

If you've correctly installed the CKEditor library, you should see a screen that lists all of the text formats on your site, along with a drop-down menu for each that currently says "No editor." If you toggle down the "Installation instructions" option, you should see CKEditor at the top, in green, with the version of the library that you installed.

If you haven't correctly installed the CKEditor library, you won't see the list of text formats, and instead the "Installation instructions" section will display all the WYSIWYG libraries compatible with the module, along with instructions for where you should put the library. If you see this screen after you've tried to install the CKEditor library, make sure that you've unzipped the CKEditor library file you downloaded (you need to upload to your Drupal code the folder you get when you unzip that file, not the file itself), and make sure that it's in the sites/all/libraries folder.

If you've successfully installed the CKEditor library and see the list of text formats, use the drop-down menu to select CKEditor for "Filtered HTML," and save (figure 8.1).

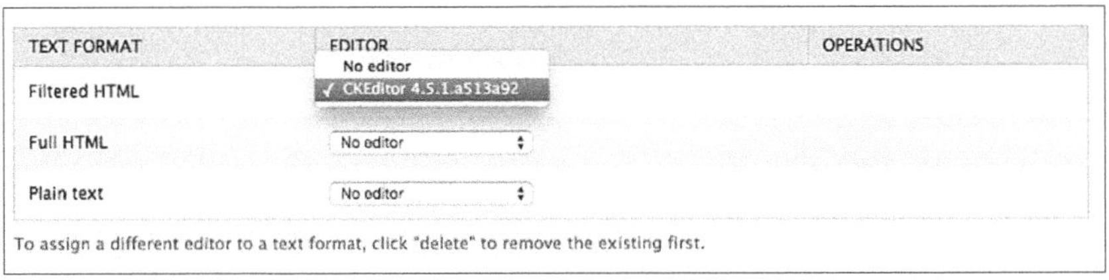

TEXT FORMAT	EDITOR	OPERATIONS
	No editor	
Filtered HTML	√ CKEditor 4.5.1.a513a92	
Full HTML	No editor ⬍	
Plain text	No editor ⬍	

To assign a different editor to a text format, click "delete" to remove the existing first.

Figure 8.1. Selecting CKEditor as the editor for Filtered HTML.

8.3.3   Configuring CKEditor for the Filtered HTML text format

Once you've selected CKEditor for "Filtered HTML," an "edit" link will appear on the WYSIWYG configuration screen. This screen lets you select which buttons will appear as part of the WYSIWYG interface. While you can check however many boxes you'd like, you may need to edit the list of permissible HTML tags allowed by "Filtered HTML" if you want to go beyond the very small default list (see section 8.2.3).

The following buttons are all compatible with the default HTML tag list for the "Filtered HTML" text format:

Bold

Italic

Bullet list

Numbered list

Outdent

Indent

Link

Unlink

Source code

If you expect that users will be copying and pasting text from Microsoft Word, you should check the box for "Paste from Word." This will strip out much of the formatting that automatically comes with text that's been copied from Word which would otherwise make the text display in an odd way.

Save the configuration, and go to *Configuration > Content authoring > Text formats > Filtered HTML*. Enable the "Convert Media tags to markup" filter, and save the configuration (figure 8.2). This filter makes it possible

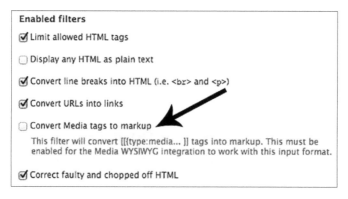

Enabled filters

☑ Limit allowed HTML tags

☐ Display any HTML as plain text

☑ Convert line breaks into HTML (i.e. `<br>` and `<p>`)

☑ Convert URLs into links

☐ Convert Media tags to markup

This filter will convert [[{type:media...]] tags into markup. This must be enabled for the Media WYSIWYG integration to work with this input format.

☑ Correct faulty and chopped off HTML

Figure 8.2.
Check the box for "Convert Media tags to markup."

to display inline images uploaded by means of the Media module, even without adding <img> to the list of acceptable tags.

Now, return to *Configuration > Content authoring > Wysiwyg profiles > Filtered HTML*. Select the "Media browser" checkbox, to enable integration with the Media module, and uploading and displaying inline images. If you don't see this checkbox, make sure you've enabled the WYSIWYG Media module, part of the Media module package.

If you want a fuller range of formatting options to be available (for instance, to administrators), you can repeat the process for the "Full HTML" text format. First select CKEditor from the drop-down list for "Full HTML" on the WYSIWYG configuration screen (*Configuration > Content authoring > Wysiwyg profiles*), then check the boxes for things you want to include. Because there are no limits on the supported HTML tags for the "Full HTML" text format, you can choose any of the options. If you include "Media browser," you'll again have to edit the "Full HTML" text format itself to include the "Convert Media tags to markup" filter.

8.3.4   Facilitating internal linking

Most of the pointers from one node to another on the example site (e.g., from an Event to a Person) will be by means of node reference fields, which provide an autocomplete interface for creating such pointers. Sometimes, though, it can be useful to be able to link to other pages on your site just as links within text. If this is something you expect you'll need to do often, you might want to use the CKEditor Link[14] module, which provides a more sophisticated interface for the CKEditor "Link" button and makes it easier to link to other pages on the same site.

Install and enable the CKEditor Link module, then go to the WYSIWYG configuration screen (*Configuration > Content authoring > Wysiwyg profiles*). Edit the profile where you want to use the CKEditor Link module, and check the box for "CKEditor Link." Save.

This doesn't create a new button, but rather, improves the interface for the "Link" button (which you should also have enabled). Now when you click the "Link" button, it defaults to "Internal path," and provides an autocomplete box for choosing the page you want to link to. You can

---

14. https://www.drupal.org/project/ckeditor_link

also change the "Link type" to URL to put in an external URL. There are additional configuration options for the link interface if you go to *Configuration > Content authoring > CKEditor link*, including making it possible to link to taxonomy terms within a particular vocabulary, or menu items within a particular menu.

8.4 Adding content

Finally, it is time to begin adding content to your site. If possible, use real content (not fake placeholder text) when trying out the content types—at least for the content types that are meant to store the core "data" of your site (e.g., information about people, events, places, etc. where there are multiple fields, in contrast to blog posts and narrative essays where the content types consist mostly of a title and body field).

Go to *Content > Add content > Your content type* for each content type you will use on the site, fill out the form, and save. Depending on the node reference fields used by each content type, you may need to do this in a particular order (e.g., creating Person nodes before creating Event nodes so the Events can have a Person to reference).

The *Drupal for Humanists* site has example data that align with the content types for the example site, available both as text that you can copy and paste, and as a spreadsheet that you can use for a bulk import, as described in chapter 14. Be sure to create at least two Person nodes, a handful of Event nodes for each person, and a few Image nodes before starting chapters 12 and 13 on Views.

8.4.1 Configuration options

When creating a new piece of content, take note of the set of options at the bottom of the content creation/editing form. These should all be available to you if you're logged in using an account with the Administrator role.

> **Menu settings:** Allows you to add the content you're creating to one of the menu(s) specified on the content type editing screen (see section 11.3 for more on menus).
>
> **Revision information:** Drupal can store multiple revisions of a piece of content, allowing you to compare and revert to previous versions. This

isn't really relevant when you're creating a new piece of content, but it does matter when you edit content: should Drupal simply overwrite the old version, or store your changes as the new version? See section 8.7 for more about revisions.

URL path settings: Once you've configured Pathauto (see section 6.9), a box will be checked here for "Generate automatic URL alias." If you want a page to deviate from the pattern you set up in Pathauto, you can uncheck the box and type the URL path you want to use in the box below.

Comment settings: Defaults to the setting defined for the content type, but you can change it on a node-by-node basis (e.g., turning off comments for a blog post on a particularly sensitive topic).

Authoring information: By default, the user who is logged in is set as the author of nodes they create. This section allows you to specify some other user as author instead. The autocomplete field for "Authored by" is based on a user's login name for the site, which you may not know. Using the Real Name module[15] (discussed in section 10.4.1) can let you search by a field you've created to store a user's actual name.

The "Authoring information" section also allows you to change the date stored in the database for when the node was authored. If you leave this blank, it will store the time and date when you first hit "save." Note that putting in a future date does not postpone publication until that date, as you might expect from WordPress. Prescheduling the future publication of nodes requires the Scheduler module.[16] For more complex scheduling and workflow needs, the Workflow module[17] is an alternative; see the *Drupal for Humanists* site for details.

Publishing options: The "promoted to front page" and "sticky at top of lists" options aren't very useful, but the "published" checkbox is quite important. A node that is saved with the "published" checkbox checked is, by default, publicly available. You can configure the permissions settings so that only authenticated users can see content on the site; see section 10.5.1 for details. A node that is saved with the "published" checkbox *unchecked* is a draft. By default, drafts are only visible to the user who created them (whose username is in the

---

15. https://www.drupal.org/project/realname
16. https://www.drupal.org/project/scheduler
17. https://www.drupal.org/project/workflow

"Authored by" field). If you want other users (or some subset of other users, such as instructors or project managers) to be able to view drafts, install and enable the View Unpublished module,[18] which provides a new set of checkboxes on the Permissions screen to allow people to view unpublished (draft) nodes. By default, unpublished nodes are filtered out of Views of content (see chapter 12 for more on Views).

8.4.2 Previewing content

Once you've entered data and made any changes to the node configuration, you can choose to either save the node, or preview it. The "preview" is a bit deceptive: while it will show things like text formatting (e.g., whether your text format has been configured correctly so as to not filter out the formatting done in your WYSIWYG editor) and the presence, absence, and/or alignment of field labels (see chapter 9), it is far from an accurate representation of what your content will look like once it has been saved. Many things, from the positioning of images uploaded to image fields to the font and color of text, are determined by your site's theme (see chapter 18), and the node preview doesn't reflect your site's theme. For a more representative preview, you can install and enable the Page Preview module,[19] which replaces the default preview (using an iframe— a webpage embedded within another webpage) that comes much closer to an accurate preview. Page Preview is currently only available as a developer (-dev) version, but because of the limited way it interacts with the database, it should be safe to use.

8.5 Viewing and editing content

When you save your first piece content, you will probably be disappointed with how it looks—particularly for content types with many fields. By default, field labels appear above the content, which leads to a very awkward-looking display. Chapter 9 will cover how to improve content display.

---

18. https://www.drupal.org/project/view_unpublished
19. https://www.drupal.org/project/pagepreview

When you're logged in as an administrator (or a user account with the right set of permissions) and looking at a saved node, you'll see a set of tabs right above the content: "View" and "Edit." If you're looking at a node with at least one revision, you'll also see a "Revisions." To edit a node, click the "Edit" link; this will make the editing form appear as an overlay.

8.6 Accessing saved content

After you have created a piece of content, it may not be immediately clear how you can find it again. Users who have the "Administer content" permission (see section 10.5 for more on roles and permissions) can click on *Content* in the administration bar, or go to /admin/content to see the content administration screen. This screen presents a table that can be sorted by any column. Filtering options at the top are another way to sort through the content, though keep in mind that filters are "sticky" and will remain active even after you leave the content administration screen, until you hit the "Reset" button.

8.7 Revisions

To make it easier to track changes on your site, particularly with multiple project collaborators, it may make sense to install the Revision All module. While you should still make adding a revision log message (in the "Revision information" tab at the bottom of the node creation/editing page) part of your data entry workflow, "Revision All" ensures that each change is saved as a new revision whether or not people remember to include a log message.

Install and enable Revision All and click the "Settings" link for the module (or go to *Configuration > Content authoring > Revision all*). There, you can choose to enable revisions for all content types, or only individual content types. There are also options for proactively enabling Revision All for all future content types, and preventing individual content types or individual nodes from disabling saving as a revision. If you don't check "Prevent Node Revisioning Overrides," the "Create a revision" box on the node creation/editing form is checked by default, but a user can uncheck it. If you do check it, the "Create a revision" box is both checked and grayed out, with a note indicating that it is disabled due to Revision All.

When viewing an individual node with revisions, the "Revisions" tab lists all revisions, the author of each revision, and the date of the revision. Clicking on the date allows you to view the revision. There are also links for deleting revisions, and reverting to a previous revision. However, by default Drupal lacks the ability to usefully compare revisions, the way you might find on Wikipedia.

The Diff module[20] provides this missing feature by adding a column to the "Revisions" tab where you can select two revisions, and click the "Compare" button to see the changes highlighted.

8.8 Summary

This chapter has described various ways to improve the appearance and functionality of Drupal's input forms, including adding a WYSIWYG editor, facilitating internal linking, and making it possible to view past versions of nodes. It has also covered the process of adding new nodes, as well as viewing nodes you've already created. Consult chapter 14 for instructions on how to import content in bulk if you have a lot of data to enter and the data already exist in a structured form (such as an Excel spreadsheet). Otherwise, continue to chapter 9 for a discussion of how to improve the appearance of nodes once you have created them, including positioning labels and configuring the display format for different kinds of data.

20. https://www.drupal.org/project/diff

CHAPTER 9

Node Display

9.1 Overview

The way fields are displayed by default in Drupal—with the field label above the content—is usually not what you want. Additionally, depending on the kinds of fields you're using (images, dates, locations, etc.) there may be a variety of options to choose from in terms of how the data you enter are displayed.

This chapter will cover how to improve the display of content stored in nodes, including hiding or changing the alignment of field labels (section 9.2.1), defining and using image styles (section 9.2.5), and repositioning fields into sidebars or other areas of a page (section 9.3.1). It will also briefly discuss advanced node display configuration using Display Suite (section 9.3.1), and how to use blocks created by Views to display related information (section 9.3.2).

9.2 Configuring node display

Node display is configured on a per-content-type basis. To configure the display of the Person content type on the example site, for instance, go to *Structure > Content types > Person > Manage display*.

9.2.1   Label and field visibility

On this configuration screen, you can specify whether the label (the title of the field) appears *above* the corresponding data, *inline* (next to it), or whether it's *hidden*. Similarly, you can hide the content of various fields. This is useful for our example site, where the person's given name, middle name, and surname already appear as the node title (as we configured it using the Automatic Nodetitle settings). We don't need them to additionally appear as individual fields, so we'll hide the "Given Name," "Middle Name(s)," and "Surname" fields. The most efficient way to do this is to immediately set the "Format" to "<hidden>." This automatically pulls the field to the "Hidden" section at the bottom of the screen. When you hide the content of a field, the label for the field is automatically hidden as well, but the same does not hold in reverse, and for good reason. In many cases, you might want to hide the label of a field (in fact, this is the default behavior for the body field, even if you rename it) while still displaying the contents.

9.2.1.1   Labels and visibility for Person content type

All labels should be inline, with the exception of "Biography" and "Image," where the label should be hidden.

The given, middle, and surname fields should be hidden.

Arrange the visible fields in the following order:

Image

Birth date

Death date

Profession

Specialization

Medical institution attended

Biography

9.2.1.2   Labels and field visibility for Event content type

In a sense, the display of the event content type doesn't matter. The event content type is intended to store data that will be primarily displayed to users through a View, rather than by itself. If you were to configure events for individual display, you'd want to hide the "Year" field (because the "Date" field would have a more complete representation of the date) as well as the "Main timeline" field. "Date," "Person," "Event type," "Location," and "Institution" should have inline labels.

9.2.1.3   Labels and field visibility for Image content type

The label should be hidden for the "Description" field (this is configured by default, since "Description" is a renamed "body" field) and the "Image" field. "Profession," "Institution," "Person," "Source collection," and "Source URL" should have an inline label.

Arrange the visible fields in the following order:

Image

Person

Profession

Institution

Description

Source collection

Source URL

9.2.2   Configuring date fields

Date fields ("Birth" and "Death" in our "Person" content type) have a number of display options to configure. The format "date and time" is a good fit here, although there are additional options such as "time ago" (which will state how long ago the event took place, in years and months by default, though you can add additional units) and "plain" (which simply provides the format "1872–05–13 00:00:00," for May 13, 1872, with no time specified). Using the "date and time" format, you can specify which of the default formats to use, or a custom format if you've created one.

9.2.2.1   Date fields in the example site

To get Drupal to display the date in a full, written-out format (such as May 13, 1872), go to *Configuration > Regional and Language > Date and time > Formats > Add format* and enter: F j, Y which is the PHP date shorthand corresponding to "May 13, 1872." Then go to the Date and Time settings

(*Configuration > Regional and Language > Date and time*) and use the drop-down menu to change the "Long" date type to use that format.

Because date fields are automatically configured to use the "Long" format, updating the "Long" format to the setting you want fixes the display of all your date fields. If you wanted to use a date format other than "Long," you'd just need to click on the cog on the far right of the date field you were configuring, and select the date format from the drop-down list that appears.

The exception is the "Year" field in the Event content type. That date field is only part of the content type in order to give you more flexibility in your choice of time line modules to use. The date field that will be displayed is the partial date "Date" field, and the "Year" field is redundant. For that reason, hide both the label and the content of the "Year" field.

9.2.3   Configuring partial date fields

You can set up "short," "medium," "long," and "custom" partial date formats at *Configuration > Regional and language > Date and time > Partial date formats* (/admin/config/regional/date-time/partial-date-formats). For each one, you can configure the following attributes:

Uppercase or lowercase for AM/am and PM/pm in times.

Whether to use BC/AD or BCE/CE notation for years, and whether to mark only dates prior to the year 0, or both those before and after.

How different components should be separated (e.g., through the use of "/" to separate month, day, and year, and ":" to separate hours and minutes).

The order in which the components should appear, arranged through a drag-and-drop table.

How each component should be formatted; for instance, for "Day" the options are:

Day of the month, 2 digits with leading zeros, 01 through 31.

Day of the month without leading zeros, 1 through 31.

Day of the month, 2 digits with leading zeros with English ordinal suffix.

Day of the month without leading zeros with English ordinal suffix.

A full textual representation of the day of the week.

A textual representation of a day, three letters.

Numeric representation of the day of the week 0 (for Sunday) through 6 (for Saturday).

Back on the "Manage display" screen for a content type with a Partial Date field (such as Event), clicking on the cog for that field allows you to choose a date format other than "Medium" (the default), or choose the short description, long description, short or long description (either one, preferring the short if available), or long or short description (either one, preferring the long if available). The nondate options only make sense if you selected "Short date text" and/or "Long date text" as possible components when you created the Partial Date field. In most cases, you will simply select the "Use date only" option and choose one of the date formats.

9.2.3.1   Partial date field in the example site

The example site has a partial date field as part of the Event content type which, as noted earlier, is not meant to be seen by users by itself. For that reason, the default display for the partial date field (using the "Medium" format) is fine.

9.2.4   Configuring geospatial fields

There are two geospatial-related fields in the configuration we have used: the text field that is used for geocoding (where you enter the name of the location), as well as the geofield that stores the coordinates. In most cases, it makes sense to display both of them: the text field can provide a label of sorts for the geofield, which will display as a map.

In many cases, it makes sense to keep the label for the text field, and have it display inline. The format of the text field can remain set to "Default." The label for the geofield should be hidden. The default format for geofield display is "Well-Known Text," which provides one kind of textual representation for the geographic coordinates. Instead, choose "Geofield map"; if you don't see this option available, enable the "Geofield map" module that is part of the Geofield module package. The default settings provide a map that takes up 100% of the width of the screen, and is 300 pixels high. You may wish to adjust this depending on how you want the node to display (for instance, to 600 px wide and 400 px tall for a medium-sized rectangular map display). You can also change other configuration settings, for example, if you want the map to be zoomed farther in or out.

The "Geofield map" display is based on Google Maps, and the standard Google Maps configuration options (e.g., choosing between a street map, terrain map, and satellite map) are available if you click on the cog for that display type. If you have the Leaflet[1] module enabled, you can choose a "Leaflet" display which provides a different set of options, including choosing from among a much broader array of map types. You can install the Leaflet More Maps[2] module to access additional maps, including a number of artistically rendered maps.

9.2.4.1   Geospatial fields in the example site

On the example site, geospatial fields appear only in the Event content type, which won't be displayed to users. For the sake of practice, set the label for the "Location" text field to be inline. Hide the label for the "Location coordinates" field, and set it to display as a Geofield map, 600 px wide and 400 px tall. Leave the rest of the settings with their default values.

9.2.5   Configuring image fields

The configuration of the display of image fields is closely connected to the concept of image styles. By default, the version of the image displayed as part of the node is the version that was uploaded. This is often inconvenient, particularly if you want to upload the highest-resolution version of the image, but display something smaller and more manageable as part of the node itself. Or perhaps you want to standardize the display, ensuring that the image is the same dimensions across all Person nodes. If you click the cog next to the image field, a drop-down list appears with a set of image styles to choose from. However, you are not limited to the default set of options.

---

1. https://www.drupal.org/project/leaflet
2. https://www.drupal.org/project/leaflet_more_maps

9.2.5.1 Configuring image styles

Drupal comes preconfigured with three image styles: Thumbnail (100 × 100 pixels), Medium (220 × 220), and Large (480 × 480). The Media module adds another image style, Media thumbnail (also 100 × 100 pixels, but cropped to a square). The three default formats use the "Scale" transformation effect—the largest dimension (either horizontal or vertical) is scaled to the largest acceptable size (100, 120, or 480 pixels, respectively), and the smaller dimension is whatever value retains the original proportions. Media thumbnail uses "Scale and crop," resizing the smaller side of the image to 100 pixels, and cropping the larger side to the same. When configuring the display of an image field, you can choose from one of these four options, or you can configure additional image styles.

To modify these default image styles, or add your own, go to *Configuration > Media > Image styles*. To add a new style, click the "Add style" text, or you can use the Administration Menu to go directly to *Configuration > Media > Image styles > Add style*. Give the style a name; in this case, we'll choose "Medium square." On the next configuration screen, you can start adding effects. In order to attain a square image style of a uniform size, regardless of the dimensions of the original image, choose the "Scale and crop" effect from the drop-down list and hit "Add." Define the maximum height and width, 300 pixels each, and click "Add effect." The preview image with the hot air balloons shows what will happen: the

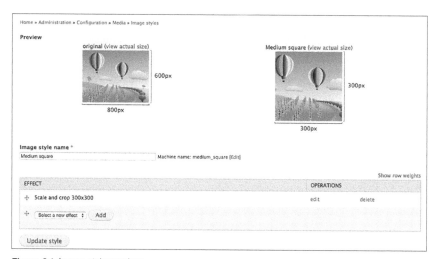

Figure 9.1. Image style preview.

smaller dimension will be scaled to 300 pixels, and the larger dimension will be cropped, resulting in a 300 × 300 square (figure 9.1).

After you've finished defining this image style, it will be available among the options for displaying the image field on your content type.

9.2.5.2   Advanced image style configuration

The Imagecache Actions[3] module provides additional effects that you can use when defining image styles, including watermarking with a transparent image, overlaying text (including text from tokens, as used in Pathauto and Automatic Nodetitle configuration), color shifting, desaturating (making the image black-and-white), posterizing (limiting the number of colors), and others. Depending on your project, this module can save you a considerable amount of time on image preparation, since you can define image styles that can automatically process all images in multiple ways.

9.2.5.3   Colorbox

The Colorbox module[4] provides a way to display larger images in an overlay over the page when you click on a smaller version of the image. Its overlay functionality can also be used to display video, audio, external links, etc., but here we will focus primarily on its use for images.

After you have installed and enabled the Colorbox module, you can choose it instead of the "Image" format on the "Manage display" page. Colorbox has the following configuration options:

> **Content image style:** The image style used to display the image on the node page.
>
> **Content image style of first image:** Should be the same as "content image style" in most cases. If you are configuring an image field where you can upload multiple images, you can use this field to make the first image appear bigger (e.g., using the Medium default style), while setting the "Content image style" to be something smaller (like the Thumbnail default style), to avoid having too many big images on the page.

---

3. https://www.drupal.org/project/imagecache_actions
4. https://www.drupal.org/project/colorbox; note that this module requires a library as well as the Libraries API module; see section 4.5.2.2 for more on installing libraries.

Colorbox image style: The size the image should be when it appears in the overlay, after a user clicks on the image. Should be a size larger than the "Content image style."

Colorbox gallery type: By default, Colorbox is set up to provide a gallery—allowing users to click through to the next image from within the overlay. In the context of configuring the display of a single node, "per post gallery" and "per page gallery" will both create a gallery based on all the images uploaded to all the fields in the node. There are other circumstances where you can use Colorbox (e.g., in Views or Panels) where a "page" may draw content from multiple nodes. If you have a content type with multiple image fields that each allow multiple image uploads, and you want each image field to have its own gallery, use the "per field in post/page" gallery setting. If you don't want the gallery option, set it to "No gallery." If there is only one image, this setting is irrelevant.

Caption: When you hover over an image in a colorbox overlay, by default, a text caption appears. This setting specifies the source of that caption. When you're using the Media module for image upload, "Title text" is the best option.

9.2.5.4   Image fields on the example site

In the Person content type, for the "Image" field, use the Image format and the "Medium square" image style.

In the Image content type, for the "Image" field, use the Colorbox format. Set the content image style to "Large," and the colorbox image style to "Original." Use "Title text" for the caption. Since there is only one image uploaded per image field, you can ignore the gallery setting.

9.2.6   Configuring file fields and multimedia

File fields (i.e., fields where you upload PDFs, Word documents, spread-sheets, audio, video, or embedded content from third-party providers like YouTube, etc.) have an extensive, but not particularly useful, set of display options by default.

Generic file: Provides an icon associated with the type of file, with the title of the file linked.

Table of files: Creates a table with an "Attachment" column that looks like the "Generic file" setting, and a "Size" column that shows the size of the file.

URL to file: Provides the text of the file's URL. It is not linked, so it's a poor choice for using to display the file; it is useful in other contexts, particularly Views.

Rendered file: Looks the same as the "Generic file," but allows administrative users to edit or delete the file without having to edit the node first. Hover your mouse over the link to the file, and a small cog appears that you can click to choose "edit" or "delete."

Download link: Allows you to choose the text for the link users will click to download the file.

The Media module provides some additional options:

Audio: Provides an audio player; if the file is not an audio file, however, this will appear blank.

Video: The same as audio, but for video files.

Large filetype icon: A large, gray icon that differentiates between documents, audio, and video.

In most cases, the Generic file option is a sensible choice, because its icon indicates the file type, and users can easily download the file.

If you want to make it easier for users to preview files, or simply view them in the browser, the PDF reader module[5] provides that functionality. Once you install and enable the module, a "PDF reader" format becomes available for many file types[6] on the Manage Display page. You can specify how big the viewer should appear, the renderer (Google Viewer is the default, but two other viewer options are available), whether to show a download link, and whether to use Colorbox to have the viewer appear in an overlay (if Colorbox is installed). If you select Colorbox, be sure to include text in the "Colorbox text" field; this is the text users will click on to access the overlay. There is currently a bug in the PDF reader module that hides the download link if you select both it and colorbox, so don't use the colorbox option if you want people to be able to download the file.[7]

---

5. https://www.drupal.org/project/pdf_reader; see also this comparison list of modules with similar functionality: https://www.drupal.org/node/1781960.

6. .PDF, .DOC, .DOCX, .XLS, .XLSX, .PPT, .PPTX, .PAGES, .AI, .PSD, .TIFF, .DXF, .SVG, .EPS, .PS, .TTF, .XPS, .ZIP, .RAR

7. A user in the forums has provided a snippet of code that you can manually add to the module that purports to fix this: https://www.drupal.org/node/2315113.

9.3 Advanced configuration of node display

9.3.1 Display Suite and CCK blocks

Not all the elements of a node page can be configured through the "Manage display" interface for the content type. There is no option for configuring where and how the Drupal title is displayed, for example, nor for configuring where and how the author/date information (if enabled) appears. Comments will appear at the bottom of the node, regardless of any configuration done here. To configure your node displays with that level of granularity, the Display Suite[8] module provides you with significantly more options (including setting up different displays in different contexts, such as search results vs RSS feed teasers), albeit with a steeper learning curve. Display Suite gives you the flexibility to create tabs, columns, or other organizing elements as part of your node display, and display blocks as if they were regular fields. The *Drupal for Humanists* site includes a tutorial on Display Suite, as well as links to external resources for learning how to use this powerful module.

Another module that may be useful when configuring node displays is CCK Blocks.[9] CCK (Content Creation Kit) was the module that allowed you to add fields to your content types in Drupal 5.x and 6.x; this was incorporated into Drupal core as of Drupal 7. When you enable CCK Blocks, it provides an additional option as part of your field configuration screens, allowing you to indicate whether or not you want that field to be provided as a block. (For more on blocks, see section 11.2.) If you choose to use the block display for a field (for instance, in order to put that field's content in a sidebar), you'll want to set both the label and the field to "hidden" when configuring the node display, so the content isn't repeated.

If you need data from multiple fields to appear as a block (e.g., birth date *and* death date), you can use the Views module (discussed in chapters 12 and 13) to generate a block that combines both types of data, rather than creating two blocks with CCK Blocks.

---

8. https://www.drupal.org/project/ds
9. https://www.drupal.org/project/cck_blocks

9.3.2   Blocks created by views

The Views module allows you to create displays (lists, tables, maps, slide-shows, timelines, etc.) of content. If you make one of those displays available as a block, you can configure it to appear on the node pages for a particular content type. Section 13.3 describes how to create a map of all the event nodes connected to a particular person, and section 13.5 describes how to create a time line for events in a person's life. Both displays are made available as blocks, and are configured to appear on Person nodes, as part of a person's profile on the site. Using blocks created by Views is a good way to pull in related content, particularly content that is connected to a particular node using a node reference field; for instance, on the example site, the Event content type includes a node reference field that points to an individual Person node.

Unless you use Display Suite, you will have to assign blocks that appear with a content type to one of your theme's predefined regions (see section 11.2.1), such as a sidebar, or under the main content. Display Suite provides options for creating a more integrated display, where you can freely mix and match and arrange fields from the content type itself along with blocks created using Views.

9.4 Summary

This chapter has described how to improve the display of nodes that you have added to your site, by configuring labels and formatters for individual field types that have advanced configuration options, such as dates, geospatial data, and images. It has also briefly covered how to go beyond the simple node display configuration, using CCK blocks and Views.

Chapter 10 discusses users, user profiles, and permissions; chapter 11 addresses the configuration of menus and blocks. While you should explore both topics at some point in your site development process, at this point you may instead choose to work on importing (chapter 14) or exporting (chapter 15) your data, creating new displays of content using Views (chapters 12 and 13), configuring search (chapter 16), managing taxonomies (chapter 17), or changing the design of your site (chapter 18).

CHAPTER 10

Users and Permissions

10.1 Overview

Almost all sites have more than one user account, if only because it's good practice for every person who works on the site to have their own. There are a number of options you should configure that relate to the creation of user accounts (section 10.3). While Drupal offers very minimal user profiles by default, they can be built to be almost as complex as content types. The skills you developed when creating content types can be applied directly to user profiles (section 10.4).

To give users access to content or administrative functionality, you can create *roles* as a way of grouping users by the level of permissions they should have (section 10.5). This is accomplished using the *permissions* screen, an enormous table that grows bigger with each module you install, and every content type, taxonomy, and file type on your site.

If you have anything on your site open to the Internet at large, you should also install some kind of spam protection before launching your site (section 10.6).

10.2 User configuration settings

Configuration settings related to users can be found in two different places. Under *People* (admin/people) you can view all the user accounts on the site, make changes to them, create and configure roles (groups of permissions), and assign roles to users.

Under *Configuration > People* (admin/config/people) you can change the site's "account settings," which include everything from who can create an account to what fields appear (and how) on user profiles. There are important changes to make in both groups of settings, and each will be addressed individually.

By default, Drupal has very lax password requirements for user accounts, and user authentication is not particularly secure. You can improve the password requirement using modules like Password policy,[1] but particularly if most or all the users are from your institution, you should look into whether your institution provides a Drupal module that integrates with your campus authentication system. See the *Drupal for Humanists* site for more about improving the security of user authentication.

10.3 Account settings

The account settings area (*Configuration > People > Account settings,* or /admin/config/people/accounts) allows you to specify how user registration can happen, the wording of various automated system emails related to users, user signatures, user pictures/avatars, and a few other miscellaneous settings.

The default configuration for anonymous users, contact settings (if you have the core "Contact" module enabled), and administrator role are fine in most cases. To cut down on spam, it is essential that you change the default configuration under the "Registration and cancellation" section (described in section 10.3.1.1).

10.3.1   Registration and cancellation

This section of the "Account settings" page lets you configure the process for user registration, as well as account cancellation.

---

1. https://www.drupal.org/project/password_policy

10.3.1.1 Account registration

These settings are very important. If your site isn't one where most people should be creating user accounts (e.g., a public web presence for an organization, where only the people who administer the site have any reason to log in), you should change the settings so that only administrators can create an account. Even if you have no visible link to the user registration page on the site, spammers know the URL for the Drupal user registration page, and you may receive emails from spammer-created user accounts that are pending administrator approval.

On the other hand, if you have a site where you want people to create accounts, having administrator approval is an additional burden on you and on them. In those cases, you may want to change the setting to allow anyone to create an account, but before you do so, make sure the user registration form is protected by an anti-spam module; see section 10.6.

10.3.1.2 Account cancellation

The most common reason to cancel an account is because it's a spam account. If you have site assistants who are no longer working with you, it's better to change their account status to "blocked"—which prevents them from logging in, but doesn't do anything to content they've created. The option "Delete account and its content" will remove both the spam account and any spam the user has created.

10.3.2 Personalization (user avatars)

This section allows you to enable signatures and user pictures (i.e., avatars) for users.

The signature option is of very limited utility, and only appears appended to comments that the user posts—and not any other kind of content they create.

The user picture option allows users to upload a photo as part of their profile. By default, that photo will appear on nodes that the user creates, along with their name and the date, if you've enabled "Display author and date information" for that content type. You can also make use of user pictures as part of views you create (see chapters 12 and 13).

The configuration options here allow you to specify a default user picture for users who don't upload their own picture, as well as the default display style, maximum file size and resolution for pictures, and a subdirectory where user pictures should be stored. A help box is available where you can put guidelines for photos, which will appear near the photo upload interface when the user is editing their profile.

This area is the "right" place to configure user pictures. In general, user profiles work a lot like content types, insofar as you can create and associate any number of fields with the site's user profiles. But if you want users to upload a picture that will be associated with them on the site, be sure to configure it here—NOT by adding an image or file field to the user profile. Depending on how you use the image, the difference may be trivial (e.g., if you're only displaying the user picture in the context of views you've created, it doesn't really matter where the picture is coming from), but Drupal core and other modules assume that user pictures will be uploaded using the interface generated by the settings you configure here. As a result, having the user picture automatically appearing along with the user's name on nodes they create only works if you use the user picture feature as intended.

10.3.3   System emails

The text of emails that Drupal sends to users (e.g., when an account is created for them, or if they forgot their password) can be managed through "Account settings."

The default text for each of these is fairly sensible, but you may want to customize it. At the bottom of the screen, you can click on "Browse available tokens" to get a list of the bits of variable text (like the site name, or the user's name) that could be used in those emails. If you click in the *editing* window for the text of one of the emails, and click on a token from the "browse available tokens" pop-up menu, that token will be inserted into the editing window.

10.4 Creating user profiles

The user profile configuration is a set of submenus under *Configuration > People > Account settings: Manage fields* (/admin/config/people/accounts /fields) and *Configuration > People > Account settings: Manage display* (/admin/config/people/accounts/display). The configuration of these two sections works exactly the same way as the corresponding sections when editing content types. The only difference is that you have an option to check whether a field you've added should be displayed on the user registration form. Fields that aren't displayed on the user registration form aren't available when creating a new user, but become available when the user subsequently edits his profile.

10.4.1 Real Name

There are many places on a Drupal site where user names are displayed. For instance, if you choose to leave the "Show author and date information" box enabled for any content type, the user name will appear at the top of nodes belonging to that content type. In most cases, however, the default configuration is *not* an accurate representation of the user's real name, because it uses their login name (i.e., what they use along with their password to sign in).

The Real Name module[2] can fix this by drawing on data stored in fields you've added to the user profile. After you've installed and enabled Real Name, ensure that you have added a field or fields to the user profile (by going to *Configuration > People > Account settings > Manage fields*) that can be used to store the person's real-life name. You might want to add a "Name" field, or you may want to add separate names for "Given name" and "Surname," for instance, if you ever want to be able to sort users alphabetically by surname.

To configure Real Name, go to *Configuration > People > Real name* (/admin/config/people/realname). Toggle down "Browse available tokens," click once in the "Realname pattern" field, and select the tokens corresponding to the name fields, just like how you configured Automatic Nodetitles or Pathauto. If any users haven't filled in the fields you defined for the "Realname pattern," their login name will be used until they do. It may be simpler to make the fields used for the person's real name required in the user profile.

2. https://www.drupal.org/project/realname

10.5 Roles and permissions

Drupal has an extremely granular permission system. Almost every module comes with a set of permissions associated with it, in addition to numerous permission settings associated with Drupal core. There are even modules (like Content Access[3] and Field Permissions[4]) that provide even more granular permissions.

Drupal doesn't let you assign permissions to individual user accounts. Instead, permissions are granted to roles, and roles are given to users. The "administrator" role is automatically granted full permission to do everything on the site; every time you add a new module, the administrator role gains extra permissions. Drupal also automatically creates roles for "authenticated" and "anonymous" users.

In general, you should be very careful about who you assign to the "administrator" role. Anyone with this role can make a mess of the site, accidentally or deliberately. You also should probably put strict limits on what the anonymous users can do (e.g., anonymous users probably shouldn't be able to post any content), or else spammers will take advantage of it. It's best to think through what the real-world roles are for site development and maintenance (e.g., content creator, data entry assistant, Drupal site builder) and create Drupal roles with permissions to match.

To create a role, go to *People > Permissions > Roles* (/admin/people/permissions/roles). Once you've created a role, go to the permissions page at *People > Permissions* (/admin/people/permissions) to check the boxes for the permissions that role should be granted. If you have a lot of roles, and it becomes awkward to read the titles of the permissions and see the role you want to edit, you can go to the Roles page and select "edit permissions" for that role.

If you have the Module Filter module installed (one of the modules on the recommended list in section 4.4), a search field at the top of the permissions screen will be enabled. If you type the name of a module, the permissions list will be filtered to only the permissions available for the

---

3. https://www.drupal.org/project/content_access
4. https://www.drupal.org/project/field_permissions

module. You can also use syntax like "perm:access" or "perm:view" to show the corresponding kind of permission (access or view) for all modules where it is relevant. The Fast Permissions Administration[5] module provides an interface for configuring permissions similar to what Module Filter provides for the modules screen.

10.5.1 Content permissions

By default, the Drupal permissions table has options for:

Viewing published content (of all content types).

Viewing one's own unpublished content.

Creating new nodes of a specific content type.

Editing one's own nodes of a specific content type.

Editing anyone's nodes of a specific content type.

Deleting one's own nodes of a specific content type.

Deleting anyone's nodes of a specific content type.

While there are many options related to creation, editing, and deletion, viewing is still all or nothing: either you can view all published content, or none of it. The Content Access module[6] addresses this imbalance, and also allows you to add per-node permissions, so that individual nodes can have different settings from the defaults for their content type.

After you install and enable the module, a warning message will appear at the top of the modules screen that the content access permissions need to be rebuilt. Click the "rebuild permissions" link to do this. The same will happen if you disable the module.

Next, go to *Structure > Content types > [the content type you want to edit] > Access control*. This page will display the view, edit, and delete options for the content type, along with a list of the roles on your site. If you make changes to edit and/or delete permissions, these will be reflected on the overall site Permissions page, where you can also edit them. Specific

---

5. https://www.drupal.org/project/fpa
6. https://www.drupal.org/project/content_access

viewing permissions for content types can only be edited on the "Access control" screen for each content type.

If you check the box for per content node access control settings, next time you view or edit a node of that content type, you'll see an "access control" tab at the top, next to "view" and "edit" and "revisions," if there have been revisions saved of the node. This tab has the same options as the access control page for the content type, and it has the same values as the content type access control setting by default. Changing the settings on an individual node's access control page only affects that node.

10.5.2 Field permissions

The Field Permissions module[7] lets you define the visibility and editability of individual fields within a content type, based on role. For example, you might want to have a "completion" field that only project leaders can change, but all users can see. Or, if your site collects information about members of an organization, you might want to have a field that only the member and administrators can edit and view, such as contact information.

Once you enable the field permissions module, a new option for "Field visibility and permissions" appears on the editing form for every field, towards the bottom under the "field settings" section (figure 10.1). By default, all fields are public, but you can also select "private" to make the field only viewable and editable by the author of the node. For more specific sets of permissions, select the "custom" option and a table will appear that displays all the roles on the site, where you can grant for each of them any of the following options:

Create own value for field.

Edit own value for field.

Edit anyone's value for field.

View own value for field.

View anyone's value for field.

7. https://www.drupal.org/project/field_permissions

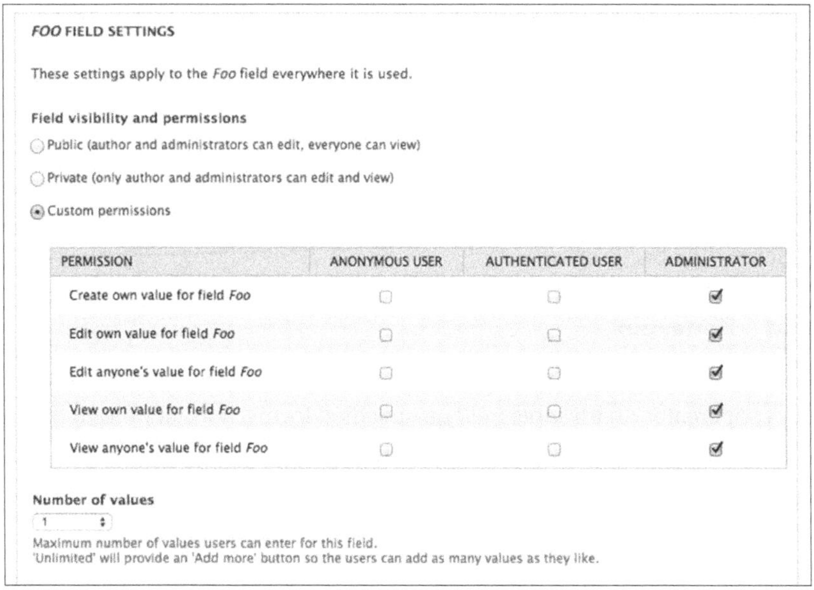

Figure 10.1. Field permissions settings for a field called Foo.

These field-level permissions don't override the viewing or editing settings set at the content type level. If a user doesn't have permission to view or edit the content type where the field appears, they won't be able to view or edit the field even if you grant them the field permission.

10.5.3 Permissions for unpublished nodes

The only default permission setting available for unpublished nodes is "View own unpublished content." This may be problematic for sites where less-experienced assistants do a first pass at data entry, and more-experienced project staff review and publish those drafts. Only people with "administrator" permission (i.e., full permission for all configurations on the site) can view unpublished nodes.

The View Unpublished module[8] provides options that allow users to view unpublished content of a particular content type. All these options are available on the Permissions page, grouped under a "View Unpublished" header.

---

8. https://www.drupal.org/project/view_unpublished

10.6 Spam prevention

If unauthenticated users are allowed to create anything at all on the site—including submitting a request for a user account, creating a new user account, commenting, filling in a survey/webform—you should install a module that can inhibit spam. Without it, even sites that aren't widely publicized will battle spam.

10.6.1 Honeypot

For the greatest accessibility, a module like Honeypot[9] is the best approach. Honeypot creates an invisible field on specified forms. No real human user can fill in the field, because it doesn't visibly appear on the page, but it appears in the code. Because most spambots are automated and access the form code directly, they will likely fill in the hidden field. Any submission that includes a value in the hidden field has revealed itself to be spam, and can be safely discarded.

Once you install and enable Honeypot, a message will appear asking you to configure it. You can click the link in that message, or go directly to *Configuration > Content authoring > Honeypot configuration.*

To activate Honeypot, either check the box for "Protect all forms with Honeypot," or select individual forms towards the bottom of the page. If you directly control the creation of accounts on the site and are confident that no spam accounts can be created, you can limit Honeypot to only those forms available to unauthenticated users. Protecting all forms is easiest, as long as no form has a field with the same name as the "Honeypot element name." By default this is "url," but you can change this to another generic term (email, webpage, etc.) if necessary. If you're interested in tracking spam attempts, you can also check "Log blocked form submissions."

There's also a time limit option. Any form submitted before the specified number of seconds passes after the page loads will be thrown out as spam. This can add another layer of defense against spam, but it interferes with page caching. If server load is a concern for your site, you may want to set this to 0.

---

9. https://www.drupal.org/project/honeypot

10.6.2 CAPTCHA

Another popular anti-spam tactic involves the use of CAPTCHAs, puzzles that a human user should be able to solve, but a spamming program should not. The most popular module for this is the CAPTCHA module,[10] which provides a framework that supports many different kinds of CAPTCHAs in addition to the ones that are included with the module itself. Add-on modules for CAPTCHA (including Google's reCAPTCHA,[11] which uses distorted book scans or image-recognition tasks) are also available.

Install and enable CAPTCHA, as well as the Image CAPTCHA module included with it. Image CAPTCHA provides images with distorted letters and numbers that users have to type in. After you enable CAPTCHA a notice will appear at the top of the modules page with a link indicating you can now configure CAPTCHA. Click on the link, or go to *Configuration > People > CAPTCHA* (admin/config/people/captcha).

On this page, you can set a default CAPTCHA, choosing from the available options (by default, "Math" and "Image CAPTCHA"). The setting for each form defaults to "no challenge" (i.e., unprotected by CAPTCHA), but you can use the drop-down menu to choose the default challenge, or a specific challenge from among the available options. The CAPTCHA module uses the database name for each form, which is less intuitive than the Honeypot interface, but the names should be relatively transparent (e.g.,"contact_site_form" is the sitewide contact form; "user_register_form" is the form where users can sign up for a new account; "user_pass" is the password reset form).

The rest of the default settings are fairly reasonable, though you may want to change the prose in the description of the CAPTCHA or turn it off. You can also check the box for "Log wrong responses" to monitor the number of spam attempts on your site.

If you'd like more CAPTCHA choices, there's a list on the CAPTCHA module page. The process for configuring each one differs slightly, and for some (like Google's reCAPTCHA) you may need to register with the CAPTCHA provider and obtain an API key (a unique string of characters that grants you access to the CAPTCHA service). Be sure to read the

---

10. https://www.drupal.org/project/captcha
11. https://www.drupal.org/project/recaptcha

module documentation for each one. When additional CAPTCHA modules are installed, they appear as options alongside "Math" and "Image CAPTCHA" on the CAPTCHA configuration screen.

10.7 Summary

This chapter has covered the creation and configuration of user accounts, as well as roles, groups of permissions that can be assigned to user accounts. It has also briefly described how to create user profiles, as well as some of the modules that enable even more granular permissions options, such as content permissions, field permissions, and permissions for unpublished nodes. Finally, it has described two common approaches to spam prevention. There are many more modules that improve the security of user authentication, spam prevention, and granular access controls; please see the *Drupal for Humanists* site for more information.

Chapter 11 will address blocks and menus. Much like this chapter, chapter 11 contains important information if you are going to run a real Drupal site, but does not directly continue the development of the example site. If you want to continue making progress on the example site immediately, you can move ahead to chapters 12 and 13, on Views, or chapter 14, on data import.

Blocks and Menus

11.1 Overview

Before moving on to creating new displays of the content that has been added to the example site (using Views, in chapters 12 and 13), it is useful to better understand two more aspects of Drupal's architecture: menus and blocks (bits of content or functionality that can be positioned somewhere on a page, like a list of recently published blog posts, a snippet of text crediting a funding agency, or a login interface).

11.2 Blocks

Blocks are generally small containers of content or site functionality (such as a user login box, or a menu) that can appear in different places on the site, like a footer, the right sidebar of blog posts, or the top right corner of the front page. Drupal core provides some blocks (like a list of users currently logged into the site), some modules create blocks (e.g., Superfish,[1] which provides a block intended to be placed in region designed for a menu, and lets you display a menu as a drop-down list), you can create blocks using Views (see chapters 12 and 13), and you can create custom blocks with any arbitrary content. Block layout is on a theme-by-theme basis, because Drupal can't guarantee that the regions where you've

---

1. https://www.drupal.org/project/superfish

put blocks will exist in the next theme you switch to (figure 11.1). If you change themes you'll need to reconfigure your block layout.

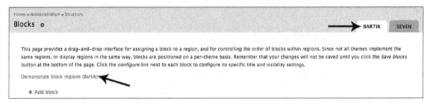

Figure 11.1. The Blocks configuration interface.

To manage blocks, go to *Structure > Blocks* or /admin/structure/block. What appears by default are the regions for your currently active theme (region labels appear in bold), and all the blocks available to you, most of which will be under the header "Disabled" at the bottom (figure 11.2). Other themes that are enabled but not set as default appear as tabbed options at the top of that interface.

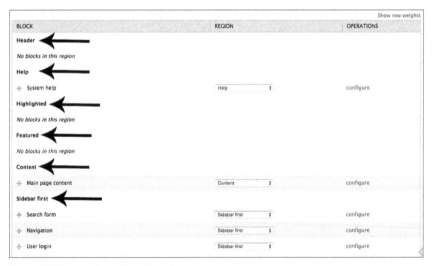

Figure 11.2. The block configuration interface. Arrows indicate regions abailable for placing blocks.

11.2.1 "Demonstrate block regions" and positioning tricks

At the top of the Block configuration page, if you click the link under the descriptive paragraph that says "Demonstrate block regions (Your Theme Name)" you will see a blank, generic page where the general location of each region will appear highlighted in yellow.

This doesn't always work well, particularly with groups of regions that form columns together—for instance, a footer may have three different regions (left, center, right), but they'll only show up the way you expect if you first put a block in the left region, then the center region, then the right region. In the "demonstrate block regions" preview, they may appear stacked on top of each other. Putting a block in the right region without content in the center or left may make that block appear as if it were in the left region; an easy way around this, if you only want a block to appear on the right, is to create custom blocks with no content and use them to fill in the "slots" for the left and center regions.

In short, while "demonstrate block regions" can be a useful tool, the most reliable way to see what a block will look like in a region (and where exactly it will appear) is to assign it to that region, save, and take a look at the results.

11.2.2 Assigning blocks to regions

You can drag and drop blocks from "unassigned" into the region where you want them to appear, by grabbing the "+" sign to the left of the block name and dragging the block into place, just as you did to rearrange fields for content types. If you do this, be sure to hit "Save" afterwards, before you go do any other configuration. If you drag and drop blocks to different regions, then hit the "Configure" link next to one of the blocks, it will take you to the configuration page for that block without saving your changes, and you'll have to redo the drag-and-drop positioning.

11.2.3 Block configuration

The options that appear when you choose "Configure" for a given block depend on the nature of the block. All blocks will have a "title" field and many will have a "description." The title will generally display in some stylized way above the block content; if you don't want a title, you have to enter *<none>*. Leaving the title blank will use whatever title the module or view that generates the block has indicated as the title.

The description is what appears on the list of blocks on the block administration page (*Structure > Blocks* or /admin/structure/block), to identify that particular block. For blocks created by Drupal core or many modules, you won't have the option of changing the description.

11.2.4   Region settings

The configuration page for a block will also list all enabled themes for your site, and in which region the block appears on each of them. You can use this interface to change the position of a block without having to go back to the drag-and-drop interface.

11.2.5 Visibility settings

The block configuration page provides multiple options for fine-grained visibility configurations. If you don't make any changes in this area, the block will always appear in the specified region, on every page. Making changes in the "visibility settings" area allows you to have blocks that only appear for users with certain roles, blocks that users can choose to turn off, blocks that appear on nodes of certain content types, and/or blocks that appear on pages with certain URLs.

In the "Content types" section, you can specify that a block should only appear on nodes of a given content type; this is particularly useful for CCK blocks, as discussed in section 9.3.1. In the "Roles" section, you can indicate that a block should only appear for users with a specific role; this can be useful for blocks that provide menus of options for adding new

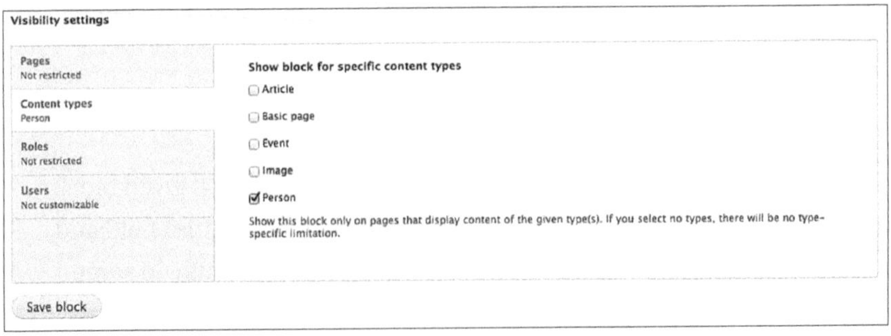

Figure 11.3. Visibility settings interface.

content, if you only want certain roles to be able to add content (figure 11.3). The "Users" option is less useful; it allows users to specify in their account settings whether or not they want a block to be shown.

The most complex set of options is under the heading "Pages." To change these settings, you need to put down a series of paths, one per line. What exactly you put down will generally depend on what you've done for your Pathauto settings (see section 6.9). Maybe you want a block to appear on all user-related pages. In those cases, you would use whatever (fixed) text you put down in the Pathauto configuration (e.g., "users"), then an asterisk, which matches any page (users/*). You can put things after the asterisk, too, if you want a block to appear only on the interface when a user edits their profile (user/*/edit).

It's worth noting that you can't use tokens here the way you can in the Pathauto configuration. You have to put down actual values, rather than placeholders (with the exception of the asterisk). If there's no fixed text that you use as part of the taxonomy path (e.g., if you use the default *[term:vocabulary]/[term:name]* for taxonomy terms), but you want a block to appear on the term pages for terms from all vocabularies, you'll have to list each vocabulary separately, by entering, for example, *tags/*, another-vocabulary/*,* and "*third-vocabulary/*,* each on separate lines.

11.2.6   Custom blocks

The block administration page also has a link for "Add block," or you can go to *Structure > Blocks > Add block* (admin/structure/block/add). This is a way for you to create a block with any content—a copyright notice, an acknowledgement of a funding organization, a sponsor logo, etc. Don't forget to check that you have the right text format selected—depending on what you're using it for, you may need to make sure that the block body is set to "Full HTML" if you are going to be using extensive formatting. See section 8.2 for more on text formats.

11.3 Menus

Drupal allows you to create any number of menus: lists of links intended to be used for site navigation. Every menu is available as a block, and where the menu is displayed depends on where you put the block; how it's styled largely depends on your theme. Some modules provide additional menu display options, such as drop-down menus (i.e., menus where, when you hover over a menu item, any subitems appear below or to the side. An "About" menu item on a center's website might have subitems including "History," "Staff," etc.).

11.3.1 Default menus

A standard Drupal 7 installation provides three menus. You don't have to use any of them, but they might be a convenient starting point.

> **Main menu:** Starts off with just a "home" link that will take you to whatever the front page of the site is. Go to *Configuration > System > Site information* to specify what node, view, etc. should be the front page, if you want it to be something other than a blog-like display of the most recent nodes. You can add other links to this menu and use it as the main navigation menu for your site.
>
> **Management:** This is a less-functional alternative to the administration menu; you can ignore it.
>
> **Navigation:** This menu is a grab bag of various things. It starts off with menu items for adding content, and various modules add their own links here (e.g., a link to the Feeds import page appears here and only here; see chapter 14 for more on Feeds). Because it's not always clear what impact installing a new module will have on this menu, and unpredictability is not a desirable trait in a menu, it is generally best to not display this menu, at least not to the public.
>
> **User menu:** Provides a "my account" menu item that takes an authenticated user to their profile, and a menu item for logging out. Potentially useful, though you might want to incorporate those links into your main menu.

11.3.2 Adding a menu

You may want to simply add your own menu items to Drupal's default menus (particularly the "Main menu"), but if you need an additional menu, you can create it by going to *Structure > Menus > Add menu* (admin/structure/menu/add). Once you create it, it will appear alongside the default menus on the menu configuration page (*Structure > Menus* or admin/structure/menu). You can delete any menus you've added, but you can't delete default menus.

11.3.3   Adding items to menus

There are two ways to add menu items: by editing the node (see section 11.3.3.1) or a view-generated page (see section 12.8.1.2) that you want to provide access to through the menu, or by adding a link directly to the menu. Adding a link is one of the options for each menu on the menu configuration page, *Structure > Menus* (admin/structure/menu). If you want to add a taxonomy term, user, or something else that isn't a node or views-generated page to the menu, you have to use the "add link" option.

"Add link" provides additional configuration options as well, such as "Show as expanded," which always shows the links nested beneath the current link. You can also uncheck the "enabled" checkbox for a link to hide it in a menu, which can be useful if you're preparing pages for inclusion in a menu before you're done creating their content.

11.3.3.1   Editing a node

When you create a new node or edit an existing node, at the bottom of the editing interface, there's an option labeled "Menu settings" with a checkbox, "Provide a menu link." If you check the box, a new set of options appear, including "Menu link title"—the text that actually appears in the menu. This defaults to the title of the node, if the node has already been saved; otherwise, you have to enter the title manually.

"Parent item" is a drop-down set of options that shows all available menus and the menu items that already exist. If you want the node to be a top-level

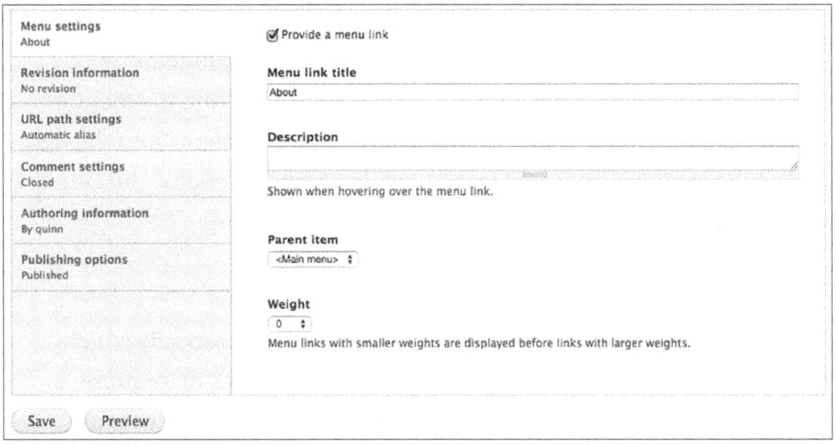

Figure 11.4. Menu settings in node editing interface.

menu item, just choose the name of the menu (e.g., "<Main menu>"); if you want it to be a subitem, choose the name of the parent item. By default, only "Main menu" is available (figure 11.4), but you can change that by editing the content type that the node corresponds to (*Structure > Content types > Content-type-name*). Towards the bottom of the content type configuration page, there's an option for "menu settings" that lets you choose menus in addition to "Main menu" to make available when editing a node.

Once you've edited a node to make it a menu item, that menu item will show up when you "list links" for the menu (an option on *Structure > Menus* or admin/structure/menu). From there you can edit the menu item, for example, by changing the link title.

11.3.3.2   Add link

From the menu configuration page (*Structure > Menus*), there's an "add link" option for each of the menus. Using that interface, you can put in the text that will display for the menu item, along with the path. This could be a Drupal path like "node/123," or you can use the more user-friendly Pathauto alias like "content/my-first-page"; you can also put in external links here. Like on the node editing page, you can select a parent item if you don't want the menu item you're creating to appear at the top level.

11.3.4   Arranging menu items

While careful use of the "weight" field (which allows items with a lower number to "float" to the top) can allow you to arrange your menu items in your preferred order, it's much easier to use the drag-and-drop interface. This interface also allows you to turn menu items into subitems by moving them under a parent item. Click on "list links" from the menu configuration page (*Structure > Menus*), drag and drop items into the right order, then save. On this same screen, unchecking the "enable" box for any menu item makes it not display as part of the menu.

11.3.5   Displaying menus

Some themes include a configuration setting where you specify which menu will appear as the primary navigation; see chapter 18 for more on themes. Other themes rely on blocks, and provide a specific region

(see section 11.2.1) for the primary menu bar. Still other themes have no
particular menu region, but are configured in such a way that you could
reasonably add menu blocks to a sidebar or header region. You might also
use a sidebar, header, or footer for additional menus, such as a menu for
site editors that isn't visible to the general public. Some themes support
the display of at least one level of menu subitems (Bartik, the default
theme, is one example), but in most cases, you'll need to use a module like
Superfish or Nice Menus, which provide drop-down menus, to be able to
see subitems.

To make a menu visible, go to the Block configuration page *(Structure >
Blocks* or admin/structure/block). If you want to use the default menu
block, just look for a block with the same name as the menu (there's no
label indicating specifically that it's a menu block), assign it to a region,
and save.

While the first menu you think about may be the menu that appears
towards the top of your site and provides the primary navigation, placing
an additional menu in the sidebar can be useful particularly on complex
sites with many nested subsections. Menus in sidebars—or anywhere else
where they aren't stretched out horizontally—display the menu hierarchy,
and expand and contract sections as you navigate, so that you can easily
see the "children" menu items of the page you're currently viewing (i.e.,
those nested beneath the current page). Links where you've checked
"show as expanded" when adding or subsequently configuring the link
will always appear expanded, even if you're currently in another section of
the site.

11.4 Summary

This chapter has provided an overview of blocks and menus, as well
as their basic configuration. Both of these concepts will be relevant in
chapters 12 and 13 as you learn to use the Views module.

Before you start working with Views, ensure that you have created
at least some dummy content on the site. Alternately, you might first
go through chapter 14 on data import, using the example data on the
Drupal for Humanists site.

CHAPTER 12

Views

12.1 Overview

The power of the Views module is one of the best reasons for developing well-structured content types for your site. Views allows you to select what data to display, from which content types, and how those data should be displayed, filtered, and sorted. Views can do the same for data stored as part of user accounts, taxonomy terms, comments, files, and there may be many more options depending on what other modules you have installed.

A full explication of all the settings and configuration options available in Views—not to mention the many modules that extend it—could easily fill an entire book; in fact, there are books available that focus primarily on Views. This chapter will provide a tour of basic Views configuration settings by walking through the case study of creating and modifying a "People" page for the example site. Each section includes additional notes on configuration options that aren't needed for this particular case study, but may be of use for future views you create.

The best way to develop proficiency with Views is through exploring and experimenting with it yourself. Once you have completed this chapter, you may find it worthwhile to create additional experimental views, choosing different options than those indicated here. It is easy to delete a view that didn't turn out the way you expected, or that you no longer want on the site. Views are, fundamentally, just ways to display your data, and changes you make to a view won't impact the actual data stored on your site, so don't hesitate to make changes to views that you've created for experimental use out of concern for harming your site.

Chapter 13 will build directly on chapter 12 by introducing the "advanced" Views configuration section, as well as demonstrating how to create different kinds of Views output, including tables, maps, time lines, and slide shows.

Before proceeding with this chapter, make sure you have created at least three nodes of the Person content type, and filled in at least their full name, birth date, death date, and image. If you want to bulk import Person nodes, you can work through chapter 14 before returning to chapter 12.

12.2 A very simple view using "Add a new view"

The most basic Views configuration settings are available without even accessing the full Views interface. We will first use it to create a list of all the historical figures on the example site.

Go to *Structure > Views > Add a new view* (or /admin/structure/views/ add). Give the view a short but informative name, like "People." For views that will be a permanent part of your site, you should check the "Description" box and provide more information about what the view shows, or what function it plays on the site (e.g., "Displays all historical figures in the database.").

12.2.1 Choosing what to display

The next option allows you to choose what kind of data you want to display. The options in the drop-down menu include the following by default, though additional options may be available depending on what modules you have installed:

> **Content:** This is the default option, which refers to content created using a content type form. The "of type" drop-down is set to "All" by default, which doesn't limit the content in the view to any particular content type. You might want to use this if you're creating a list of all recently updated content. The simple configuration screen only lets you choose

"All" or a single content type; if you want to choose two or more content types (e.g., all new events and all new blog posts), you'll have to hit the "Continue & edit" button at the bottom of the screen and use the full Views interface to set this up. In this case, we need to limit this to just the "Person" content type, so choose that from the drop-down list.

Users: This refers to user accounts on the site. If you want to display information that's stored in a user's profile, this is the right option.

Files: This refers to files uploaded to the site, or files from a third-party hosting provider embedded using the Media module. While you can also access uploaded files if you go to *Content > File* (if you have the Media module installed), creating a view gives you a lot more flexibility in what information is displayed about each file, as well as how many files are displayed per page.

Taxonomy terms: You can use this option to show taxonomy terms; you can also limit the list to one particular vocabulary. If you want to choose multiple vocabularies, you'll need to hit the "Continue & edit" button and use the full Views interface.

Comments: This option shows data stored as comments.

12.2.2   Displays

By default, the "Add new view" interface has enabled the option for creating a page to display the view contents. This is what we want for the example view, but not all views make sense as a page, such as those that create a slide show of content meant to appear as part of another page. In such cases, you would uncheck the "Create a page" box, and check the "Create a block" box, and continue with a similar set of configuration options.

Since we do want our example view to be available as a page, configure the following settings:

Page title: This text appears in the same place, color, style, etc. as node titles on a node page. For the example view, use the page title *People*.

Path: This is the URL (the part after your main site URL) where the page will appear. For the example view, use the path "people."

Display format: These options vary depending on what kind of data you're displaying. The options provided by the Views module are listed below; additional modules may provide other options. For the example view, use "Unformatted list" of "Titles (linked)." The various options available are described below:

Unformatted list – The default; it displays the content in a list, without bullet points or other accents, and a blank space between each item.

Grid – Each item appears in an invisible box, and there are multiple rows and columns of these boxes. In the full Views interface (though not the "Add new view" page), you can specify how many columns the grid uses.

HTML list – An HTML bulleted list (using the <ul> element).

Jump menu – A jump menu is a drop-down menu where each of the drop-down items is a link; this is rarely used.

Table – A table of fields from the data type you specified under "show"; each field specified (using the full views interface) is a column, and each item is a row. If you choose this option, Drupal will automatically choose "fields" and you'll have to use the full views interface to configure it. Section 13.8 discusses how to configure a table in Views.

Display format options: Depending on the data type you've chosen, each of the display formats can be paired with one or more of the following options (using the drop-down next to the heading "of"). For the example view, choose "Titles (linked)."

Comment – All the content stored in a comment.

Fields – Uses fields that you set up as part of content types.

Full posts – The entire content of the node, including the values of all fields.

Teasers – A shortened form of the node content; the exact nature of what the teaser contains can be configured by going to *Structure > Content types > [select the content type] > Manage display > Teaser*. This is selected by default.

Titles – The Drupal title.

Titles (linked) – The Drupal title, linked to the node or comment itself.

User – All the content in a user's profile.

Items to display: While it may seem like the inverse of what you want, for the example view, enter 0 in order to display *all* people. Uncheck the "Use a pager" box; using a pager only makes sense if you are displaying fewer than all the results. A pager provides a row of numbers at the bottom of the view, each representing another page of results, along with options for next/previous and first/last.

Create a menu link: For the example view, check the box for "Create a menu link." The default text of People is fine, and the menu should be the default "Main menu." As an alternate way of adding a view to a menu, you can use the menu configuration interface to create a custom link (see section 11.3.3.2).

Include an RSS feed: For the example view, check the box for "Include an RSS feed." The default path of people.xml is fine, and the feed row style should be set to the default "Content." This will add an RSS icon to the bottom of the page, and will create an RSS feed corresponding to the content displayed in the view.

Once you have finished configuring the page, check the box for "Create a block" as well. We also want to display a random person on the front page of the site. This is best accomplished by creating a block. The title, like that of the Page display, should be "People," and also like the page, it should display an unformatted list of linked titles. For items per page, enter 1, and leave "Use a pager" unchecked.

12.2.3   Next steps for new views

The configuration options on the "Add new view" page may be sufficient, and you can always come back and edit the view you've just created using the full Views interface. However, there is no way to return to the simple view creation interface after you've saved a newly created view. If there's nothing more you need to change now, you can hit the "Save & exit" button, which will save the view. The "Continue & edit" button takes you to the full views interface, where you have many more configuration options. Keep in mind, though, that your view is not saved when you hit "Continue & edit," and you have to be sure to save it on the next page.

For the example view, choose "Save & exit." Drupal will take you to the new People page. This view, as we have created it, has numerous shortcomings, described below. Each will be addressed later in this chapter.

12.2.3.1 Sort order

The sort order may seem somewhat random.[1] In fact, the default sort order displays the most recently created node first. For this People view, the order in which Person nodes were created is an unimportant artifact of the data entry process, and we do not want to use it to determine the sort order. Instead, the People page should show person nodes sorted alphabetically by the person's last name.

However, the block display we created (which won't be visible anywhere on the site until you enable it) needs a different sort order. Instead of always showing the alphabetically first person in the database, it should select a person node based on a random order.

12.2.3.2 Format

The format of the page could be more inviting. Instead of having a vertical text list, the view would be improved by using the "Grid" display format, in order to take advantage of the horizontal space on the page. We will also add an image thumbnail to each listing, as well as the birth and death dates of the person.

12.2.3.3 Editing a view

To make these changes, you will need to edit the view you just created. If you're looking at the page that displays the view, the fastest way to edit the view is by hovering your mouse towards the upper right corner of the view, to the far right of the name of the view (here, "People"). A small cog with an arrow will appear, and a dotted line will appear around the view itself (figure 12.1). Click on the cog, and select "Edit view."

Alternately, you can go to *Structure > Views > People* (if it doesn't appear in the administration menu, clear the cache first), or go to *Structure > Views* and click on the "Edit" button next to the listing for "People." This will take you to the full Views configuration interface. We will walk through the Views interface first from top to bottom, then from left to right.

---

1. If the only Person nodes on your site were created using the Feeds importer described in section 14.4, the people will be listed alphabetically by last name, but only by coincidence. Unless the feed took a long time to import, the creation date for all the Person nodes will be identical.

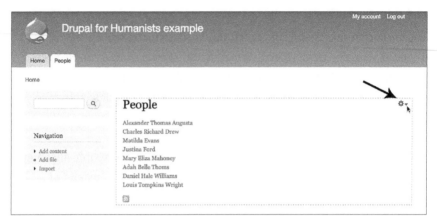

Figure 12.1. Hover in the upper right of the view for the cog to appear.

12.3 Displays

Grouped at the top of the Views configuration interface, in a gray box, are the different "displays" for your view. Displays are manifestations of the view (e.g., as a page, as a block, as an RSS feed), and a view can have one or more displays. Displays answer the question "In what form will this view appear on the site?"—not in terms of what the view will look like, but the manner in which it appears.

The example view has three displays, as you already configured on the simple view-creation interface: Page, Feed, and Block (figure 12.2).

By default, each display is named by the display type (e.g,. Page, Feed, etc). A single view may have multiple page or block manifestations, in which case it may be helpful to rename one or more of them to indicate

Figure 12.2. The full Views configuration interface.

what's unique about each one. Immediately below the gray bar of displays, there is a section called "[Display type] details." On the left side of the screen, you can click on the name of the display next to "Display name" to change the name of the display (figure 12.3). This only appears within the Views interface, as well as other places that display the administrative name of a display (e.g., the blocks overview page), and won't impact what's shown to users. You might use display names like "Block-5" for a block that lists 5 people, or "Gallery" for a page that provides a gallery-like display.

Figure 12.3. The arrow indicates where you can click to change the display name.

On the right side of the screen within the "[Display type] details" section, there is a set of options for modifying the display you currently have selected (figure 12.4).

Figure 12.4. The options for modifying the Page display, with the menu expanded.

Some displays have a "View [display type]" option, which shows you how the output of the display will look on your site; this works better for some display types (e.g., Page) than others (e.g., Feed).

If you hit the small arrow, you'll see options like "Clone," "Delete," and "Disable." Clone is useful if you want to provide a variant of the display, while keeping most of the configuration the same (for example, if you have a block that displays an MLA-formatted bibliographic citation for works with two authors, and you want to also create one that displays the citation for works with three authors). Disable is a way to "turn off" a display you think you won't need, before fully committing to deleting it. Deleting a display removes it entirely, but only after you save the view. Before you save the view, the display appears with a line through it, and you can click on it to undo the deletion.

12.3.1   Titles, and overriding and reverting display settings

When you make changes to the configuration of a view, you can choose whether the new configuration should apply to all displays, or whether it should only apply to one particular display, thereby *overriding* the default setting.

For the example view, the need to have different settings for different displays first occurs with the view title.

This title appears wherever a title would be appropriate for the display in question—e.g., as the page title, as the block title, etc. By default, the title is the same as the name you created for the view (figure 12.5).

Figure 12.5. The title for the Feed display.

Different displays can have different titles; in fact, this extends to all views settings. The ability to create different variants of the view in different displays is very useful, but it's easy to make mistakes that can impact multiple displays and require significant cleanup work.

By default, when you make a change to a setting in Views (other than in the display-specific settings area; see section 12.8), it impacts all the displays where relevant. For instance, adding fields to a Page display won't impact an RSS feed display that doesn't use fields. If you want to make a change that only impacts a single display, you need to use the drop-down option at the top of the configuration screen to change the setting from "All displays (except overridden)" to "This [display type] (override)" (figure 12.6). This will change the "Apply (all displays)" button at the bottom to "Apply (this display)." If you make a change to a display and indicate it should apply only to that display, all other displays will retain the previous value.

Figure 12.6. Overriding the title for only the Feed display.

Overriding happens at the section level; a display can have its title overridden, but its format, fields, filter criteria, etc. can remain unified with the other displays. All of the settings within a section that has been overridden, and/or the name of the section itself will appear in italics. Overriding represents a fork in the road for the configuration of a given section. Once you've overridden a setting within a section for a particular display, that display is no longer impacted by changes that you make to displays that aren't overridden within that section. For instance, if you override the Format section of one display in order to show a "Grid" rather than the default "Unformatted list" and later edit the default display so that it shows "Content" rather than "Fields" (using the "Show" option within the Format section), the display you previously overrode will not be impacted by this change because the entire Format section has been overridden (figure 12.7). For that reason, it's best to do all configuration that should be shared by all displays before you start overriding displays to address unique configuration needs.

Figure 12.7. Overriding one setting within a section causes all the settings in the section to appear in italics.

If you have overridden a display in a particular section and later realize you need to make a change across all your displays, there are two ways to approach the situation. You can either make the change separately for the overridden displays as well as those displays that have not been overridden (if the overridden displays already have extensive changes in the section in question), or you can revert the overridden displays to the default settings, make the changes across all displays, then re-override the displays as needed. To revert an overridden display, click on any setting within the overridden section, and in the drop-down at the top, choose "Revert to default" (figure 12.8). This will change the "Apply (this display)" button into a "Revert to default" button. Click to restore the settings to those shared by other displays.

Figure 12.8. Reverting settings to the default.

For the example view, go to the Feed display, and override the default title. The default title "People" makes sense for the page and block, but if you leave the Feed title as "People," that won't be very informative when a user adds the feed to an RSS feed reader. Change the title for the Feed display only to "CHAAMP: People."

12.4 Format

This section refers to how the content is displayed. Clicking the name of a particular format ("unformatted list") allows you to choose a different option (such as "table"). Clicking on "settings" allows you to change the configuration for the option that is currently selected (e.g., how to group the items in the unformatted list, which columns in a table should be sortable, etc.). The settings under "Show" refer to the format of the content that will be displayed in the table, unformatted list, etc.

For the example view, make sure you have selected the Page display, then click on "Unformatted list." Change the display to "Grid." The grid format is useful for a gallery-like display, filling up horizontal as well as vertical space. Making this change will impact both the page and the block displays, though there will be no visible difference in the block display, since it is only displaying a single Person node. If you scroll to the bottom of the Views interface, you can immediately see the impact of this change in the "Preview" area (figure 12.9). This isn't a perfect representation of how the view will look, since it does not use the site theme and does not incorporate elements of multiple displays (for instance, the RSS icon generated by the Feed display does not show up here), but it can give you a general sense of how your view is shaping up.

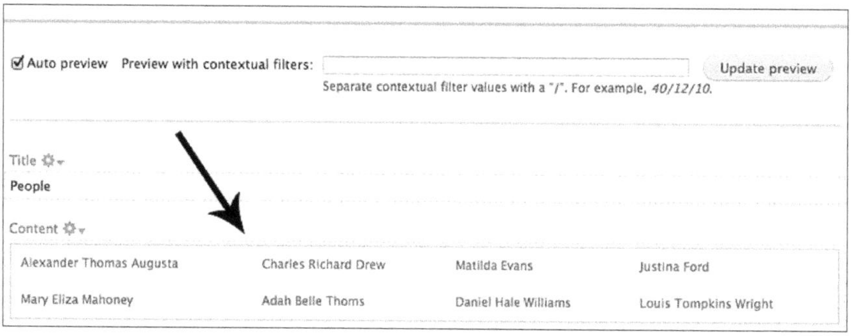

Figure 12.9. The preview of your view after you have set the format to "Grid."

If you click on the "Settings" next to "Grid" once you have selected that display format, you can define the number of columns in the grid, and whether you want to use horizontal or vertical alignment. Horizontal alignment (where the first four results appear in the first row of the grid) is more intuitive if you are trying to create a gallery-like display. Vertical alignment makes more sense if you are displaying a large quantity of titles (or some other set of 1–2 lines of text from each node) and you want them to fill up multiple columns that are defined arbitrarily. The default number of columns, four, is fine in this case.

While we will not need this feature for our example view, the "Grouping field" option available under "Settings" here is extremely useful in many cases, and is worth discussing briefly.

12.4.1   Grouping fields

Under "Settings" for any of the default Views formats (grid, HTML list, jump menu, table, unformatted list), you can choose one of the fields you've added (see section 12.5 or more about fields) as a "Grouping field." This allows you to organize the nodes based on a particular parameter. For instance, if you added a "Profession" field to this view (see section 12.5), you could use it here as the grouping field to create a display of people grouped by profession (figure 12.10). Note: this is just an illustration; you don't need to make these changes on your example site.

Figure 12.10. The effect of using a Profession field as a grouping field.

Once you've added a grouping field and saved the setting, you can click "Settings" again to add a second grouping field, which further groups the results within the first grouping using a different parameter. If you set "Profession" to be the first grouping field, and "Specialization" to be the second, Views would display all the physicians together (separate from the nurses and medical researchers), then, where applicable, it would group together all cardiology specialists, all neurology specialists, etc. Any field can be used as a grouping field, but it's best to choose a field where multiple nodes will share a common value—birth date fields, for instance, are not usually a good choice.

Fields that you wish to use as grouping fields are good candidates for excluding from display (see section 12.5.6.2; figure 12.11). If you don't exclude them from display, they will be repeated: once as the header,

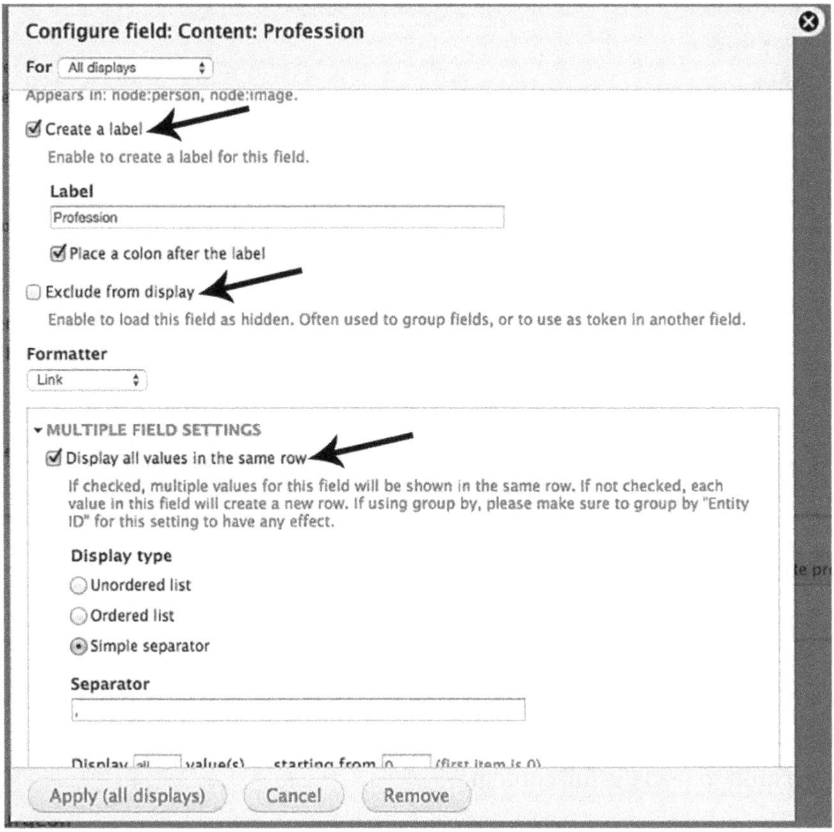

Figure 12.11. The field settings for the Profession field.

and once in every single record grouped under the header. Excluding them from display removes them from each record under the header. In addition, if you are using a grouping field that can accept multiple values, you may want to uncheck the "Display all values in the same row" box under "Multiple field settings." This default option is useful when you are not using a grouping field, in order to avoid duplicate listings for a person who has a multivalued field as part of their profile, but when you are using a grouping field, it is desirable to have a listing for the person under each value (figure 12.12).

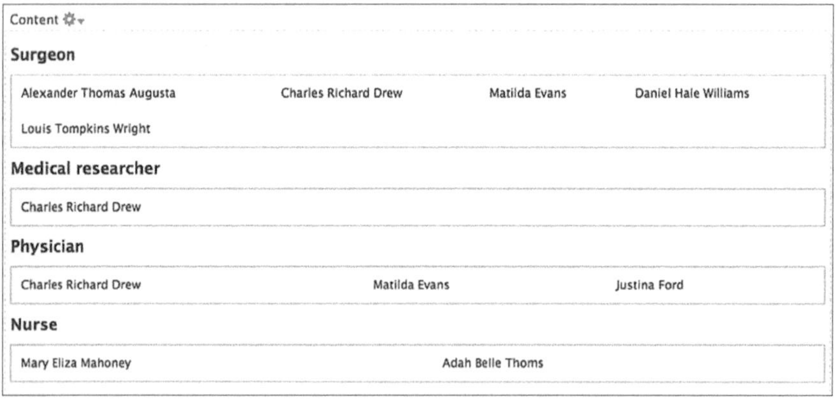

Figure 12.12. The effect of modifying the Profession field as described in figure 12.11.

12.4.2   Show

The "Show" setting refers to the format of the content itself. For a view of nodes, you can choose between "Fields" (where you can specify in the "Fields" configuration section which fields you want to display) and "Content." If your view is based on users or files instead of nodes, there will be an option that corresponds to that entity type available in lieu of "Content."

In most cases, you will use "Fields," just as our example view is currently configured. Choosing "Content" or the equivalent is good in situations where you want to create a blog-like view, either of full posts or of teasers with links to read the full content.

12.5 Fields

In the "Fields" configuration section, our example view currently has one field, "Content: Title." This will display the Drupal title of the nodes that appear on our view. Because of the way we configured Drupal's title field for the Person content type, it displays the full name of all the people in the database. We want this view to display an image of each person, along with their birth and death dates.

12.5.1 Adding fields

In order to pull an image, birth and death dates into the view, click the "Add" button to the right of the "Fields" label (figure 12.13).

TITLE	PAGE SETTINGS	▶ Advanced
Title: People	Path: /people	
FORMAT	Menu: Normal: People	
Format: Unformatted list | Settings	Access: Permission | View published content	
Show: Fields | Settings	⊘ (Add)	
⊘ (Add ▾)	**HEADER**	
FIELDS	⊘ (Add)	
Content: Title	**FOOTER**	

Figure 12.13. The "Add" button for adding more fields.

This will open an overlay where you can check the boxes corresponding to each field you want to add (figure 12.14). In most cases, you'll be adding fields from the "Content" section, so the "Filter" option isn't particularly useful here. The search box, which automatically updates the list as you

Add fields   ⊗

For (All displays   ⬍)

Search [bi]   Filter (- All -   ⬍)

☐ Content: Birth date
   Appears in: node:person.

☐ Content: Body
   Appears in: node:page, node:article, node:person, node:event, node:image. Also known as: Content: Body,
   Content: Biography, Content: Description.

☐ Content: Biography
   This is an alias of Content: Body.

Figure 12.14. Searching for the "Content: Birth" field.

type, is much more helpful here. If you don't want to scroll through the whole list, type "birth" into the search field, and check the box for the "Content: Birth" field. Click the "Apply (all displays)" button at the bottom of the screen, and move on to configuring the birth field.

Adding and configuring one field at a time as described here is easiest as you are learning how to use the Views module. As you gain experience, you may prefer to add all the fields you'll need at the same time. To do this, you can search for each field you want, check the corresponding box, and repeat for the next field before hitting "Apply (all displays)." If you select multiple fields, you will be presented with a sequence of field configuration screens, one for each field. They will be arranged in alphabetical order by field name (e.g., "Content: Birth date," "Content: Death date," "Content: Image") regardless of the order in which you checked the boxes.

12.5.2   Configuring date fields

Most of the parameters for configuring fields are the same regardless of the field type, but there are some important unique configuration settings for some specific fields.

We do not want a label for this field (i.e., we want to just display the date, not "Birth: November 22, 1913"), so uncheck the "Create a label" box.

Under "Formatter," the default "Date and time" is generally the right choice, though you can also choose "Time ago" or "Plain" (which stores the data as it is stored in the database, including "00:00:00" for the hour, minute, and second information that we are not capturing with the field).

Under "Choose how users view dates and times," you can choose from the date formats that you previously configured in section 9.2.2.1. For this view, we just want to display the year, to prevent the birth and date displays for a person from getting too long. This means revising the date format configuration.

Click the "Apply (all displays)" button. The birth date of each person, using the default date format, will now appear under the person's name. Save your view by clicking the "Save" button towards the upper right of the screen.

Now, go to *Configuration > Regional and Language > Date and time > Formats > Add format* and enter "Y," which is the PHP date shorthand corresponding to a year (such as "1872"). Then, go to the Date and Time settings (*Configuration > Regional and Language > Date and time*) and use the drop-down list to change the "Short" date type to use that format. (This recapitulates the steps you took in section 9.2.2.1 to configure the "Long" date format.)

Go back to your view by going to *Structure > Views > People*. Click on the "Content: Birth" field and select "Short" under "Choose how users view dates and times" (figure 12.15). Click "Apply (all displays)," and the view preview should update to just show the year of people's birth.

Figure 12.15. The "Content: Birth date" field after configuration.

Repeat this process for the "Death" field, adding "Content: Death," removing the label, and setting it to only display the year. At this point, your view should show the name of each person, and their birth and death years, in a list.

12.5.3   Configuring image fields

Add the "Content: Image" field to your view. If you use the search box to find it, you'll get numerous results in addition to the one you want. This is due to the fact that you have a content type on your site called "Image," and the search box also searches the metadata of where each field appears, along with any aliases.

This field does not need a label. The formatter should be the default "Image," and the image style should be the "Medium square" (300 pixels, scaled and cropped) that you configured in section 9.2.5.1 (figure 12.16). Under "Link image to," choose "Content," so that when people click on the image, it will take them to the corresponding person's profile. Hit the "Apply (all displays)" button to apply the changes you've made.

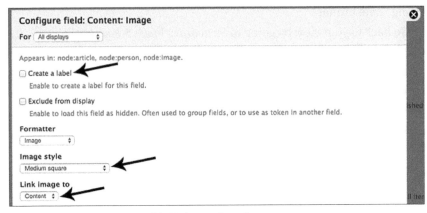

Figure 12.16. The "Content: Image" field after configuration.

12.5.4 Rearranging fields

Now your view should display the name, birth date, death date, and image for each person, arranged in that order. Next, arrange the fields so they appear in the order that you want. Click the little down arrow next to the "Add" button for Fields, and select "Rearrange" (figure 12.17).

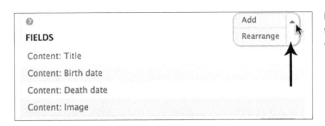

Figure 12.17. Accessing the "Rearrange" option for fields.

Using the little "+" sign to the left of each field name as a handle, drag and drop the fields in the following order: 1) Content: Image, 2) Content: Title, 3) Content: Birth, and 4) Content: Death.

If you want to remove multiple fields, going into the "Rearrange" screen is the fastest way to do it, as you can simply click the "Remove" link, rather than editing each field individually and hitting the "Remove" button at the bottom.

12.5.5 Style settings

To clearly differentiate the names from the other text in this view, click on the "Content: Title" field to edit it. Toggle down the "Style settings" section. Check the box for "Customize field HTML," and set the HTML element to H2 using the drop-down list (figure 12.18). Click "Apply (all displays)" and take a look at the view preview. It's not a perfect representation of how your view will display once you save it, because it doesn't use your site's theme, but it gives you some sense for the effect you've created.

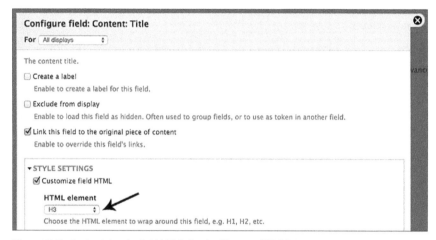

Figure 12.18. Customizing the field HTML for the "Content: Title" field.

There are separate style settings for the field HTML and the label HTML in the "Style settings" section. If you ever have a view where you include a label as part of a grid, unformatted list, or HTML list display, by default the label will appear above (rather than next to) the field content. The easiest way to put the label and field content on the same line is to customize the field HTML (as you did above) and choose <span>.

12.5.6 In-line fields and rewriting fields

We don't want the birth and death fields to display on separate lines. Instead, we want them to display like (1872–1935). There are two ways of accomplishing this; the second is recommended, but the first can be faster in situations where you simply want two fields to appear next to one another.

12.5.6.1 Using "Format" to display in-line fields

To simply put fields on the same line and separate them using a hyphen, click on "Settings" next to "Fields" in the "Format" section of the Views configuration screen. Under "Inline fields," check the boxes of the fields that should appear on the same line (Content: Birth and Content: Death), and put the hyphen in the separator field (figure 12.19).

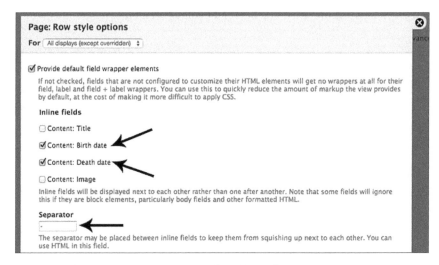

Figure 12.19. The settings configuration next to "fields" in the "Format" section.

This almost has the result that we want, other than the parentheses. We can add the parentheses to the birth and death fields, respectively, by *rewriting* them.

Click on the "Content: Birth" field and toggle down the "Rewrite results" section. Check the box for "Rewrite the output of this field" (figure 12.20). A text box will appear. Below it, toggle down the "Replacement patterns" section. The replacement patterns will show the syntax you can use to pull in the value for the current field, as well as any field that appears before it in the fields list. Sometimes there are multiple options for a single field, as in this case: [field_birth_date-value] will give you the "raw" value (the date as stored in the database, as if you'd chosen the "plain" formatter when you first set up the field), and [field_birth_date] will give you the value of the field, respecting the configuration options you've already selected (e.g., using the "date and time" formatter, displaying it as only a year, etc.) Type into the text box: `([field_birth_date]` (i.e., an opening parenthesis and the replacement pattern for the value of the field). Then click "Apply (all displays)." Configure the "Content: Death" field the same way, putting a closing parenthesis at the end.

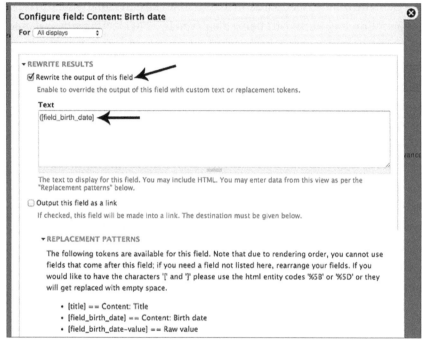

Figure 12.20. Rewriting the birth date field.

12.5.6.2   Excluding and rewriting fields

An alternate approach is useful when you want different groups of in-line fields to be separated in a different way (e.g., for birth and death dates to appear together separated by a hyphen, but for first and middle names to appear together separated by a space), or when you want to have separating punctuation appear immediately next to a field value, rather than with a separating space.[2] It's also faster to configure than the approach described above.

---

2. See the *Drupal for Humanists* website for a case study on using Views to create MLA bibliography listings for an example where this could be relevant.

Edit the "Content: Birth" field and check the "Exclude this field from display" box, which appears towards the top of the configuration interface; if you previously checked the "Rewrite results" option as described above, uncheck it. The field will disappear from your view as soon as you click "Apply (all displays)." Next, edit the "Content: Death" field and toggle down the "Rewrite results" section, as well as the "Replacement patterns." Even though "Content: Birth" isn't being displayed by your view, it's still available as a replacement pattern because it appears *before* "Content: Death".[3] In the text field, type: ([field_birth_date] – [field_death_date]) and click "Apply (all displays)." The result will look the same as the result using the approach described above.

The *Drupal for Humanists* site includes an example view from the World Shakespeare Bibliography that extensively uses field rewriting. If you have a lot of fields that are excluded from display, and particularly if you have duplicates of individual fields that are rewritten or configured in different ways, you may want to toggle down the "More" setting at the bottom of the configuration screen for those fields, and give them a more descriptive name. For instance, if you had two birth fields, one rewritten using a parenthesis and displayed, and another excluded from display, you might name the latter "Birth – no paren, rw" as a shorthand for a birth field that doesn't have parentheses and is to be used for rewriting. There is no standard set of shorthand conventions, so you can use whatever makes sense, as long as you document the conventions you establish for your project.

12.6 Filter criteria

Filter criteria restrict what content is displayed. By default, even if you don't limit your view to a particular content type, Drupal adds a filter to only display published content, "Content: Published (Yes)." This is important because, by default, only site administrators and the person

---

3. For comparison, you can open the rewriting interface for the "Content: Birth" field. [field_title] and [field_image] appear as options, but "Content: Death" will not, because it appears *after* "Content: Birth." When arranging fields, it is important to position all fields you want to use for rewriting *before* the field where you actually do the rewriting.

who drafted the unpublished content would be able to see it, and everyone else would see an error message if they tried to access the unpublished content.

On the example view there is an additional filter, "Content: Type (= Person)." If you click on it, you could check the box for showing other content types as well, in contrast to the simple view creation interface which only allowed you to select one content type.

While we already configured the filters we need for the example view when we first created it, you could potentially add any number of other filters. A few examples:

> If you had a site with an "Event" content type, you could add a filter that limits the results to those where the event date is greater or equal to the current date, in order to only show events that have not yet taken place.
>
> If you wanted to create a gallery, you could add a filter to only show those nodes where a particular image field is not empty using the File ID option, "Content: Image (field_image:fid)," to avoid gaps in the display.
>
> If you're using the Flag module[4] (see the *Drupal for Humanists* site for more on Flag), you could add a filter in order to only show nodes that at least five people selected as a favorite.

The *Drupal for Humanists* website includes many examples of views that use different filter criteria. Filter criteria can be *exposed*, or made visible to users, allowing them to dynamically update the results list based on criteria they select. Section 13.6.4 will describe how to configure exposed filters.

If you need to create a one-off display of all the events in the life of a particular person (as a way to quickly gather material for a blog post about that person, for instance), you can set up a filter where you limit the results to event nodes that reference the person in question. In general, though, if you're trying to create something like a block that you can use on an individual person's profile, showing all the events in his or her life, filter

---

4. https://www.drupal.org/project/flag

criteria are *not* the right approach, because you would have to create a new block display for each person, with the filter set to pull in only one person's events. Under the "Advanced" views settings, there is a section called "Contextual filters" that you can use to accomplish such a thing much more easily. Contextual filters are discussed in section 13.3.5.

12.6.1 And/or options

By default, all filters that you add to a view are connected by "and": an item must meet all the criteria listed, or it will be excluded. If you click on the small down arrow next to the "Add" button for filters, you can rearrange filters and create new groups of filters that can be separated by either "and" or "or."

12.7 Sort criteria

By default, Views sorts nodes by the order they were published, with the most recent nodes appearing first, using "Content: Post date (desc)." To define a different sort order, you'll need to add criteria, and rearrange them so they appear before the "Content: Post date" sort criterion, otherwise the nodes will sort first by post date, and then (if two nodes have the exact same post date) by the criteria you've specified. You could also remove "Content: Post date (desc)," by clicking on it and hitting the "Remove" button, if it isn't relevant for how you want to sort your content.

For the example view, we want different sort orders for different displays. Let's start with the page display, and make its configuration the default. Remove "Content: Post date (desc)." If no sort order is defined, Drupal will sort the nodes by their node ID, which is to say, by post date in the opposite order, with the nodes that were added first appearing first. Add "Content: Surname" as a sort criterion, and choose "ascending" as the direction. This will sort the people in alphabetical order, by last name, which is the correct order for the page display.

Next, click on the "Block" display at the top of the Views configuration screen. Once you have selected that display, click on the "Content: Surname (asc)" sort criterion. At the top of the overlay screen that appears, using the drop-down list, choose "This block (override)" and then click the "Remove" button (figure 12.21). The "Sort criteria" header should now appear in

Figure 12.21. After you've selected the block display, choose "This block (override)" in the top left, then click the "Remove" button.

italics, without any criteria under it. If you click the "Page" display, the "Content: Surname (asc)" sort option should still be there. If you go to the "Page" display and "Content: Surname (asc)" is missing, add it to the page again, go back to the block, and make sure you've chosen "This block (override)" when removing the surname criterion.

For the overridden "Block" display, add the sort criterion "Global: Random" and click "Apply (this display)," then "Apply (this display)" again, as there are no configuration options for this sort criterion beyond exposing it to users, which wouldn't be useful since there's nothing they could configure either. A single person should appear in the view preview area. To see the effect of the random sort order, you can click the "Update preview" button above the preview area, again and again, and different people should appear below.

While it isn't relevant for the example view, the sort criteria—like the filter criteria—can be exposed for users to configure; in most cases, this amounts to selecting an ascending or descending sort for a given criterion.

12.8 Display-specific settings

At the top of the center column of the Views interface, there are display-specific settings (e.g., "Page settings," "Block settings," etc., depending on the display that you are looking at). Different displays have slightly different sets of options, and we will walk through the options for each of the three displays of the example view.

12.8.1   Page settings

12.8.1.1   Path

The path is the URL where the Views-generated page will appear; entering something in this field is required if you have a page display for your view, or for certain other displays, including feeds.

12.8.1.2   Menu

By default, Views-generated pages are not added to a menu. To add a page to a menu, click "No menu" and instead select "Normal menu entry." Enter the title (the text that will appear in the menu), an optional description, and choose the menu from the drop-down list. You can only select the top-level menu; if you want to make the Views-generated page a child page of another menu item, you need to first add the page to a menu, and rearrange it using the Menu configuration interface (*Structure > Menus > [Menu name]*).

12.8.1.3   Access

The default setting here limits access to the Views-generated page to any user who has the permission for "View published content." By default, this includes anonymous (unauthenticated) users; see section 10.5 for more about how to define permissions. If this is a view of users rather than nodes, the permission setting will be "View user profiles."

Instead of using a particular permission setting, you may want to limit access to a view to a particular role (like administrator). Click "Permission," change it to "Role," and then choose the role(s) that should be able to see the view.

Sometimes views need to be accessed by nonhuman agents, such as a Views Data Export CSV display that will be used by a Feeds importer on another site (see chapter 14 for more about the Feeds module). In such cases, you may need to change the Access setting to "None," which bypasses the Drupal permissions system entirely.

12.8.2   Feed settings

Feeds displays have a "Path" and an "Access" setting, just like the Page display. There is an additional setting, "Attach to," that applies to Feeds displays. This allows you to select other displays (such as a Page, and/or Block) that should display an RSS icon at the bottom, with a link to the RSS feed.

12.8.3   Block settings

Blocks have an "Access" setting, as well as a "Block name." The block name is the text that will appear as the title of the block.

12.9 Header and footer

The header and footer sections appear below the display-specific settings. You can add one or more text areas ("Global: Text area"; for writing custom text, like an explanation of what the view contains, or how to use exposed filters), or a View area ("Global: View area," that will allow you to embed another View in the header/footer of the view), or a result summary ("Global: Result summary," showing how many pages of results there are). You can also choose whether or not these items appear when a view has no results. The example view doesn't need a header or footer.

12.10 Pager

At the bottom of the center column of the Views interface, this section lets you specify the number of results that will be displayed, and how. By default, Drupal provides a "full pager" (that shows a number for each page of results, in addition to "next," "previous," "first," and "last" navigation options) and 10 results.

If you click on "Full" under "Use pager," you can choose to display a specified number of results, all results, or choose between the "Full" and "Mini" pager (which provides fewer navigation options, but doesn't require that the entire webpage be reloaded as you navigate through the different pages of results). If you have enabled a pager (either full or mini), you can configure how many pages you want to offer, what the text of the pager should say (other than "first," "last," etc.), whether you want to provide an option for seeing all items, etc. The example view displays all Person nodes, so a pager is not needed.

12.11 Caching

Buried in the advanced settings section is an option for turning on *caching*, which saves the results of the database query that a view executes, and /or the rendered HTML output (the results, once they've been processed through the various settings you've configured for how the view and its fields should be displayed). This is easy to overlook or forget about, but it can have a tremendous impact on your site's performance. This problem is most noticeable on sites with thousands of nodes; without any caching, Views-generated pages are excruciatingly slow to load. But even for smaller sites, turning on view caching wherever possible is a good way to guard against trouble, particularly if the site is part of a multisite setup where there may be multiple sites putting demands on the server at the same time. Loading a complex view with no caching enabled when other sites in the same multisite are also experiencing traffic can at worst bring your site down altogether, with a MySQL error about too many connections.

Toggle open the "Advanced" section in the right column, and look under the "Other" section.

Click "None" next to caching, and in the configuration box that appears, choose "Time-based." On the next page, you can choose the duration of the cache; 1 hour is default. If your site will be changing very quickly (for instance, if you expect a lot of users to be contributing content during a conference), you should set this to a shorter time period, because any new content that added since the last time the view was cached won't appear until the cache is refreshed.

For views that display content (rather than users or taxonomy terms), a good alternative is the Views Content Cache[5] module. Once you install and enable it, you can choose "Content-based" caching. This allows you to choose which content types the module should monitor. Changes to that content type (new content, deleting content, or updating content) will cause the cache to refresh. You should still set a minimum cache lifetime of 1 minute, at least during periods when you don't expect the site will be under constant use.

---

5. https://www.drupal.org/project/views_content_cache

12.12 Final result

After you have made the changes described above, save the view, and look at the resulting page, you should see something like figure 12.22.

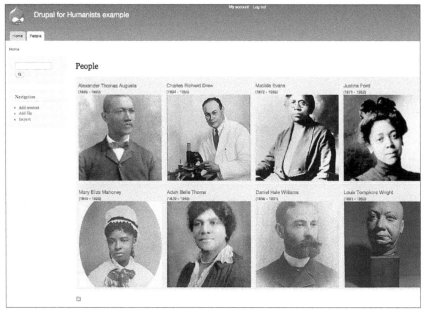

Figure 12.22. The final form of the page display of the view.

For each person in the database, Drupal displays their picture, name (in a more prominent text style), and their birth and death years. The picture and name are clickable, to take you to the person's profile. This "People" page appears as part of the main menu on the site.

12.13 Summary

The basic configuration options described in this chapter have given you a general familiarity with how to create and configure views. Chapter 13 will build on this by describing how to use the Views module to create maps, slide shows, time lines, and tables, how to pull in data from connected nodes, and how to use the contextual filter option to only show nodes that share a common node reference (e.g., all events referring to the same person). Before moving on, consider creating a new view (you can simply call it "Test" or "Example," and delete it when you're done), and seeing what happens when you add different fields, use a different format, or configure things differently. The Views module is an extremely useful module to master, and hands-on experimentation is the best way to develop your skill with it.

Advanced Views

13.1 Overview

Chapter 12 provided an overview of the basic functionality of the Views module. This chapter will provide additional case studies covering more formats (tables, slide shows, maps, time lines, and galleries), advanced configuration options (contextual filters, which allow you to easily limit results to those that share a particular node reference; and relationships, which allow you to pull in data from a different node connected by a node reference field), and exposed filters, which allow users to independently change the filtering on a view you have already created.

Before proceeding with this chapter, make sure you have created at least three Event nodes for at least two different people, as well as three Image nodes. If you want to bulk import Event nodes, you can work through chapter 14 before returning to chapter 13.

13.2 Troubleshooting Views

When creating the views described in this chapter, keep in mind these tips for troubleshooting the Views module:

> 1. To avoid a number of strange bugs (including the "drop-down" selection style for node and term reference filters failing to work), after you click "Continue & Edit" on the basic view creation screen, save the

view immediately. Until the view has been saved at least once, certain parts of the configuration interface are more liable to break. Even after you've saved the view once, remember to save the view periodically as you make changes.

2. Related to saving your view: if you've made a change to the view that messes it up in a considerable way, and you can't (or can't easily) undo it, you can hit "Cancel" (next to "Save") in the upper right corner of the Views interface. Then, when you go to *Structure > Views* and edit the view you were previously working on, it will have reverted to the last saved state.

3. Many of the views described below use additional modules to generate their display format. If you don't find the indicated format in the list of display formats, go back to the Modules page and make sure that you have the specified modules enabled. If the modules are enabled but the display format still doesn't appear, make sure you've installed any required libraries. Checking *Reports > Status report* is a good place to start, although it doesn't necessarily cover all libraries.

13.3 Maps

In this view, we will create two maps: 1) a page display with a comprehensive map that shows all events in the database, and 2) a block display that shows events that apply to a specific person. This section will cover the use of contextual filters (accessible through the "Advanced" section of Views configuration), as well as the use of the Leaflet module for creating map displays, using data stored in the Geofield associated with the Event content type.

13.3.1 Installing modules

Before creating this view, you need to install and enable the Leaflet[1] module; also enable the submodule Leaflet Views. Because many of the events will be clustered in the same general location, you should also install and enable the Leaflet Markercluster[2] module. Note that both of these modules, Leaflet and Leaflet Markercluster, require you to add a library; consult the README.txt file in each module for instructions on

1. https://www.drupal.org/project/leaflet
2. https://www.drupal.org/project/leaflet_markercluster

where to download the library and where it should go. By default, Leaflet maps defaults to the OpenStreetMap Mapnik[3] style. To increase the number of map options available to you, including Google Maps and a number of attractive and artistic map renderings, you should additionally install and enable Leaflet More Maps.[4]

This book recommends Leaflet as the mapping module largely for its relatively simple configuration interface and the number of easy-to-use, add-on modules that increase map attractiveness and functionality. There are other mapping modules (such as OpenLayers, which provides a more sophisticated set of configuration options) that one could substitute for Leaflet, though the exact configuration process varies between modules. For an up-to-date list of mapping modules for Drupal, consult the "Comparison of mapping modules" page[5] on drupal.org, and look for modules that list "Geofield" under "Supported location storage modules"; modules that do not support locations stored in a geofield would require more extensive changes to your content type to be usable.

13.3.2 Basic view creation

Once you have installed and enabled the modules indicated above, create a new view using the following settings on the basic view creation page:

> **View name "Map," description:** "Map of all events, with block of events for an individual person."
>
> Show *Content* of type *Event*.
>
> Create a page, title "Map" and path map.
>
>> **Display format:** *Leaflet map* of fields.
>>
>> **Items to display:** 0 (recall that this means "all"), uncheck "use a pager."
>>
>> Create a menu link, add to *Main menu*, link text "Map."
>
> Create a block, title "Map."
>
>> **Display format:** *Leaflet map* of fields.
>>
>> **Items per page:** 0.

---

3. http://mapnik.org/
4. https://www.drupal.org/project/leaflet_more_maps
5. https://www.drupal.org/node/1704948

Click the "Continue & edit" button, which will take you to the full Views interface. Save the view. For the Leaflet map format, no preview is available, so in order to check your work you'll need to save the view, then view the page display you've created by going to the path you've assigned it (yoursite.org/map). If you're creating a more complex map (for instance, using fields pulled in using a relationship as described in section 13.4.6), and you want to make sure the relationship is correctly configured and pulling in the right data, you may want to first choose a format other than the map (such as a simple "unformatted list"), and only switch to Leaflet map once you see that Views is pulling up the data you want.

13.3.3 Adding fields

Before you can even access the Leaflet map configuration settings, you have to add a geofield. Under the "Fields" section, add "Field: Location coordinates." The default configuration (using the formatter "Well Known Text (WKT)" and data option "Use full geometry") is correct here.

13.3.4 Configuring Leaflet maps

Click "Settings" next to "Leaflet maps" under "Format." By default, Leaflet will have selected "Field: Location coordinates" as the data source (i.e., the location information that will generate points on the map). Under "Description Content," choose "<node entity>," then select a view mode (figure 13.1). The teaser is default, but "Full content" could be another good option. This will display the content of the Event node in the style you have configured for the teaser, or the full node display, depending on which you choose. See chapter 9 for instructions on how to modify either of these display types. Hit "Apply," then save the view. Go to the path of the page you just created, /map, to look at the map.

How the resulting map looks will depend largely on the data that you've entered into the site so far (figure 13.2). The map will be zoomed out as far as necessary to display the coordinates for every event where you've added a location. If you have installed and enabled the Leaflet Markerclusterer module, locations that are relatively close together (the threshold varies depending on the zoom level of the map) will be merged into a cloud with a number indicating how many points that cloud represents. If you click on an individual point, a pop-up will appear with the teaser or full content

Figure 13.1. Configuring the Leaflet display.

Figure 13.2. The map, using Markerclusterer and OSM Mapnik.

display for that node. If you click on any of the numbered clouds, the map will zoom in until you can see individual points and pull up their details.

13.3.4.1   Troubleshooting Leaflet maps

If you visit the page that your view created and you don't see anything below the page title (i.e., just blank space), then something is either wrong with the map configuration, or the view isn't pulling in the right data.

Under the Leaflet Map format settings, you can try unchecking the "Hide empty" box (underneath "map height"), as a way to check if Drupal can successfully display a Leaflet map at all. If you still see a completely empty spot under the page title on the page you created with Views that should be displaying a map, go to *Reports > Status report* and scroll down until you see "Leaflet" to check and see if the Leaflet library is installed correctly. If not, walk through the steps in the Leaflet module's README.txt file again to install the Leaflet library.

If unchecking the "Hide empty" box does successfully display a map, but checking the box again causes the map to disappear, it probably means that the problem is with the view. One way to troubleshoot this is to change the format of your view from "Leaflet map" to "Unformatted list" and look under the Views preview to make sure that the right data are being pulled in (titles of event nodes), and under at least some of the location coordinates you're seeing something that looks like "POINT (-77.0194377 38.9226843)." If the "location coordinates" field is always blank, that suggests that something is misconfigured with the location coordinates field. Revisit section 6.5.5, and ensure that you have correctly installed and configured the necessary modules. If you are developing your site locally (i.e., with the code and database running on your own laptop), and your laptop was not connected to the Internet when you added the event nodes, it is possible that there may not be any data in the "location coordinates" field because the Geocoder module responsible for translating the text-based location into geographic coordinates requires an Internet connection to do the lookup. Once you are reconnected to the Internet, edit and resave the event nodes, and check back with the view you've created (using the "unformatted list" format) to see if values are appearing.

If you go to the page where your map should appear, and what you see is a gray square with some map pushpins on it, but no actual map, this is probably caused by an Internet connectivity issue. Drupal pulls in the map tiles from the map provider as it needs them, and if it is unable to do so (for instance, if you're building the site locally on your own computer, and aren't currently connected to the Internet), the result will be a gray square. Once you fix your Internet connection and reload the page, the map should appear.

If you only have one location on the map (e.g., because you only have created one event node), depending on your map choice, this may cause a white box to appear where the map should be. Some of the maps, particularly those provided by the Leaflet More Maps, don't offer the most zoomed-in level of resolution that the Leaflet module offers. Because having only a single point will cause Leaflet to zoom in all the way by default, the map will appear as a white box until you zoom out to a resolution it supports. You can fix this by going into the settings for Leaflet Map in Views, toggling open "Zoom settings" and reducing the maximum zoom level until the map shows up without you having to zoom out.

13.3.5   Contextual filters

The block display of this view is meant to appear on a person's profile page, and show a map containing only the events related to that person.

Select the "Block" display, and toggle down the "Advanced" settings in the right column of the Views configuration interface. Click "Add"

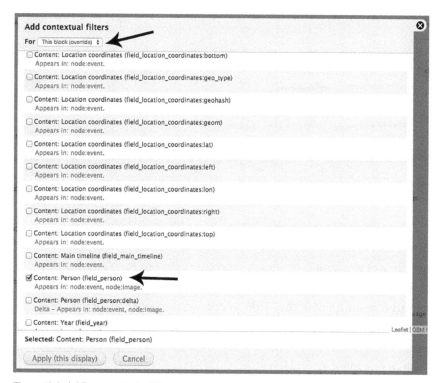

Figure 13.3. Adding a contextual filter.

next to "Contextual Filter." Override the display using the drop-down menu at the top, so it says "For this block (override)" and check the box corresponding to "Content: Person (field_person)" (figure 13.3). Take care to select the right option, and not accidentally choose "Content: Person (field_person:delta)," which deals with different data. Click the "Apply (this display)" button.

There are a number of things to configure on the next screen (figure 13.4). In the section "When the filter value is *not* available," choose "Provide default value," and in the drop-down list that appears, select "Content ID from URL." This tells Views to look at the node ID of the page where the block appears, and use that as the filter value for this block, so that only events that have, for example, Adah Bell Thoms's Person node ID in the Person field are included when the block appears on Adah Bell Thoms's profile (the Person node about her).

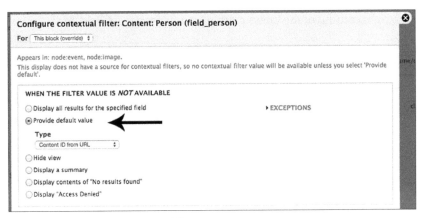

Figure 13.4. Configuring the contextual filter.

While we don't need it for this case study, it's worth looking further down the configuration screen to the section "When the filter value *is* available or a default is provided," and check the box for "Override title." By default, you define the title of this block in the same place you would for any other display, in the "Title" section in the upper left of the Views interface. Occasionally, it can be useful to override that title when you're using a contextual filter to include some data from the contextual filter itself in the title.

Once you've checked the box for "override title," you can enter the new title using "%1" as a placeholder for the value of the contextual filter—in this case, it's the name of the person referenced in the event. You could enter, for instance, "Map of %1's life" and once you enable this block, it will appear on Adah Bell Thoms's profile with the title "Map of Adah Bell Thoms's life." In this case, leave the "override title" box unchecked; in the context of a person's profile, just "Map" will suffice as a title.

13.3.6   Caching

Turn on content-based caching (as described in section 12.11; install and enable the Views Content Cache[6] module first), and check the checkbox for "Event." Set the minimum lifetime for query results and rendered display to 1 minute, and the maximum to 6 days.

13.3.7   Enabling the block

Save the view, and go to *Structure > Blocks*. Find the block "View: Map," which should be towards the bottom with the other disabled blocks. Click on the "Configure" link for it. Set the region to "Content," and under "Visibility settings" at the bottom of the page, click on "Content types" and check the box for "Person," so that the block only appears on the Person content type. This will ensure that it receives the contextual filter value it needs. If the block doesn't receive the contextual filter value for a person, it won't show up. While this is a good thing (insofar as you don't have to worry about a stray, empty map appearing on other pages when the contextual filter doesn't pull up any results), having blocks try and fail to load on pages where they don't apply will slow down your site, so it's best to limit blocks to appearing only in places where they'll successfully display.

   Once you have saved these settings, go to the profile of a person for whom you have created some events to see how the individual map looks.

13.4 Site time line

This view will create a site time line that will include events from multiple people. To do this, we will use the A Simple Timeline[7] module, which can pull in data from Partial Date fields (see section 6.5.2 for a discussion of the Partial Date module compared to the Date module). In the following case

---

6. https://www.drupal.org/project/views_content_cache
7. https://www.drupal.org/project/simple_timeline

study, which covers creating a time line for an individual person, we will use the Views Timeline JS Integration[8] module. This module has a more sophisticated display and additional configuration options, but it can't use data stored in a Partial Date field. It is because of this constraint that we also added a regular Date field to the Event content type (see section 7.3.2.2). For information on other Drupal modules that provide time line functionality, see the *Drupal for Humanist*s website.

13.4.1 Installing modules

Install and enable the A Simple Timeline module. No additional libraries are needed, and there are no module-specific configuration options.

13.4.2 Basic view creation

Once you have installed and enabled A Simple Timeline, create a new view using the following settings on the basic view creation page:

> View name "Site time line," description: "Sitewide time line of major events from all people's lives."
>
>> Show *Content* of type *Event.*
>>
>> Create a page, title "Time line" and path time line.
>>
>>> Display format: *Simple time line of teasers, without links, without comments.*
>>>
>>> Items to display: 0 (all), uncheck "use a pager."
>>>
>>> Create a menu link, add to *Main menu*, link text "Time line."

Click the "Continue & edit" button, which will take you to the full Views interface. Save the view.

13.4.3 Adding fields

The Simple Timeline format is compatible with Views preview, and when you load the full Views interface, it will pull in all Event nodes, with the most recently published item appearing first.

---

8. https://www.drupal.org/project/views_timelinejs

The configuration of a view that uses the A Simple Timeline format is unusual insofar as it combines some traits of a content display (you must select either "Content" or "Simple Timeline Item" under "Show" for the A Simple Timeline module to work; selecting "Fields" will trigger an error message), but at the same time you can and must add fields to the Fields section, which is typically greyed out when you choose to show "Content" rather than "Fields."

Add the field "Content: Date," uncheck "create a label," and under "Date format," choose "Long."

13.4.4 Adding filters

The site time line shouldn't have every event, only those deemed significant enough to appear on the main time line. Under "Filter criteria," add "Content: Main timeline (field_main_timeline)," select "On" under "Options," and apply the changes. This will remove all events where the "Main timeline" checkbox is not checked.

13.4.5 Configuring the simple time line

Under the "Format" section, click on "Content" and change it to "Simple Timeline Item." Under "Timeline Date fields," check the box for "Date." Under "Timeline text fields," check the box for "Content: Title." While there is also an image field option, the Event content type doesn't store an image. Save the configuration and look at the result.

This configuration already improves the time line, grouping events by date, with whatever granularity is available. However, there is a major shortcoming insofar as it isn't clear who each event relates to.

To address this, add the field "Content: Person," and uncheck "create a label" on the configuration screen. Rearrange the fields so that "Content: Person" appears before "Content: Title." Next, click on "Settings" next to "Simple Timeline Item." Check the box for "Content: Person" under "Timeline text fields," and in the separator box, enter <br /> to create a line break between the name and the event.

This improves the time line further, but it creates a user interface issue. Contrary to most user's expectations, the person's name and the text describing the event link to two different places: the name to the person's profile, and the event text to the event node. There is no particular reason for users to look at an event node directly; for more information about the event, they should look at the person's profile, which will display an individual time line with more details.

In order to remove the link to the event node, click on the "Content: Title" field and uncheck the box for "Link this field to the original piece of content," and apply the changes.

The site time line is almost ready; the only remaining shortcoming is that we aren't taking advantage of the option for displaying an image. While it's true that there are no images as part of the Event content type, there *is* an image field in the Person content type, and the Event content type includes a node reference to a Person node. We can use the Views Relationship option to pull in that image.

13.4.6   Relationships

In the far right column of the Views interface, toggle down the "Advanced" section. Under Relationships, add "Content: Person (field_person)." This will allow you to pull in fields from the nodes referenced in the "Person" node reference field.

Be careful not to accidentally choose "Content: Person (field_person) – reverse." *Reverse* relationships allow you to pull in fields from all the *nodes that point to* the selected node using that particular field. This isn't relevant for a view displaying nodes of the Event content type, since there are no node reference fields on this site that point to events. If, however, you had a view of Person nodes, and you wanted to include their birth and death locations as part of the view, you could add the "Content: Person (field_person) – reverse" relationship, and use that to pull in data from the Location field stored in event nodes that point to the person.

The "identifier" needs to be something that you'll recognize when you have to select the relationship as part of a field configuration screen in the next step. By default, Drupal uses the name of the field. If you only have one or two relationships, based on different fields, you can leave this as the default value.

A section "Delta" will appear if the node reference field you used for the relationship can accept more than one value. Leave this with the default setting "All" for now; we will revisit this in section 13.4.6.1.

Save the configuration, and under the "Fields" section, add the field "Content: Image." A new option, "Relationship," will be available at the top of the configuration screen (figure 13.5). Select the relationship you just created, choosing the identifier from the dropdown. If you used the default value, this should be "field_person." If you don't select a relationship, nothing will appear in the view for this field, because for fields that don't specify a relationship, Views looks for that field within the nodes represented by the current set of results, which in this case are Event nodes that don't have an image field. Selecting the "field_person" relationship here tells Views to look for the image field in the node that's connected to each of the current set of results (Events) using the field specified in the relationship (the "person" field, which does exist in the Event content type).

For the Image field, uncheck "create a label", set the image style to "Thumbnail", and change the configuration so that the "Link image to" drop down list says "Content". Apply the changes.

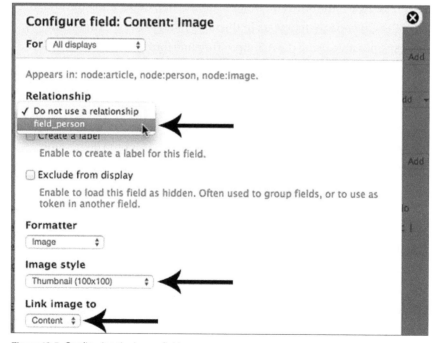

Figure 13.5. Configuring the Image field.

Because we are using the A Simple Timeline view, one additional step is needed to make the image appear in the display. Click "Settings" next to "Simple Timeline Item," and under "Timeline Image field," select "(field_person) Content: Image." Now, the images should show up as part of the time line.

13.4.6.1   Relationships and duplicate results

If you have imported the event data as described in section 14.5 before creating this view, if you look closely at the time line you may notice something odd. The event "Co-founded the National Association of Colored Graduate Nurses (NACGN)" appears *twice*, once with each woman's picture. Because of the format of the simple time line renders events in a vertical sequence with the same amount of space between each item (regardless of whether two items share a date, or whether several millenia transpired between the events), the end result is misleading.

This is caused by the default setting for the "Delta" configuration when you created the relationship. Ideally, there would be a way for Views to return a single entry with two images, rather than duplicating the entry for each Person node that appears in the node reference field. Unfortunately, that isn't possible using the A Simple Timeline format as the module is currently written (figure 13.6).

If you were creating an ad hoc time line (a list of events using the "unformatted list" of fields format, for instance) you would have more flexibility to work around this problem. You could change the configuration of the relationship you already created to specify "1" for the delta value. This would make it a relationship to the *first* person listed in the Person node reference field. You could then add "Content: Person" a second time as a relationship, specify "2" for the delta value, and change the identifier in some way to ensure you can distinguish between the two relationships (for instance, changing it to "field_person_2", or more transparently, "second person"). Then, you could add "Content: Image" as a field again, and use the same field configurations as above, but this time set the relationship to the second Person. Then, you could rearrange the fields so that the two "Content: Image" fields are next to each other. You could then click on "settings" next to "fields" in the "Format" section, and check the boxes so that the two image fields are in line with one another (similar to the

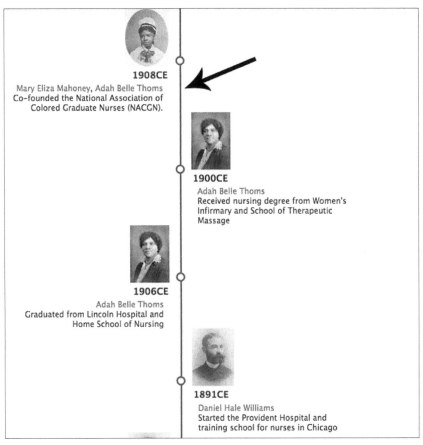

Figure 13.6. Final result of site time line.

scenario in section 12.5.6.1). This would achieve the desired result, but it's only possible because the unformatted list of fields places no restrictions on what fields you can have, or how you can arrange them.

If you want to continue to use the A Simple Timeline format for your time line, the easiest way to work around this issue is to disregard the image of the second person by specifying "1" for the delta value of the relationship you already created. Doing this will eliminate the duplication. The names of both people will still appear on the time line, each with a link to their respective person profile.

This scenario is highly representative of many situations you'll encounter when developing Drupal sites, particularly if your projects lack the resources to fund the development of module improvements to address shortcomings like this. While costs can vary significantly, adjustments to existing modules by experienced developers can fall in the range of $4,000–$7,000, and new module development generally begins around $7,000. Is it better for your site to have a time line that's clearly formatted to look like a time line (in contrast to the unformatted list format, which looks more like a list of historical events), or does the module requirement that there be only one image create too much liability for your project in opening you up to claims of historical erasure? Different projects will make different decisions based on their own communities and needs.

13.4.7   Caching

Turn on content-based caching (as described in section 12.11), and check the checkbox for "Event." Set the minimum lifetime for query results and rendered display to 1 minute, and the maximum to 6 days.

13.5 Individual time line

In this view we will create a more sophisticated time line of all the events related to an individual person, which will appear as a block on their profile page.

13.5.1   Installing modules

Install the Views TimelineJS Integration module, and enable only Views TimelineJS. This module requires you to download a library from Github, unzip that folder, rename it as "timeline" and move it to your libraries folder, so it can be found at sites/all/libraries/timeline.

13.5.2   Basic view creation

Once you have installed and enabled Views Timeline JS Integration, create a new view using the following settings on the basic view creation page:

> View name "**Individual time line**," description: "Time line block of all events in a person's life."
>
> Show *Content* of type *Event*.
>
> Uncheck box for creating a page.
>
> Check box for creating a block.

> **Block title:** Time line.
>
> **Display format:** *TimelineJS* of fields.
>
> **Items per page:** 0 (all).

Click the "Continue & edit" button, which will take you to the full Views interface. Save your view at this point. When the Views interface reloads, it will give you a preview that starts with the word "Array," and includes additional indented text, including a warning about "Insufficient field mapping." This will be addressed by adding fields and pointing to them in the TimelineJS Views settings. The only preview available through the Views interface is this array, which shows the data as it will be sent to the time line module. To see what the time line actually looks like, you'll need to enable the block and look at it on a page where it appears.

13.5.3   Adding fields

TimelineJS can't parse dates that are stored in a Partial Date field, so for this time line we'll need to use the Year field (which stores the year in a Date field) as the source of the date. Add the field "Content: Year," uncheck "create a label," and choose the "Short" format, then apply the changes. Also add the "Content: Body" field, and uncheck "create a label," and apply.

13.5.4   Configuring TimelineJS

Under "Format," click on "Settings" next to TimelineJS.

You can skip the "General configuration" section at the top; the default settings are fine.

Scroll down to the "Field mappings" section. For "Headline," choose "Content: Title." For "Body text," choose "Content: Body." For "Start and end date," choose "Content: Year." Leave the rest of the fields empty; unlike on the site time line, it makes less sense to pull in an image from the corresponding person node, because every image will be the same (since this time line will only show events related to a single person), and the image that would be pulled in will already be on the same page as this time line, since it will be part of the person's profile.

Under "Display configuration," enter 400 and choose "px" for the width of the time line (in order to make it match the width of the map described in section 13.2). Set the height to 400 pixels; if you were using images as part of the time line, you might want this to be larger to accommodate the image size you selected when configuring the image field, but setting the height to less than 400 px cuts off the display of the text of each event. The "%" option allows you to define the time line as a percentage of available screen space, but depending on your site theme, this may or may not work. If you try the "%" option and if no time line appears when you enable the block, try to define it using the pixel option.

Once you apply these changes, you'll see that the preview has updated. If there are any nodes that don't have a value in the year field, you will see an error "Could not format date for field field_date_field in node [node ID #]. It won't be shown in time line." While the formatting of the preview isn't the most user-friendly, it is fairly readable. You should see dates next to "[startDate] =>," titles of event nodes next to "[headline] =>," and fuller descriptions next to "[text] =>." The view currently displays all events, so there's a lack of clarity surrounding who each event relates to. In this case, though, we do not need to pull in the name of the person to clear this up, because we'll be applying a contextual filter to limit the results to one individual at a time.

13.5.5   Enabling the block

Follow the steps in section 13.3.7 to enable the individual time line block on Person nodes. Go to any Person profile to see how the time line looks so far.

13.5.6   Contextual filter

Toggle down the "Advanced" section in the far-right column, and under "Contextual filters," add "Content: Person." Under the section "When the filter value is *not* in the URL," choose "Provide default value" and select "Content ID from URL," then apply the changes.

You may notice that the information in the preview section disappeared as soon as you added the contextual filter; this was not an issue when we previously configured a contextual filter in section 13.2.5 because no preview was available to begin with. The automatic preview has disappeared because there is nothing providing the view with the node ID of a person node, which it needs to display results.

Save your view, and go to the content overview page (by clicking *Content* in the administration menu). Find a Person node corresponding to a person who you know has events in the database; if you have entered the example data, look for Matilda Evans. It may be easiest to use the filter at the top of the page to show only items where type = Person. Once you see the person you're looking for in the list, hover your mouse over the "edit" link, and look at the bottom left of your screen. In many browsers, you will see a URL appear there; look for the number after /node/ (figure 13.7). This number is the node ID of that person node. Make note of it, and return to editing the individual time line view. If your browser doesn't display the URL, right-click on the "edit" link, copy the link location, paste it into a plain-text editor, and look for the node ID.

	TITLE	TYPE	AUTHOR	STATUS	UPDATED ▼	OPERATIONS
☐	Matilda Evans	Person	admin	published	2015	edit delete
☐	Charles Richard Drew	Person	admin	published	2015	edit delete
☐	Justina Ford new	Person	admin	published	2015	edit delete
localhost:8888/dfhexample/node/23/edit&destination=admin/content		admin	published	2015	edit delete

Figure 13.7. Hover over the "edit" link on the right, and look for the node ID.

Once you're editing the individual time line view, insert the node ID you just found into the "Preview with contextual filters" box, immediately above the (currently empty) preview area. This should pull in all the events related to the person. Save the view, and go to the profile of an individual person for whom you have created events to see the result (figure 13.8).

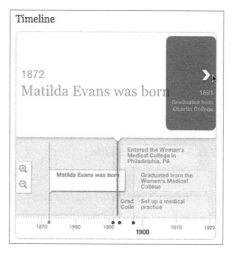

Figure 13.8. The time line block for Matilda Evans.

13.5.7 Caching

Turn on content-based caching (as described in section 12.11), and check the checkbox for "Event." Set the minimum lifetime for query results and rendered display to 1 minute, and the maximum to 6 days.

13.6 Image gallery with exposed filters

This case study involves creating an image gallery, with exposed filters so users can easily sort through the content.

13.6.1 Installing modules

If you installed and enable the Colorbox module as described in section 9.2.5.3, you won't need to install additional modules for this case study. Otherwise, install Colorbox, as well as its library, and enable the module.

13.6.2 Basic view creation

Create a new view using the following settings on the basic view creation page:

> **View name "Gallery," description:** "Gallery of all image nodes."
>
> Show *Content* of type Image.
>
> Create a page, title "Gallery," and path gallery.
>
> **Display format:** *Grid* of fields.
>
> **Items to display:** 20, use a pager.
>
> Create a menu link, add to *Main menu*, link text "Gallery."

Click the "Continue & edit" button, which will take you to the full Views interface. Save the view.

13.6.3 Adding fields

Add the field "Content: Image," and uncheck "create a label." For "Formatter," choose "Colorbox" (figure 13.9). For "Content image style," choose "Medium." For "Colorbox image style," choose "Large." "No special style," the default value, is correct for "Content image style for first image." Under "Gallery (image grouping)," choose "Per page gallery." You can keep the caption set to "Automatic," which pulls from the image file the first non-empty value of the title, the alt-text, or the content title. Apply the changes, and save the view.

Figure 13.9. Configuration of the Image field.

The colorbox effect does not work correctly in the view preview, so after you save the view, visit the page itself to test this. If everything is configured correctly, clicking on an image should trigger an overlay box with a larger version of the image and a caption.

13.6.4 Exposed filters

The view as it is currently configured shows all image nodes. While this is fine while the number of images on the site is small, as the collection grows it will be helpful for users to be able to sort through the images in some way. Exposed filters are a good way to do this.

Under the "Filter criteria" section, add a filter for "Content: Institution." Set the selection type to "Dropdown" (figure 13.10). On the next configuration screen, check the box at the top labeled "Expose this filter to viewers to allow them to change it." This opens up additional options. Change the text under "Label" to just read "Institution" (without the "(field_institution)" since this will be visible to users). If you only want people to select one institution at a time from a drop-down list, click the "Apply (all displays)" button at this point. However, at some point it is worth experimenting with some of the other options available on the exposed filter configuration screen; these have fairly intuitive descriptions. To get back to that configuration screen later, click on the "Content: Institution" filter under "Filter criteria."

Figure 13.10. The gallery view with an exposed Institution filter.

"Content: Institution" is an example of an exposed filter using a term reference field. Node reference fields work similarly. You can also create an approximate search box by adding "Content: Title," renaming it "Search," and setting the operator to "Contains."[9]

---

9. You can also add a proper search box by adding the exposed filter "Search: Search Terms," but if you're using the default Drupal search functionality, it may not be much more effective than simply searching the titles. See chapter 16 for more on search.

In principle, exposed filters can be added to any view, but many views that use a format provided by a module other than Views itself (e.g., time lines and maps) aren't compatible with exposed filters.

If you toggle open the "Advanced" settings, there's a section called "Exposed form" (figure 13.11). This is where you can specify that any block displays of the view should display exposed filters; by default, they don't. If you click "Settings" next to "Exposed form style," you can tweak the labels used for the exposed form, and choose whether or not to include a "Reset" button. You can also check the "Autosubmit" box if you want the view results to automatically update as people make selections, rather than waiting until they hit the "Apply" button.

Figure 13.11. The Exposed Form section within the Advanced section of the Views interface.

The Better Exposed Filters[10] module provides additional options for improving the interface of exposed filters in Views. Install and enable the module, then return to editing the view. (Refresh the Views editing interface if you had it open in another tab while installing Better Exposed Filters.) Click on "Basic" next to "Exposed form style," and choose "Better Exposed Filters." The following configuration page provides a wide range of new options, including allowing you to choose a different selection widget for each of your exposed filters. The best way to explore these settings is to try different settings, see the effects in the Views preview area, and try another option if a particular arrangement is not to your liking.

10. https://www.drupal.org/project/better_exposed_filters

13.6.5   Caching

Turn on content-based caching (as described in section 12.11), and check the checkbox for "Image." Set the minimum lifetime for query results and rendered display to 1 minute, and the maximum to 6 days.

13.7 Slide show

Slide shows are commonly used to highlight multiple pieces of content on landing pages and as part of other overviews. For Drupal sites, the Views Slideshow[11] module is the most widely used for creating slide shows. In this case study, we will create a slide show that displays a random selection of image and person nodes, but the same approach could be used to highlight the three most recent blog posts on the site, or any other set of content that can be isolated using a combination of filter and sort criteria (e.g., all nodes that have a particular taxonomy term associated with them, the three users who have logged in most recently, the five files that have been viewed the greatest number of times). While it's not described here, the Nodequeue[12] module is one way you can group pieces of content for use in a slide show or other view display, even if they don't share any common metadata (e.g., for a "Project staff picks" slide show). See the *Drupal for Humanists* website for an example of how to use Nodequeue.

13.7.1   Installing modules

Install and enable the Views Slideshow module as well as the Views Slideshow: Cycle submodule, following the instructions in the documentation[13] on drupal.org. Note that this includes installing a library—in this case, it's a single file rather than a whole package that needs to be unzipped. The file, "jquery.cycle.all.min.js," needs to go in the folder /sites/all/libraries/jquery.cycle. While the documentation does not specify it, you should create an additional folder in the libraries directory, /sites/all/libraries/json2. Download the zip file from the JSON-js Github repository,[14] unzip it, take

---

11. https://www.drupal.org/project/views_slideshow
12. https://www.drupal.org/project/nodequeue
13. https://www.drupal.org/node/903244
14. https://github.com/douglascrockford/JSON-js

the file "json2.js," and put it in that directory. Without this file, you will have fewer choices of slide show animation, and the slide show may not show up at all.

13.7.2   Basic view creation

Create a new view using the following settings on the basic view creation page:

> **View name "Slide show," description:** "Slide show of person and image nodes."
>
> Show *Content* of type *All* (recall that you can only choose one content type on this screen; since we want to select nodes from two different content types, we'll add the filter on the full Views interface).
>
> Uncheck box for creating a page.
>
> Check box for creating a block.
>
>> **Block title:** make this blank; you won't need a title for this slide show.
>>
>> **Display format:** *Unformatted list* of *Fields*; it will be easiest to first set up this view using a very basic display format, and later switch to the slide show.
>>
>> **Items per page:** 5.

Click the "Continue & edit" button, which will take you to the full Views interface.

13.7.3   Fields, filters, and sort criteria

Let's first limit the results to the Person and Image content types. Under "Filter criteria," add "Content: Type" and check the boxes for "Person" and "Image."

Next, we want Drupal to select a random assortment of person and image nodes. Under "Sort criteria," click on "Content: Post date," then "Remove." Then, still under "Sort criteria," add the criterion "Global: Random," then apply. Every time you hit the "Update preview" button, it should give you a different collection of nodes.

Now, under "Fields," add "Content: Image," which should exist in both the "Person" and "Image" content types. Uncheck "Create a label," set the

"Image style" to "Medium square," and use the drop-down list below that to specify that the image should be linked to the content. You may want to go into *Configuration > Media > Image styles* later and create a new image style specifically for your slide show, and use that instead of the "Medium square" style.

Also add "Content: Body," and uncheck "create a label." Set the formatter to "Summary or trimmed." The default trim length (600 characters) is fine.

Click on "Content: Title" and toggle open "Style settings." Check the box for "Customize field HTML" and set the HTML element to H3.

Rearrange the fields so that the order is "Content: Image," "Content: Title," "Content: Body."

13.7.4 Configuring the slide show

Click on "Unformatted list" in the "Format" section, and change it to "Slideshow." The default options are generally good here. There are options for changing the animation effect when transitioning between slides (a fade effect is used by default), as well as for adding "next/previous/pause" links at the top or bottom of the slide show. The default styling for these and the other widget options is fairly unattractive, and they're best omitted unless you plan on doing some theming work on your slide show. See the *Drupal for Humanists* website for links to tutorials on theming slide shows.

Once you apply the changes, the preview should update to only show one node at a time. After a few seconds, it should switch to another node. If you don't see the preview switching, check the location of your mouse; the default configuration makes the slide show pause when the mouse is hovering over an item. Move your mouse into the configuration area (outside the Views preview area), and the items should resume rotating.

In section 19.2.3, we will include this block as part of the front page; don't worry about positioning it for now.

13.7.5 Caching

Turn on content-based caching (as described in section 12.11), and check the checkboxes for "Person" and "Image." Set the minimum lifetime for query results and rendered display to 1 minute, and the maximum to 6 days.

13.8 Table with exposed filters

This case study covers creating a table display of event nodes in Views, with exposed filters to help browse the content. In this case, the view isn't meant to be part of the public interface for the site, but could be used as a research tool for the project team, or a way for the project director to assess the data entry progress of assistants. No additional modules are needed.

13.8.1 Basic view creation

Create a new view using the following settings on the basic view creation page:

> **View name "Event table," description:** "Table of event nodes."
>
> Show *Content* of type *Event.*
>
> Create a page, title "Event table" and path event-table.
>
> **Display format:** *Table* of fields.
>
> **Items to display:** 20, use a pager.

Click the "Continue & edit" button, which will take you to the full Views interface. Save the view.

13.8.2 Adding fields

The table display format is one of the only formats where it is useful to keep the label for each of the fields you add, as this serves as the table's column header. Add the following fields: "Content: Person," "Content: Date," "Content: Location," "Content: Event type," "Content: Main timeline." The default configuration settings are fine for each of those.

If this table will be used to monitor the activity of data entry assistants, it might be useful to include date and author information as well. Add the field "Content: Post date." If this is a content type that you expect will frequently be edited and updated, you may wish to use "Content: Updated date" instead. For the date format, choose "Long format."

Click on the button to add another field, and use the search box at the top to look for User. You'll find that the only field available that is relevant for what you're looking for is "Content: Author uid"; the user ID, however, is not a very informative datum. The configuration interface suggests adding the "Content: Author" relationship. Cancel adding the field, and go to add that relationship first.

Toggle open the "Advanced" section of the Views interface, and under "Relationships," add "Content: Author." Helpfully, this relationship includes some explanatory text, "Relate content to the user who created it." The default configuration settings for this relationship are fine.

Return to the interface for adding another field, and again use the search box to look for User. Many more options are available now that you have added the "Content: Author" relationship. Choose "User: Name"; if you have the Real Name module configured (see section 10.4.1), this will display the user's full name. If not, it should still provide the username of the creator of each Event node, and if you have fairly transparent account naming conventions, it should be understandable. Change the label to "Created by."

13.8.3   Configuring the table

Click on "Settings" next to "Table" in the "Format" section. Check the "Sortable" box for every row where it is available; note that it won't be available for "Person" because the "Person" field can take more than one value, and multivalued fields are not sortable (figure 13.12).

Change the "Default sort" from "None" to "Post date," and change the default order for Post date to "Descending." Apply the changes.

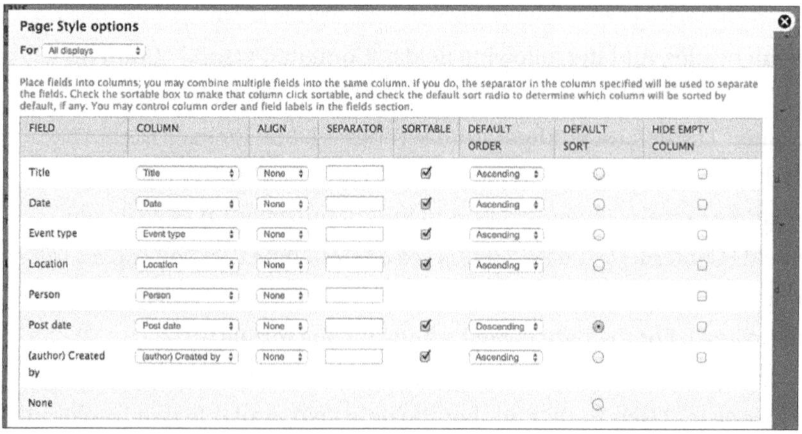

Page: Style options

For [All displays ‡]

Place fields into columns; you may combine multiple fields into the same column. If you do, the separator in the column specified will be used to separate the fields. Check the sortable box to make that column click sortable, and check the default sort radio to determine which column will be sorted by default, if any. You may control column order and field labels in the fields section.

FIELD	COLUMN	ALIGN	SEPARATOR	SORTABLE	DEFAULT ORDER	DEFAULT SORT	HIDE EMPTY COLUMN
Title	Title ‡	None ‡		☑	Ascending ‡	○	☐
Date	Date ‡	None ‡		☑	Ascending ‡	○	☐
Event type	Event type ‡	None ‡		☑	Ascending ‡	○	☐
Location	Location ‡	None ‡		☑	Ascending ‡	○	☐
Person	Person ‡	None ‡					☐
Post date	Post date ‡	None ‡		☑	Descending ‡	◉	☐
(author) Created by	(author) Created by ‡	None ‡		☑	Ascending ‡	○	☐
None						○	

Figure 13.12. The table configuration interface.

Now, the table is sorted to show the most recently entered events first. The headers of almost all the columns (excluding Person) are also clickable, as a way to change the sorting of the table. The default order when you click on a table header is for it to sort alphabetically, but you can click on the same table header again to reverse the sort order.

13.8.4   Exposed filters

Manipulating the sort order can be helpful for navigating the data, but in some situations it may be easier to first use exposed filters to narrow the set of data displayed, and then use the sort order. Add exposed filters for "Content: Person" (name the exposed filter "Person") and "User: Name" (name the exposed filter "Created by") as described in section 13.5.4.

13.8.5   Other configuration

If this view were to be used as part of an operational project site, you may want to make some additional adjustments. If it's intended for internal use by the project, you may want to configure the page access based on role, and limit it to specific groups of users (or at least exclude anonymous, which is to say, unauthenticated, users); see section 12.8.1.3.

You may also want to make it easier for the right groups of people to access this page. To do this, you might create a new menu (see section 11.3.2), add this view-generated page to that menu (section 12.8.1.2 or 11.3.3.2), and then enable the block for that menu only for certain roles (section 11.2.5).

13.8.6   Caching

Turn on content-based caching (as described in section 12.11), and check the checkbox for "Event." Set the minimum lifetime for query results and rendered display to 1 minute, and the maximum to 6 days.

13.9 Other noteworthy Views modules

There are numerous modules that extend Views through providing additional display formats, fields, or other functionality. A few modules that may be particularly useful for digital projects are listed below; the

Drupal for Humanists site includes examples for each of these modules, as well as others.

13.9.1   Editview

Editview[15] provides a display format where the fields you add to the view appear as an editable table. It works for fields attached to content types, taxonomies, and user profiles, and you can also add new nodes or taxonomy terms. Editview is compatible with exposed filters, and it's very effective for building data entry and editing interfaces that are more efficient than adding (or editing) one node at a time. The end result has some similarity to the FileMaker Pro data entry interface, but with the flexibility and customizability of Views.

13.9.2   Views Conditional

The Views Conditional[16] module provides a new kind of field that you can add to a view. In the configuration of the "Views: Views Conditional" field, you can tell Views to display one thing if a certain field has a particular result (or is empty, or is greater/less than some value, etc.), and another thing if the condition is not met. This is particularly useful if you are creating a view for a content type where you use conditional fields (for instance, to differentiate "person" into "instructor" and "student" subtypes without creating two completely different content types), and you might want to show one field if it contains data, but provide another field as a "backup."

13.9.3   Views Bulk Operations

The Views Bulk Operations module[17] (often abbreviated to VBO) is a way to make bulk changes to nodes, users, files, or other content that you can display using Views. This can include adding new tags, changing the author of nodes, or changing the value of a field.

---

15. https://github.com/agile-humanities/agile_editview
16. https://www.drupal.org/project/views_conditional
17. https://www.drupal.org/project/views_bulk_operations

13.9.4   Views Autocomplete Filters

By default, Drupal provides an autocomplete widget for exposed filters that are based on term or node reference fields. In some cases, it can be useful to have autocompletion for simple text fields as well. Views Autocomplete Filters[18] adds a "Use autocomplete" checkbox to text fields that are used as exposed filters, as an alternative to a plain text search box.

13.10 Summary

This chapter has covered a wide range of Views use cases that leverage different display types, field configurations, relationships, and contextual filters. If you'd like to consult additional examples, visit the *Drupal for Humanists* site. From here, the best thing to do to continue to build your skill with the Views module is to modify the views you have created in this chapter, or start from scratch and pick an entirely new set of options, and see what happens.

Chapters 14 and 15 shift focus, addressing data import and export, respectively. Chapter 16 covers search, and chapter 17 discusses managing taxonomies. If you have already populated your site with data and want to move on to the next step that directly applies to building the example site, proceed to section 17.2 where you will use Views to configure the display of taxonomy term pages.

---

18. https://www.drupal.org/project/views_autocomplete_filters

CHAPTER 14

Importing Data

14.1 Overview

If you already have data for your project in another format, you can use the Feeds module to import it into Drupal without manually reentering everything. Perhaps data entry was already underway in a spreadsheet before you started building a Drupal site, or maybe you're migrating your project from different software, like FileMaker Pro. There is even a module that allows you to import data from XML, like TEI-encoded texts. This chapter will cover how to import data from a spreadsheet via a CSV (comma-separated values) file, using our example site. The *Drupal for Humanists* website contains additional use cases of pulling in items from RSS feeds, and importing data from a TEI file, as well as information on other relevant modules that extend Feeds.

14.2 Essential modules for data import

The most widely used module for importing data is Feeds.[1] Feeds allows you to specify the type of file you're importing from, whether you want to upload it or point to a URL, how often you want to run the import, what kind of Drupal "thing" it should create (users, nodes, taxonomy terms,

---

1. https://www.drupal.org/project/feeds

etc.), and how to map the source data into Drupal's fields. To install Feeds, you must also install its prerequisite, the Job Scheduler module.[2]

If you need to modify or clean up the source data before importing it into Drupal, you may be able to simply use the Feeds Tamper module.[3] Feeds Tamper offers a wide range of transformations that can be applied to any source data that have been mapped to a Drupal field (see section 14.3.5 for field mapping, 14.3.6 for Feeds Tamper).

By default, Feeds supports CSV files (comma-separated value, a plain-text representation of a spreadsheet) and RSS feeds. If you want to import from XML or HTML files, you need to also install and enable the Feeds Extensible Parsers module.[4] A fairly comprehensive list of all plug-in modules for Feeds is maintained on Drupal.org.[5] If you install and enable any of these plug-in modules for Feeds after you've already installed and enabled Feeds, be sure to clear the cache (by hovering over the house icon in the upper left of the administration menu, and choosing "clear all caches"), or the new options provided by the Feeds plug-in module may not appear when you go to the Feeds interface.

14.3 Overview of Feeds settings

Install the Feeds module, and enable Feeds and Feeds Administrative user interface (UI), along with Feeds' prerequisite, Job Scheduler. Go to *Structure > Feeds importers > Add importer*. Provide a name for the importer; this should usually include information about what kind of data the importer creates, and optionally, what kind of source data it draws from. For instance, "TEI to poem" for an importer that creates "Poem" nodes out of imported TEI files, or "User import." You can include more details in the "Description" field.

The next page is the main configuration screen for Feeds, and is broken up into a number of sections.

2. https://www.drupal.org/project/job_scheduler
3. https://www.drupal.org/project/feeds_tamper
4. https://www.drupal.org/project/feeds_ex
5. https://www.drupal.org/node/856644

14.3.1 Basic settings

This section allows you to change the name and description of the Feeds importer. For the "Attach to content type" setting, the default "Use standalone form" option is almost always correct, with very rare exceptions (e.g., pulling in RSS feeds from multiple different websites, on an ongoing basis). While it may seem intuitive to select the content type for the nodes you want to import, that setting occurs later, as part of the processor settings (see section 14.3.4).

The stand-alone form is always the right option if your importer is meant to pull in data from one particular CSV file[6]—even if you expect you may end up uploading multiple revisions of the CSV file, or different versions of it corresponding to different sources.

If this is an import that should happen on an ongoing basis (e.g., importing from a file on a remote server that is frequently updated), you can specify how often the import should happen. If the importer you are creating is meant to be run once, just to get data on the site so that it can be managed there, you can set "Periodic import" to "off."

You should choose between "Import on submission" and "Process in background." For most imports, "Import on submission" is correct. That setting immediately carries out the import as soon as you hit "Submit" on the import page. If you choose "Process in background," Drupal will import 50 records every time cron (a series of automated site actions, including indexing new content for the site search and importing data in the background) runs. By default, cron runs every three hours; you can modify this by going to *Configuration* > *System* > Cron (admin/config/system/cron). If you have an import of thousands and thousands of nodes, you may want to increase the number of records imported per cron run. There is no easy, UI-based way to configure it, but it can be done with a small tweak to the settings.php in your site's code base, as discussed in this Feeds module issue.[7]

---

6. Note that you can also import data from an entire folder of source files, as mentioned in section 14.3.2.2. This doesn't change the applicability of the stand-alone form.

7. https://www.drupal.org/node/1551246

14.3.2   Fetcher

The "Fetcher" is how Drupal acquires the source file. The default fetcher is the "HTTP Fetcher," which allows you to put in a URL pointing to the file. If you click the "Change" link next to the "Fetcher" header, you can choose "File upload," which allows you to upload a source file.

14.3.2.1   HTTP Fetcher

There are configuration options for attempting to detect an RSS feed if you submit an HTML page. This works, for instance, on most WordPress sites: if you were to put in the URL of a WordPress site to a Feeds importer where you've checked the "Auto detect feeds" box, Drupal should be able to identify the site's RSS feed and import based on that.

By default, Drupal waits 30 seconds to get a response after sending a request to an external website. If you want it to wait longer (for instance, if you know that the server that hosts the source for the feed is slow to respond), you can indicate a larger number of seconds in the "Request timeout" field.

14.3.2.2   File upload

You can add file extensions to the "Allowed file extensions" field, but the default set should cover most cases. The default upload directory is fine.

If you want to import a directory of files (for instance, if you have a directory of TEI-encoded poems uploaded to your site, and want to import content from each file into a "Poem" node), check the "Supply path to file or directory directly" box.

14.3.3   Parser

The "Parser" setting lets you specify the kind of source file you will be using.

14.3.3.1   Common syndication parser

This parser is used for importing RSS feeds, which are widely used to disseminate web-based content like blog posts or notifications of updates to websites. There are no configuration settings.

14.3.3.2   CSV parser

This parser is used for importing CSV (comma-separated value) files. CSV files are used to store tabular (spreadsheet) data in a format that isn't dependent on any piece of software—unlike, for instance, XLS files from Microsoft Excel. You can export data from any spreadsheet software, and from individual tables in database software (like FileMaker Pro) as a CSV file. Be sure to choose "UTF-8" or "Unicode" encoding, if possible, to ensure that any non-Latin characters are stored correctly.

If you choose the CSV parser, there are a couple configuration options that you can almost always leave with the default settings. If your CSV file uses something other than a comma to separate the columns of the spreadsheet (such as a tab), you can select it from the drop-down menu. If there is not a header row on your CSV that indicates what each column is (e.g., "Project name," "Disciplinary field," "Surname," etc.), you can check a box for that, and use the number corresponding to each column instead of a label. If you do this, note that the first column is number "0," the second column is "1," etc. If your CSV file does not have headers when you export it from the source software, it may be easiest to open it in a plain-text editor (e.g., Notepad or TextWrangler, *not* Microsoft Word or any other editor that includes text formatting options) and add headers rather than dealing with the numbers.

14.3.3.3   HTML Xpath parser and XML Xpath parser

If you've installed the Feeds Extensible Parser module, this option will be available. The configuration for the parser allows you to define XPath expressions that will pull out the data that you want to map to Drupal fields. First, you must define the context. This is the expression relative to which all subsequent expressions will be evaluated. In XSLT, this is similar to the expression used in <xsl:template match="some-expression-here">. Then, you can add one new source at a time, give it a name (which will be used in the mapping interface), and an expression. After each new source, hit "Save" at the bottom of the screen. You can choose to display errors and/or use the debugging mode if you're testing the feed or if you experience problems.

14.3.4 **Processor**

The Feeds settings described so far deal with the data source. How often should it be imported? How can Drupal access it? What is its format? The Processor section, in contrast, deals directly with the connection between the source and what you want the source to become once it's imported into Drupal. The default processor options are "Node," "Taxonomy term," and "User." Work is underway on the Feeds module to support a more generic processor that would make it possible to import content into the "File" entity created by the Media module; in the meantime, importing Files can be done as part of importing nodes, users, or taxonomy terms (if there is a file field associated with one of those).

14.3.4.1 Node and taxonomy term processor

In the settings for the node processor, "Bundle" refers to the content type that should be used for each entry in the source file. For the taxonomy term processor, there is an option that is labeled more intuitively, "Vocabulary." Note that you have to choose only one; if you want to import nodes from multiple different content types or terms from multiple vocabularies, you need to create multiple source files and Feeds importers.

You can specify what should happen if Drupal imports content that matches existing content. (In the "mapping" configuration section, you define how Drupal should find matches.) The options are fairly intuitive. If you choose "Update existing nodes/terms," only the fields that match the mappings you have defined will be updated. If you've made other changes to the node/term (e.g., comments, or adding data to other fields that don't match a mapping), those will remain untouched.

The text format should be "plain text" (the default), unless the source data itself includes HTML, in which case you should choose one of the text formats that accommodates HTML ("filtered text," "full HTML," or a text format you have defined; see section 8.2 for more on text formats).

The node author you set on this screen is the default author. On the mapping screen, you can indicate that some aspect of the source data indicates the author, and that will supersede the default setting. It's best to assign imported nodes to an actual user (even if it's the "admin" user). If you use the default "anonymous" value for the author, you should uncheck the default "authorize" box, because if you've configured permissions correctly (see section 10.5) anonymous users shouldn't be able to create new nodes.

If you're importing data that should be a permanent part of your site, you can use the default "Expire nodes: Never" setting. If you're importing data that you want to display on your site for a short period of time (e.g., the latest RSS feed items from another site, which will quickly be replaced by newer items), you can choose a shorter time period. For example, if you expect that new RSS feed items are published every five hours, you might want to expire nodes after 6 or 12 hours, so your site doesn't get cluttered up with data that will never be displayed again.

14.3.4.2   User processor

The user processor has a similar setting for updating existing users. You can define which role the users should have; this is not configurable as a field mapping, so all imported users should have the same role, or you should add roles later (using Views Bulk Operations, which is discussed in the context of modifying taxonomies in section 17.5, but can be applied to other situations as well).

Feeds does not send email notifications to users when creating accounts. One way to work around that is to import user accounts with the "Blocked" status. When you change their status from "Blocked" to "Active," they will receive an email with their username, password, and the login URL.

14.3.5   Mapping

Mapping is a setting under "Processor," but it is nearly identical for nodes, taxonomy terms, and users, with the exception of the specific options available under "Target." "Target" options are the Drupal fields (user-created, like "Given name" or "Surname" or system-internal, like "Created date") into which the data will be imported. The mapping interface is where you indicate how different components of your source data should be mapped onto the different fields (targets) within Drupal.

The "Source" section is where you specify where Drupal should look in the source file for the data that will be imported into each field. Source options vary based on the parser you selected. If you are using the CSV parser, you will be presented with a text field where you can type in the label of the column in your source file corresponding to the data you want to import. You must type this in exactly as it exists in the source CSV file for it to match; it may be easiest to copy and paste it directly from the CSV. If you are using the HTML or XML parser, the source options will be a drop-down list drawn from the configuration you entered on the parser settings page (where you defined XPath expressions to find different pieces of data in your source file). If you are using the Common Syndication parser (for RSS feeds, for instance), the source options are drawn from the properties defined for RSS feeds (e.g., title, author name, publication date, etc.).

You can map a source to more than one target, but you can only create one Feeds Tamper configuration for each source. Mapping multiple sources to a single target depends on the nature of the target, but in most cases, Feeds Tamper will be required. See section 14.3.6 for how to address both of these scenarios.

14.3.5.1 Unique targets

Some "Target" options can be "used as unique." This means using that field as a way to identify unique nodes, in order to determine whether an existing node matches a node represented in the CSV. For instance, say your site has an existing node with the title "Crime and Punishment," and your CSV has a row where the data in the "Title" column is "Crime and Punishment." If you are using the node processor, enter "Title" in the source field, choose "Title" from the target drop-down list, and indicate that it should be used as unique (by clicking the cog under "target configuration" and checking the "Use as unique" checkbox), when Drupal starts importing the "Crime and Punishment" row, it will recognize that a "Crime and Punishment" node already exists, and will proceed as you specified in section 14.3.4.1, by skipping, updating, or replacing that node.

14.3.5.2 Term reference fields

When used as a target, term reference fields have target configuration options. The default setting searches taxonomy terms by term name (i.e., it matches a term in the source to a term stored in Drupal based on the term name, rather than a system-internal ID number), which is correct in almost all cases. If you are importing data that use terms that don't already exist on your Drupal site, and you don't want to first run another feeds importer in order to preimport the new terms, you can click the cog icon under "target configuration" for the term reference field in question, and check the box for "Auto create."[8]

14.3.5.3 Node reference fields

There are numerous target options available for node reference fields, but the most common setting is "Node reference by node title." If you are importing data into a node reference field that accepts multiple values, instead choose "Node reference by node title—allow duplicate nodes." For multivalued node reference fields you will need to add a Feeds Tamper plug-in for it to work; see section 14.3.6.

14.3.5.4 Image targets

The easiest way to import images is to upload them directly to the server, and include a pointer to them in the spreadsheet. Unless you're using private file storage (see section 6.6.1), the pointer should start with *public://* and continue with the name of the file (if it's stored directly in the files directory) or the subdirectory the file has been uploaded in, then the name of the file.

You should generally upload images into the place they would appear if you had uploaded them via Drupal's UI; if you've configured a field so that any image uploaded into it goes into a subfolder (for instance, on the example site, the thumbnail images of each person go in the subdirectory people, as described in section 7.2.2.7), you should upload images of people whose profiles you will create using Feeds into the same directory. For instance, if you are going to import a set of "person" nodes into the example site, the source data should have a column where the values look like public://people/person_1.jpg, and that column should be mapped to the "Image" field.

---

8. Due to a bug in the Feeds module (https://www.drupal.org/node/2026543), for this to work correctly and not create duplicate terms, you need to use Feeds Tamper and add the "Trim" plug-in to the term reference field. Leave the field blank to trim white space, and choose "both." Note that if your source file has more than one term to import into the term reference field, you should also add the "Explode" Feeds Tamper plug-in, and run that before the "Trim" plug-in.

14.3.5.5   Date targets

Even if you did not configure it to have "start" and "end" values, every field created using the Date module has those two variants as part of the feed importer. Choose the "start" variant if your date field is configured to only take a single value.

The Partial Date module[9] has a target for every component that is included in the partial date field that is part of a particular content type— year, circa, short text description, etc. If the field is not a partial date range, all targets will say "from"; if it is a range, there will be "from" and "to" options.

14.3.6   Feeds Tamper

After you have saved the mappings for your Feeds importer, you may need to use Feeds Tamper to manipulate your source data. Install and enable both Feeds Tamper and Feeds Tamper Admin UI. You can then access Feeds Tamper through the "Tamper" tab in the upper right of the Feeds configuration interface, or by using the administration menu: *Structure > Feeds importers > [Feed importer name] > Tamper.*

Feeds Tamper lists each source you defined in the Mapping interface, along with the target(s) it is mapped to. If a source is mapped to multiple targets, they all get grouped together. Under each source is a table with an option to "Add plugin." Feeds Tamper comes with a set of plug-ins that can transform your data; there are many more besides the common ones discussed below. Be sure to explore the full list if you need to manipulate your data to see if there is an option that fits.

14.3.6.1   Adding a plug-in

To add a plug-in to a source, click the "Add plugin" link. On the next screen, select the plug-in from the drop-down list. If you are only going to use the plug-in once for a given source, you can keep the default description and machine name. If you need to apply the same plug-in more than once (for instance, you might use the "Find replace" plug-in multiple times

---

9. Be sure to use a version of the module released in 2015 or later; previous versions did not include Feeds support.

to modify the data in different ways), you will need to at least provide different machine names for each instance. The available configuration options vary from plug-in to plug-in.

14.3.6.2   Explode

If you are importing data from a CSV into a field that accepts multiple values, and your CSV spreadsheet has cells that contain more than one value (e.g., a person with an appointment in multiple departments might have a spreadsheet cell under "Department" that looks like "English, Interdisciplinary Studies"), you need to use the "Explode" plug-in so that Drupal recognizes the values as distinct. The string separator is the character(s) used to delineate the different values in the source file. If you are importing data into a multivalued taxonomy term field, node reference field, or user reference field, you should add the "Trim" plug-in after the "Explode" plug-in.

14.3.6.3   Trim

Importing into multivalued fields that are supposed to match existing nodes, terms or users may malfunction if you don't trim spaces before and after each value. Leave the "Characters to trim" field blank in order to trim spaces, and leave the "Side" setting on "Both."

14.3.6.4   Rewrite

This plug-in is useful if you want to take multiple pieces of source data, and map them to a single Drupal field—for instance, if your source file has "given name" and "surname," and you want to map them to the Drupal "title" field. If you also want to store each value separately in Drupal, you can simply map the "given name" source to a "Given name" field target, and the "surname" source to a "Surname" field target. To create the mapping to the title field, you can add a new, empty column to your CSV source, by putting something in the header row (for instance, "Title," if that isn't already used by another column). Map the "title" source to the "Title" target, and add the "rewrite" plug-in in Feeds Tamper. In the rewrite plug-in configuration options, you can specify the "replacement patterns" (i.e., other imported source data) to use. Enter "[given name] [surname]" (or the equivalent, depending on your source data) and save.

If you want to import "given name" and "surname" into the title field, but you do *not* want to store the data separately, you can directly map one of the sources to the title (for instance, mapping the "given name" source to the "Title" target). For "surname," create a mapping to a "Temporary target." This will temporarily store the data from the source, just long enough for you to use it in Feeds Tamper, before discarding it. On the mapping list, temporary targets will display as "Missing," which is not a problem. In Feeds Tamper, go to the configuration for "given name," and add the "rewrite" plug-in. For the values, enter "[given name] [surname]" (or the equivalent) and save. This will put the values of the given name and surname in the title field, but they won't be imported anywhere else.

14.3.6.5   Find replace/find replace REGEX

The "find replace" filter allows you to specify the text to search for in the source, along with the replacement text. There are checkboxes for making this case sensitive, respecting word boundaries, and matching whole words/phrases.

To do more complex find and replace queries, you can use the "find replace REGEX" plug-in, which lets you use regular expressions, a particular kind of syntax for doing find and replace that allows you select things like all dates within a text that are formatted a certain way, or all email addresses. Many programmers are familiar with at least the basics of regular expressions. If you need to do sophisticated find and replace work on your source data, it might be helpful to show your data to a programmer and explain what data you are trying to capture. Because the details of regular expression syntax vary by programming language, you may want to point the programmer to the documentation for the particular flavor of regular expressions used by Drupal.[10]

14.3.6.6   HTML entity decode

Depending on how your source file was created, you may notice that punctuation shows up strangely after you've imported the data. If you see things like "&" and """ in your imported data, you should

---

10. http://php.net/manual/en/reference.pcre.pattern.syntax.php

reimport it using the "HTML entity decode" Feeds Tamper plug-in, which will restore the actual punctuation marks.[11]

14.3.6.7 Convert case

If the text in your source uses, for instance, all capital letters, and you want to normalize that before the import, you can use the "convert case" plug-in. This provides a choice of converting the text to all capital letters, all lowercase letters, "title case" (every word capitalized), or "sentence case" (the first word capitalized).

14.3.6.8 Strip tags

Particularly if you are using the HTML Xpath parser source, you may want to strip out the HTML tags embedded in your data, if you are importing the text into a plain-text field. (See section 8.2 for more on text formats.) You can specify which tags, if any, should remain after running this plug-in.

14.3.6.9 Keyword filter

If you import data from a spreadsheet that you have prepared specifically for your site, you can be confident that all the data in the source belongs on the site. The keyword filter plug-in is useful if your source isn't specific to your import—for instance, if you are importing data from another site's RSS feed, but not all items they publish are relevant. You can define words and/or phrases that must occur in the source; if those words do not occur in the field where the feeds tamper plug-in is assigned, the corresponding item won't be imported. You can also invert the filter to turn it into a blacklist, so that the terms in the list cause items to be rejected, rather than accepted.

If you want to require a source to have *all* of a certain set of words, include them all on a single line in the text box. If you want to require a

---

11. Note: this problem may not always be caused by the source data. If you are using Automatic Nodetitles, using tokens provided by the Entity Token module (i.e., tokens that use underscores in their names), you may see things like "&" in the titles of nodes, even when the data in the fields that Automatic Nodetitles is pulling from has the correct punctuation. If that is happening, replace the tokens with the equivalent entity tokens (the variants with a hyphen in their name). See the *Drupal for Humanists* site for more on entity tokens.

source to have *any* of a certain set of words, include each on a separate line. See section 14.5.4 for an example.

14.3.6.10 Boolean filter

If you are importing data into a Boolean field, the best way to ensure that it comes through correctly is to use the Boolean filter. This filter lets you specify what text in the source field should count as "true," and what to do if that value is not found (e.g., mark the node's value for the field as "false," or leave it blank.) For this to work, your data need to be consistent, so you may want to apply other filters, such as find and replace, before the Boolean filter to make sure that all the "true" values are identical in the source, if you know you were not completely consistent with your source data.

14.3.7 Importing data

After you have gone through all these configuration settings, go to the "Import" page. This page is not part of the administration menu, and as such you have to type it into the URL bar yourself by going to /import. Note that *Structure > Feeds importers > Import importer* does *not* take you to the import page, but rather, to a different page where you can copy and paste the exported configuration settings for a feed importer.

Click on the name of the importer you want to run. Only importers that use the "use standalone form" configuration under "basic settings" appear on this list, but this should cover all cases with very rare exceptions.

Once you've selected the importer to run, you will be presented with a field where you must specify the source, either by putting in a URL or by uploading a file, depending on your choice of fetcher in section 14.3.2. Once you've indicated the source, click the "Import" button to start the import.

14.3.8 Import page options

The import page for each Feeds importer has a set of tabs along the top that present additional options. If an import didn't yield the results you wanted (for instance, if your Feed Tamper plug-ins didn't work as expected), you might want to delete all the items you created in the import, in order to make subsequent imports go more quickly than if Drupal has to look for existing node matches in order to update or replace content. The "Delete items" tab allows you to do this. Note that it deletes all items that were ever imported using that particular Feeds importer, not just the items from the most recent time you ran the importer.

The "Log" tab shows you how many items were created each time the importer has been run, as well as how long the import took to run.

The "Unlock" tab can be useful if you are running a large import and it gets stuck, failing to make any more progress. In those cases, you can unlock the importer, delete the nodes that have been imported (or not, if you prefer), and restart the import.

14.4 Example: Importing People nodes

To illustrate importing data from a CSV, we will bulk-import Person nodes on the example site, and follow this by bulk-importing Event nodes that relate to those Person nodes. Data for these imports (both the CSV files and the image files you'll need to upload to the server) are available for download from the *Drupal for Humanists* website.[12]

14.4.1 Source data

Start by downloading the DFH-data.zip file from the website. Unzip it; inside you will find two CSV files and a set of image files. If you want to take a look the source data for this import, open Drupal-for-humanists-people.csv in a plain-text editor like TextWrangler on Mac, or Notepad on Windows—*not* Microsoft Excel, which can corrupt data in a CSV if it gets saved in Excel. The header row contains the following fields:

Given name

Middle names

Surname

Biography

Birth date

---

12. http://drupal.forhumanists.org/drupal-humanists/chapter-14-importing-data

> Death date
>
> Image
>
> Medical institution attended
>
> Profession
>
> Specialization
>
> GUID

All of these, with the exception of GUID, match the names of the fields where you will be importing the data. This is for convenience, but is not a requirement; the source header rows can be named anything you wish, and the data will be imported successfully as long as you correctly line up the exact name of the source header with the field where you want to import the data.

GUID (globally unique identifier) is the header of an otherwise blank column, and it's included in order to make it possible to run the importer more than once without creating a whole set of duplicate nodes. In many cases, your importer will have a mapping for the title field of the node, which you can set as a unique value, and Drupal can use those data to identify what nodes already exist, and not create duplicates (if you've set the configuration to update, rather than replace or not update, existing nodes). In this case, the titles for Person nodes are generated by Automatic Nodetitles. While you could add a mapping for Title, set it to be unique, and use Feeds Tamper to generate the same kind of titles that Automatic Nodetitles does (combining the given, middle, and surnames), on subsequent imports Feeds will fail to recognize the nodes created for the two people without a specified middle name (Matilda Evans and Justina Ford). As a result, every time you rerun the importer, it will create new nodes for Matilda Evans and Justina Ford. Creating a mapping for GUID instead of Title will successfully avoid this problem.

14.4.2 Creating the importer and basic configuration

Create a new feeds importer by going to *Structure > Feeds importers > Add importer*. For the name, call it "Person importer from DfH CSV," with the description "Imports events using the CSV file from the *Drupal for Humanists* website."

The default values under "Basic settings" are mostly fine, but change "Periodic import" to "Off" and save.

Set the fetcher to "File upload" and the parser to "CSV parser." The default node processor setting is correct. In the settings for the node processor, choose "Person" under "Bundle" (figure 14.1). Under "Update existing nodes", select "Replace existing nodes." For the author, choose your own account.

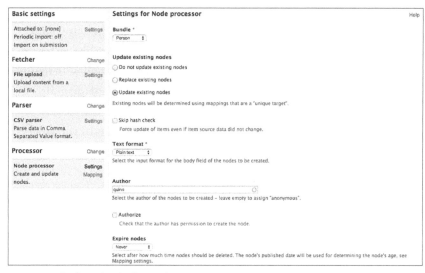

Figure 14.1. Configuration for Person importer.

14.4.3   Mapping

Create the mappings detailed in Table 14.1.

Source	Target	Target configuration
Given name	Given Name	Used as unique
Middle names	Middle Name (s)	
Surname	Surname	
Biography	field_date: from: body	
Birth date	Birth date: Start	
Death date	Death date: Start	
Image	Image	
Medical institution attended	Medical institution attended	Search taxonomy terms by: Term name; click the cog and check the box for "auto create"
Profession	Profession	Search taxonomy terms by: Term name
Specialization	Specialization	Search taxonomy terms by: Term name
GUID	GUID	Click the cog and check the box for "used as unique"

Table 14.1. Field mappings for Person importer.

14.4.4 Feeds tamper

Profession

Add the "explode" plug-in, because some of the people have more than one profession. The default settings are fine.

GUID

Add the plug-in "rewrite,", and use the replacement patterns below to re-create the full-name pattern, which should look like the following if you are using the source data from the website: [given name] [middle names] [surname] (figure 14.2).

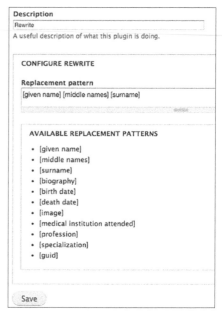

Figure 14.2. Feeds Tamper configuration for GUID -> GUID.

14.4.5 Import and cleanup

Go to /import (e.g., yoursite.org/import) and choose "Person importer from DfH CSV." Click the "Choose File" button and select the Drupal-for-humanists-people.csv file from your computer. The other default settings are fine. Click the "Import" button.

If the import is successful, you'll see a progress bar, then a notice at the top of the screen that Drupal created 8 nodes. If you previously created some of the Person nodes manually using data from the *Drupal for Humanists* website, you may see that it created a smaller number of nodes, and updated a certain number of the nodes you already created.

Click on *Content* in the administration bar at the top of the screen and take a look at the person nodes that have been created. Make sure that all the fields were imported successfully. If some of the data from the source spreadsheet was not imported, the most common cause is a mismatch between the exact heading of the column in the spreadsheet and the text you used in the mapping; you may want to open the source CSV file in a plain-text editor and copy and paste the text directly. If you have the GUID field configured correctly, you should be able to rerun the importer without it creating duplicate nodes.

You may notice that the nodes for Justina Ford and Matilda Evans look a bit odd, with [node:field_middle_names] appearing between their first and last names. Even though the standard tokens you used to configure the automatic node titles are generally hidden when empty, this isn't the case for nodes created using Feeds. To fix this, click on the "edit" link for one of those nodes on the Content page, then on the node editing form, save without making any changes. (You can make changes if you wish, but you don't need to.) This will remove the stray token text. Be sure to do this before importing the Event nodes, and only do it once you no longer need to run the Person importer; rerunning the importer will re-add the [node:field_middle_names] where you have removed it.

14.5 Example: Importing Event nodes

14.5.1 Source data

The source data for this import can be found in the Drupal-for-humanists-events.csv file, in the same zipped package as the people CSV. The header row includes the following fields:

> **Person:** Each event is associated with the life of one or more people.
>
> **Month:** The month the event happened, if available. Months are given using a numerical value, which is a requirement for importing them into a partial date field.
>
> **Day:** The day the event happened, if available.
>
> **Year:** The year the event happened.
>
> **Location:** Text describing the location where the event took place.
>
> **Description:** A longer description of the event.
>
> **Title:** A very brief description of the event, to be used in the "title" field.
>
> **Event type:** Categorizes the type of event.
>
> **Institution:** Associates an institution with an event.
>
> **Main timeline:** Uses "yes" to indicate that the event should appear on the main timeline.

14.5.2   Creating the importer and basic configuration

Create a new feeds importer by going to *Structure > Feeds importers > Add importer*. For the name, call it "Event importer from DfH CSV," with the description "Imports events using the CSV file from the *Drupal for Humanists* website."

Use the same settings as described in section 14.4.2, but in the settings for node processor, set the "Bundle" to "Event."

14.5.3   Mapping

Create the mappings detailed in Table 14.2 and shown in Figure 14.3.

Source	Target	Target configuration
Title	Title	Used as unique
Person	Person (node reference by title) – allow duplicate nodes	
Month	field_date: from: month	
Day	feld_date: from: day	
Year	field_date: from: year	
Location	Location	
Description	Description	
Event type	Event type	Search taxonomy terms by: Term name
Institution	Institution	Search taxonomy terms by: Term name; click the cog and check the box for "auto create"
Main timeline	Main timeline	
Year	Year: Start	

Table 14.2. Field mappings for Event importer.

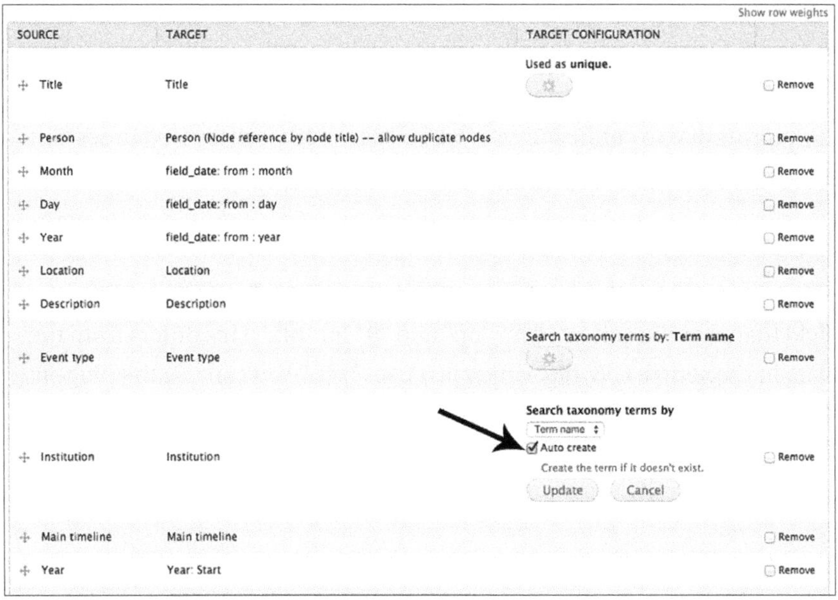

Figure 14.3. Mapping settings for event importer.

14.5.4 Feeds tamper

Person

For the Person field, add the "Explode" plug-in, in order to separate multiple values. There is one event with more than one person associated with it. The default comma is the correct separator.

Next, add the "Trim" plug-in; the default settings for that are correct.[13]

Event type

The Event type field only takes one value, so you don't need to apply the "Explode" plug-in.

---

13. The source data is already configured to accommodate a quirk in the person node title conventions, namely, that the people without a middle name actually have *two* spaces between their first and last names, even though it doesn't appear that way on the screen due to the HTML convention to collapse multiple spaces into a single space on display. (There was a space both before and after the middle name token). If the source data had only one space between the first and last names of people without a middle name, you could fix it by adding the "Find replace REGEX" plugin to the Person field, setting the "REGEX to find" pattern to /^(w+) (\w+)$/ and the replacement pattern to $1 $2 (with two spaces).

Institution

For Institution, because you are allowing it to create new taxonomy entries, choose the "Trim" plug-in to make sure that it doesn't create duplicate new terms due to confusion over white space; this is discussed in section 14.3.5.2. The default settings are correct.

Main time line

As discussed in section 7.3.2.8, the "Main time line" field is a Boolean field that uses the value "1" for "on" and "0" for "off." This differs from the data in the source CSV file, which just uses "yes." You can use the plug-in "Convert to boolean" to address this situation. Under "Truth value," enter "yes." The "False value" should simply be blank. The other default settings are fine.

14.5.5 Importing

Go to the import page (yoursite.org/import), and click on the "Event importer from DfH CSV" importer. Upload the CSV you downloaded from the website and click the "Import" button to import the events.

14.6 Summary

This chapter has covered the basic configuration of the Feeds module, with a focus on importing data from spreadsheets using CSV (comma-separated values) files. If you need to import data from RSS feeds, XML, JSON, or other sources, see the *Drupal for Humanists* site for examples that address those scenarios. The site also has example data and a description for how to import Image nodes into the example site.

Chapter 15 looks at the inverse task—exporting data *out* of a Drupal site.

Exporting Data and Settings

15.1 Overview

There are numerous reasons for exporting data out of a Drupal site, even if you aren't switching to another technical platform for your project. There are tools that may be analytically useful for your research that aren't primarily web based, like Gephi for network analysis, and exporting your data allows you to integrate those tools into your overall workflow. You may also want to periodically export your data in a standard, text-based format (such as a CSV file) for archival storage. Other project partners, such as your publisher, may expect a version of your data in a particular format, such as XML encoded using the TEI (Text Encoding Initiative) guidelines. Depending on the project, it may make more sense to enter, organize, and present your data online using Drupal, and then export the data using Drupal's XML format, and write XSLT to transform it into the required encoding.

This chapter covers the most common types of data export, as well as how to export configuration you have done on a Drupal site (e.g., content types, views, feeds importers, etc.). This may be useful as a way to move configuration work between a development site and the live version, or share some "template"-like configuration work you have done with others in your discipline who want to undertake a similar project.

15.2 Exporting data with Views Data Export

The easiest way to export your data for use with other software or for submission to an institutional repository is the Views Data Export[1] module. Views Data Export provides a new type of display (like "Page," "Block," or "Feed"), not simply a display format. This has the advantage of allowing you to "attach" a data export display to another display, to allow users to also download the data. If you create a Page display that lists all the Event nodes on the site, with exposed filters to allow users to browse the data, and you attach a data export display to that page, there will be a small icon at the bottom of the page specifying the format of the data export (e.g., CSV, XML) that a user can click to download the data in that format. Best of all, any filters they apply to the page will also be reflected in the downloaded file.

As an example, let's extend the event table described in section 13.8 by adding multiple data exports. If you haven't already created that table, follow the instructions in section 13.8 first before continuing with this section.

Install and enable the Views Data Export module, and edit the Event Table view by going to *Structure > Views > Event Table*.

15.2.1 Configuring a CSV data export display

In the top left of the Views configuration, under "Displays" click "Add" next to the Page display, and select "Data export."

Under "Data Export Settings" in the center column of the Views display, there are a number of things you must configure:

- Set the path to event-table/events.csv (or any other path you choose, ending in CSV).
- For "Attach to," check the box for "Page."
- Because the current data set includes fewer than 1000 nodes, we can leave the "Batched export" setting at "no."

---

1. https://www.drupal.org/project/views_data_export

- For "Permissions," consider whether you want to allow other sites to automatically pull in this CSV file, for example, using the Feeds module described in chapter 14. If so, you should set permissions to "none." If you only expect humans to be manually downloading the file, you can configure the permissions as you see fit.

Data export displays default to including 10 items, as defined in the "Pager" section in the center column. Click on "Display a specified number of items," and change it to "Display all items." After you do this, the Views preview will still only display a maximum of 20 items, but all items will be included in the export.

In the left column, under "Format," you can click on "CSV file" to see the other options available: DOC, TXT, XLS, and XML. If you click on "Settings" next to "CSV file," you can make additional configuration choices. In most cases, the default settings are fine, but note that by default, HTML is stripped out in a data export, but there's a box you can check under "Settings" to keep it in the output ("Keep HTML tags").

You can have more than one data export attached to a given page or block. Let's add an XML data export as well. First, in the upper left, under "Data export details," click on the link "Data export," and change the display name to CSV to help differentiate these two displays (figure 15.1). Then, add a new display, and once again select "Data export." If you didn't save your view after renaming the first data export display "CSV," the second display you add will appear with the name "Data export 2." Rename it "XML."

Figure 15.1. The event table view after adding and configuring a data export display.

15.2.2 Configuring an XML data export display

Follow the example in 15.2.1 to configure the data export settings in the center column, setting the path to *event-table/events.xml*. Don't forget to change the number of results that will be included in the data export.

Change the format from "CSV file" to "XML file." XML has extensive configuration options, like CSV; DOC, TXT, and XLS formats, by comparison, lack these settings.

The XML that is output by Views Data Export aligns with no standard; it is valid XML, and nothing more. You can specify the root element, and the element containing each node of results, but the markup of the rest of the data simply reflect the names of your fields; the data stored in the "Year" field are marked up using <year></year>, etc. RDF attributes are added to links, but attributes are not used to store field data. Once you have solidified the data model for your site, however, as long as you're storing data at a granularity that maps well to TEI, you could write XSLT that transforms the ad hoc Drupal-produced XML into TEI.

If you set the format to XML, you have the following options:

Provide as a file: This is unchecked by default, but you can check it to make the XML download as a file rather than attempting to display in the browser when a user clicks it.

Parent sort: Attempts to apply the sort order from the page to the resulting XML file.

Transform spaces: This is checked by default; it changes field labels that have multiple words into a valid XML tag, using the option you provide. A dash is selected by default, but you could also select an "underline" (_), "camelCase" (where all words after the first are capitalized), or "PascalCase" (where all words are capitalized).

Root and item node: You can specify the name of the root node, as well as the node for each item returned by the view.

Disable encoding of XML entities: By default, all HTML in a field gets encoded; for instance, an emphasis/italics tag <em> becomes "<em>". This option allows you to include HTML as-is, as a subelement of the field element, but if your HTML isn't valid (e.g., if you don't close all the tags), it will make the XML invalid as well.

> **Fields value to wrapped using CDATA:** This approach maintains the HTML tags, but doesn't treat them as subelements of the field element in the XML.

Part of the reason that the XML output format includes multiple ways of dealing with HTML in fields is because it *does not* strip out HTML from your output, the way the CSV format does by default. The XML format will export the data exactly the way it appears in the view, preserving, for instance, links from the author's name to their user profile. To remove these links from the XML output, you'll need to modify the individual linked fields (by overriding the XML display, in order to avoid losing the links on the page itself). Depending on the field, this may involve unchecking the "Link this field to its user" box, or changing the "Formatter" from "Title (link)" to "Title (no link)."

15.2.3 Output

Save your view, and go to the event table page. At the bottom of the table, you should see two small icons, labeled "CSV" and "XML" (figure 15.2). Clicking on either one should download a file with the same results as the page. To test this, download one of the file types, apply one or more exposed filters, and download the same file type again. The files should be different, with the second file reflecting the current state of the page.

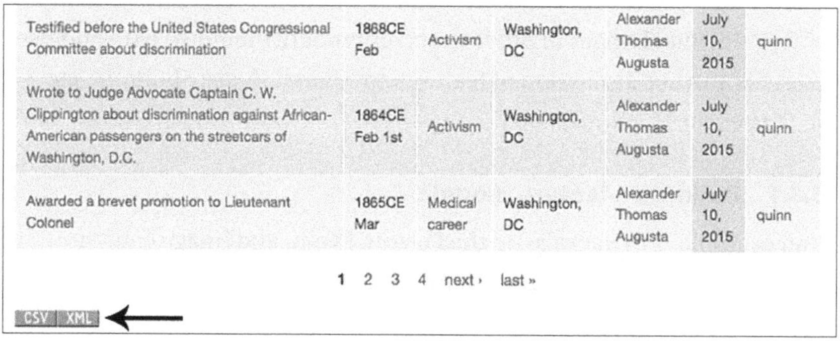

Testified before the United States Congressional Committee about discrimination	1868CE Feb	Activism	Washington, DC	Alexander Thomas Augusta	July 10, 2015	quinn
Wrote to Judge Advocate Captain C. W. Clippington about discrimination against African-American passengers on the streetcars of Washington, D.C.	1864CE Feb 1st	Activism	Washington, DC	Alexander Thomas Augusta	July 10, 2015	quinn
Awarded a brevet promotion to Lieutenant Colonel	1865CE Mar	Medical career	Washington, DC	Alexander Thomas Augusta	July 10, 2015	quinn

1 2 3 4 next › last »

CSV XML ⟵

Figure 15.2. The event table view, with icons for downloading a CSV or an XML file.

15.3 Exporting configuration using Features

Features[2] is a module that allows you to create and install other modules that encapsulate Drupal site configuration (content types, views, etc.), making it possible to move configuration from one site to another. An additional module, Node Export,[3] allows you to capture content in this way too, though the success with which Node Export can maintain relationships to terms, other nodes, and users referenced in a given node can vary.

If you are attempting to re-create an existing site on a new Drupal installation (for instance, if you have created a "template" site for others to modify and adapt), using Features to capture and move configuration and content (taxonomy terms, nodes, etc.) is the best way to do this cleanly, in a onetime way. You can provide other users with a feature that they can install and from that point on, the responsibility shifts to them to update all the modules that the site depends on (Views, Token, various field modules, etc.).

This stands in contrast to the Drupal concept of the "install profile" or "distribution" (a complex install profile), which is intended to be the "correct" way to create template sites, but it puts all derivative sites in the position of depending on the provider of the distribution to provide updates for Drupal core and the modules contained in the distribution. It isn't realistic for an individual scholar or a digital scholarship center at a single institution to download, install, test, and push out ongoing updates for a community of users, each of whom may have made their own significant changes in order to accommodate their own data and use cases. For further discussion of features compared to distributions, see the *Drupal for Humanists* site.

15.3.1 Building a feature module

As an example, let's package up the Person, Event, and Image content types, as well as the views created in chapters 12 and 13.

---

2. https://www.drupal.org/project/features
3. https://www.drupal.org/project/node_export

Install and enable the Features module, then go to *Structures > Features > Create feature*. On the left side, fill in the following information:

Name: Drupal for Humanists example content types and views.

Description: Creates a Person, Event, and Image content type, and various views for displaying these data.

Package: This is the section within the Modules page where the feature module will appear. Leaving this as "Features" is generally reasonable. You can also create an entirely new section on the Modules page for your features by putting in whatever text you would like (e.g., the name of the general kind of project this feature encapsulates, like "Documentary editing" or "Catalogue raisonné").

Version: 7.x-1.0.

The right side shows all the site components that Features knows about. Not all modules are written to be compatible with Features. Toggle down the following sections, and check the following items. Note that other items may be added to the list that you haven't directly specified; Features tries to include dependencies automatically wherever possible:

Content types: Event, Person, Image.

Menu links: Main-menu – Gallery, main-menu – People, main-menu – Time line.

Views: Event table, Gallery, Individual time line, Map, People, Site time line, Slide show.

If field bases and field instances don't immediately appear when you check the boxes for the content types, toggle open the "Advanced options" section on the left side of the configuration interface, and hit the "Refresh" button next to "Add auto-detected dependencies."

If you have incorporated any of the default Drupal fields (e.g., body, field_image) or taxonomies (i.e., the default Tags vocabulary) into your site, you need to remove them from the "Field bases" or "Taxonomy" section, respectively, otherwise when you install the feature on a new Drupal site, it will duplicate those fields or taxonomies rather than using the ones that already exist. In this case, we have not used the Tags vocabulary, but we have used the Body and Image fields, so uncheck "body" and "field_image" from the "Field bases" section. Also uncheck "Main menu" from the "Menus" section for the same reason.

15.3.2 Saving a feature module

Once you are done configuring the feature, you can simply click the "Download feature" button in the lower left to download a zip file that you can install as a module on another Drupal site. However, this leaves no trace of the configuration work you did in packaging up the feature on your source site, meaning that if you want to modify the feature in the future, you'd have to redo all that work.

To save the features configuration settings on your source site for later reuse, toggle down the "Advanced options" section on the left side of the configuration interface, and in that section, click the "Generate feature" button. This will package up the feature and place it in your sites/all/ modules folder. It will also make it available for you to edit in the future if you go to *Configuration > Features*, select the package (section within the Modules page) that it belongs to, and click "Recreate," which will take you back to the feature creation interface with all settings as you previously configured them.

"Generate feature" and "Download feature" are not mutually exclusive options: after you click "Download feature" (to have a copy of it saved locally), you can click "Generate feature" to save the configuration for future reuse.

15.3.3 Modules that extend Features

The Node Export[4] module allows you to include actual node content as part of a Feature, and it makes an attempt to maintain relationships to other nodes, taxonomy terms, and users.

The Features Extra[5] module (which can be found in the Modules list after you've installed it if you search for "FE") has submodules for enabling the export of block configuration settings and custom blocks (using the FE Blocks submodule).

---

4. https://www.drupal.org/project/node_export
5. https://www.drupal.org/project/features_extra

15.3.4 Using Features

Features largely work like any other module. They can be installed via the *Modules > Install new module* interface (or they can be placed manually in the sites/all/modules directory), and they are enabled via the Modules page. All feature modules have the Features module as a dependency, and may have many additional module dependencies depending on what the feature contains.

Once a feature module is enabled, any content types and views provided by the feature will appear on the site, and you can freely make changes to them. Once you have enabled a feature module, it generally makes sense to leave it enabled. If, however, you need to disable it in the future (for instance, if you move your site to a university-managed hosting environment that does not support custom modules), keep in mind that disabling a feature affects its components in different ways. Content types that were created using the feature remain on the site, whether or not you have modified them. Content imported using Node Export also remains on the site. However, views that were created using the feature disappear unless you've modified and saved them.

15.4 Other means of exposing data: Services, JSON, RDF

There are numerous other modules that enable you to make the data on your site available through different kinds of interfaces. The Services[6] module, supported by extensions like Services Entity API,[7] and Services API Key Authentication,[8] provides an interface for creating an API for your site.

Views Datasource[9] provides a Views display format (similar to how you configure maps or time lines, not a new display type like Views Data Export) for exporting your site's data as JSON, RDF (FOAF, SIOC, DOAP), XML, or XHTML.

---

6. https://www.drupal.org/project/services
7. https://www.drupal.org/project/services_entity
8. https://www.drupal.org/project/services_api_key_auth
9. https://www.drupal.org/project/views_datasource

Drupal has basic RDF support included among the core modules, but the RDF Extensions[10] module allows you to customize the RDF properties for individual fields. Additional modules support RDF indexing and SPARQL endpoints, though their user base is small. See the *Drupal for Humanists* site for a list of these modules as well as descriptions of how to configure them.

15.5 Summary

This chapter has covered how to export your site's data as CSV or XML files, as well as how to use the Features module to export your Drupal configuration. Chapter 16 addresses a rather different topic, focusing on search on Drupal sites.

---

10. https://www.drupal.org/project/rdfx

CHAPTER 16

Search

16.1 Overview

Searching is an indispensable functionality for any modern website. While it is hard to avoid putting a search box somewhere on your site, Drupal's built-in search capabilities are adequate at best, and could often be better characterized as "poor," particularly for very large sites.

To make it easier for your users to navigate your site content, you may want to create your own alternate "search" page using Views and exposed filters, and make it prominently available as part of the main menu. If you want your site to have robust search functionality, and you have the technical infrastructure to support it, you should consider using the Search API module (as discussed in section 16.7), which can integrate with the Apache Solr search platform for best results, but can also use Drupal's own database.

This chapter covers the configuration of Drupal's built-in search and how to modify the display of search results. It also briefly discusses some of the advanced options available if you use other search modules, like Apache Solr integration.

16.2 Search block and search pages

If you have the Search module enabled (which should happen by default when you install Drupal using the standard installation profile), Drupal provides a search block that you can enable anywhere for a simple search field. If you go to the path /search, you will find the standard Drupal search page. It presents a single search field, as well as an "Advanced search" section that you can toggle down to narrow the search to a particular content type, or refine your search using the fields "Containing any of the words," "Containing the phrase," "Containing none of the words." If you wish, you can link to Drupal's default search page from a menu using the instructions in section 11.3.3.2.

If you want to use the search block and/or search pages as part of your site, be sure to configure the permissions accordingly (by going to *People* > *Permissions* and scrolling down until you see the "Search" section), to allow anonymous and/or authenticated users to use the search. By default, only users with the administrator role are able to use the search.

16.3 Configuring Drupal's built-in search

Drupal's built-in search is set up to automatically index content, and you don't necessarily need to change the default configuration. There are a few adjustments to the ranking of results that you may want to make, depending on how your site is set up.

16.3.1 Indexing and cron runs

To configure Drupal's search, go to *Configuration* > *Search and metadata* > *Search settings*. As you create new content or update content, it goes in a queue to be indexed on the next "cron run." A cron[1] run does routine maintenance tasks, such as indexing content and checking Drupal.org for new module and core updates. Some modules also tap into cron runs, such as Feeds if you choose the "process in background" option for an import; see section 14.3.1. By default, Drupal sites execute cron runs every three hours, and index 100 items per cron run. The search settings page indicates what percentage of your content has been indexed, and under "Indexing throttle," you can change the settings to index more or fewer items per

---

1. Cron is a job-scheduler utility in Unix-like operating systems; the name comes from *chronos*, the Greek word for time.

cron run. In most cases, you can leave this with the default value. You can also modify how often the cron run occurs by going to *Configuration > System > Cron*.

16.3.2 Search modules

Further down on the search settings page, the "Search modules" area lets you specify what kind of content Drupal should be allowed to search. You need at least one search module enabled for search to work, and the default one should be "Node." If you enable the modules for users and/ or files, this will create new tabs at the top of the search screen for each of those search types; there is no way to search everything at the same time (figure 16.1).

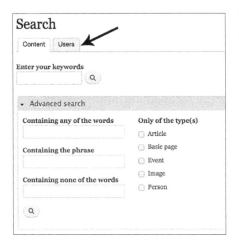

Figure 16.1. Drupal's default search page, with the "Advanced search" section toggled open.

16.3.3 Search ranking

Drupal's core search module provides a set of traits you can use to affect the ranking of search results. By default, all are set to zero, which is to say that none has a disproportionate influence on the search result ordering. "Keyword relevance" and perhaps "Recently posted" are the two factors that you may want to rank more highly than others.

16.3.4 Debugging search

Drupal's search functionality should simply work without any setup required. If, however, you have added content to your site, given the site time to index the content, and nothing comes up when you search for a term that you know appears on the site, it's possible that something has gone wrong with the indexing.

Go to the search configuration page (*Configuration > Search and metadata > Search settings*) and see what percentage of your content is indexed. If it indicates that none of your content is indexed, check to see if a default search module is specified. If not, choose "Content," save the settings, wait for cron to run (or run it manually by going to *Reports > Status report* and clicking the "run cron manually" link), and try to search again.

16.4 Customizing the search result display

You can configure how nodes of different content types appear as search results by going to *Structure > Content types > [select content type] > Manage display*. At the bottom of the page, toggle open the "Custom display settings," check the box for "Search result highlighting input," and save. This will reload the "Manage display" page with a new option in the upper right for selecting the "Search result highlighting input" display. After you click on it, you can modify the display as described in section 9.2.

16.5 Hiding content from the index

If there are content types or fields that you don't want to be indexed, you can follow the same steps as described in section 16.4 to enable the custom display setting for "Search index." Any field that is set to hidden as part of the "Search index" display will not be indexed.

16.6 Creating a custom advanced search page using Views

Drupal's built-in search page, even with the "advanced search" settings, is fairly limited; see figure 16.1. For instance, there is no way to search within a particular field. If you want to provide a more robust set of search options, create a view with a page display and add exposed filters as described in section 13.6.4. You can even provide a search box that uses Drupal's core search index by adding "Search: Search Terms" as an exposed filter. When you use Views to create an advanced search page, the "Format" area of the Views configuration interface (where you indicate whether you're displaying content or fields, and if you're displaying fields, which ones you include and how you configure them) is responsible for determining how the search results appear. Any configuration done as part of the content type display settings, as described in section 16.4, will not apply.

16.7 Search API

The Search API module is designed to be a replacement for Drupal's core search. Search API needs to be connected to a *backend*, which stores its index; it cannot use the built-in Drupal index. Configuring Search API is a fairly complex process, but it gives you much more fine-grained control over what content gets indexed and how, including specifying characters to be ignored, defining lists of stop words (words like "to" and "this" that should be filtered out of the index), and boosting the value of words in certain HTML elements (e.g., making words that appear as part of a <h2> or <h3> header tag rank more highly). Numerous add-on modules for Search API are available, including Facet API (which allows you to define and display "facets" that can be used to narrow search results—for instance, one facet block might show a checkbox for each "Institution" taxonomy term that occurs in one or more of the search results, and a user could check the box for one particular institution to show only the search results that relate to that institution), blocks that provide advanced sorting options, and modules that provide autocomplete prediction as people enter search terms.

For more on configuring Search API using the Database Search[2] backend (which stores the index in the same MySQL database as the rest of your site) and using the Apache Solr[3] search platform, see the *Drupal for Humanists site*.

---

2. https://www.drupal.org/project/search_api_db
3. https://www.drupal.org/project/search_api_solr

16.8 Summary

This chapter has briefly addressed some of the things you can do to improve Drupal's search functionality by using Views and by configuring the search result display of nodes. Particularly for sites with fewer than 500 nodes, this may be sufficient. The larger and more complex your site becomes, the greater the payoff will be for tackling the configuration of a more robust search module like Search API.

Chapter 17 will cover various tasks related to taxonomies, including configuring taxonomy term pages, tag clouds, merging terms, and making other bulk changes to taxonomy terms.

Managing Taxonomies

17.1 Overview

Section 6.4.4 covered how to create vocabularies and populate them with terms. This chapter discusses how to do more with taxonomies, including customizing taxonomy term pages (the list of nodes that appears when you click on a particular taxonomy term), creating tag clouds, editing and merging terms, and options for importing and exporting taxonomy terms.

17.2 Configuring taxonomy term pages

By default, when you click on a taxonomy term you will see a list of all the nodes that share that term, using the node title, a "teaser" snippet from the body field, and a "read more" link. The easiest way to customize this involves using Views to override the default display.

Go to *Structure > Views*, and scroll down to the bottom of the list. You will see a grayed-out view called "Taxonomy term." Click the "enable" button on the right side, and the view will move up to the area of active views. Click the "edit" button to edit the view. You can configure this view just like any other, including providing exposed filters so that users can narrow the results using other parameters.

In this case, under the "Format" section in the left column, change the view from showing "content" to "fields," and change the format from "Unformatted list" to "Grid." As soon as you change from "Content" to

"Fields," a "Master" display will appear. Click on it, and add the fields "Content: Title" and "Content: Image"; the image will always appear blank for Event nodes, but it will appear for Person and Image nodes. Neither should have a label. The image should use the "Medium" image style, and link image to content. For the title field, under "style settings," check "customize field HTML" and select "H3." Save the view.

Now, go to a Person node and click on one of the taxonomy terms under "Profession." You should see a grid of images and people that share the same taxonomy term (figure 17.1).

Figure 17.1. The "Nurse" taxonomy term page, as configured in section 17.2.

This works well if you only have taxonomy terms associated with content types that are reasonably well represented by a title and an image. If, however, you use the default Drupal content type of "Article" to maintain a site blog, your blog posts will have terms from the "Tags" vocabulary associated with them, and in those cases you might want a title and text-based teaser to show up when you click on a particular tag. The Taxonomy

Display[1] module allows you to specify a different view for the term display on a vocabulary-by-vocabulary basis. See the *Drupal for Humanists* website for instructions on how to configure that module.

17.2.1 Displaying content and users that both use a given term

If you look closely at the view that overrides the default taxonomy term page, you'll notice that it is a view of *content*. If you have a vocabulary with terms that appear as *both* a part of nodes *and* of the user profiles (such as "Institutional affiliation," for a site that includes a "Project" content type and user profiles), only the nodes will show up when you go to the term page. There's no way to display the users as well.

You can address this by creating a new view of users (rather than content), making it available as a block, and enabling the block on term pages for terms in a vocabulary that is connected with both nodes and user profiles.

Create a new view using the following parameters:

> **View name "Taxonomy users," description:** "Block of all users whose profiles use a given taxonomy term."
>
> Show *Users.*
>
> Create a block, title "People."
>
> > **Display format:** *Unformatted list* of fields.
> >
> > **Items per page:** 10, use a pager.

Add and configure fields however you would like to create the display of users. "User: Last access" may be a good choice for sorting the results, so that users who are more active on the site appear first.

Toggle open the advanced settings section. Under "Contextual filter," add the name of the field in the user's profile that stores the taxonomy terms that are also shared with a content type. For instance, "Field: Institutional affiliation" might be part of a user profile, drawing on an "Affiliation" vocabulary that is also used in a Project content type. In the section "When the filter value is *not* available," choose "Provide default

---

1. https://www.drupal.org/project/taxonomy_display

value," and in the drop-down list that appears, select "Taxonomy term ID from URL." Below that, check "Load default filter from term page." For a more general discussion of contextual filters, see section 13.3.5.

If your site has multiple vocabularies that are shared between content and user profiles (e.g., disciplinary field, affiliation, tools used), you can add additional block displays to this view, and override the contextual filter section for each one, so each block has a different contextual filter corresponding to a field in the user profiles that uses term references.

Once you have created these blocks, you can enable them (perhaps in a sidebar) on the block configuration page (*Structure > Blocks*). You should only enable each block for the taxonomy term pages related to the corresponding vocabulary, which is to say, under "Visibility settings" you should select the "Only on listed pages" option and put in the path that indicates all terms within the vocabulary that matches your block. To check on what that pattern will be, go to *Configuration > Search and metadata > URL aliases > Patterns* and scroll down to the "Taxonomy term paths" section. The default pattern for taxonomy terms is [term:vocabulary]/[term:name], meaning that unless you have configured specific alternate paths for the vocabularies in question, under "only on listed pages" you should enter "institutional-affiliation/*" for a vocabulary called "Institutional affiliation," "tools/*" for a vocabulary called "Tools," etc. See section 11.2.5 for more on configuring visibility settings for blocks, and section 6.9 for more on configuring URL aliases.

17.3 Tag clouds

Tag clouds are a common way to provide a quick view of the relative frequency of term use. The TagCloud[2] module provides a tag cloud block for each vocabulary. Once you install and enable the module, you can configure it by going to *Configuration > Content authoring > TagClouds configuration*, or by clicking the "Configure" link next to the module on the modules page. On this page, you can determine the sort order for tags (by title or count, or random), whether to use a node count or a style

---

2. https://www.drupal.org/project/tagclouds

(usually implemented as font size) difference to represent the number of nodes with a given term, how many tags should appear, and how many "levels" should be available if you're using a style rather than a node count.

On the blocks page, a new set of blocks will be available named "Tags in [vocabulary name]," one for each

Professions
Nurse Physician
Medical researcher
Surgeon

Figure 17.2. A tag cloud block for the Professions vocabulary.

vocabulary (figure 17.2). You can override this title as part of the block configuration process otherwise it will appear along with the tag cloud.

17.4 Taxonomy manager and term merge

The Taxonomy Manager[3] module provides a convenient interface for adding and modifying taxonomy terms, including making changes in bulk. If you want to be able to merge terms, you can also add the Term Merge[4] module, which adds that functionality to the taxonomy manager. Merging terms is useful if you have any uncontrolled vocabularies (vocabularies where you haven't predefined all allowable terms) on the site. Particularly if you allow users to add their own terms (for instance, entering their own institution or department name), over time your site will accumulate multiple variant terms (e.g., "Slavic," "Slavic Department," "Slavic Languages and Literatures"). Periodically, it is worthwhile to go through your taxonomies and clean up these variant terms

Install and enable the taxonomy manager and term merge modules. Using the administration menu, go to *Structure > Taxonomy Manager > [Select a vocabulary to edit]*. In this case, we'll edit Institutions. Click on any term to open a panel where you can edit its text, description, and parent term(s). You can also check individual terms to make bulk changes, or use the small icons to the left of the vocabulary name to select (check mark) or deselect (x icon) all the terms on the list.

---

3. https://www.drupal.org/project/taxonomy_manager
4. https://www.drupal.org/project/term_merge

The "Up" and "Down" arrows change the *weight* of a term, the property that determines the order in which terms appear, if you want an ordering other than alphabetical. The "Add" button allows you to add one or more new items, and includes help text about the syntax to use to add child nodes. The "Delete" button allows you to delete the selected term(s), and optionally, their child nodes as well. The "Move" button allows you to specify a new parent term for the selected terms. The "Double tree" button adds another column to the interface. If you choose the same vocabulary as in the left column, you can drag and drop terms into new parent-child relationships. If you choose a different vocabulary, you can move terms to a different vocabulary. You can switch vocabularies using the drop-down menu in the upper right.

To merge terms, check all the *unwanted* terms that you want to merge into a single preferred term (figure 17.3). Then, click the "Term merge" button. Use the autocomplete to enter the preferred term. If the preferred term is identical to the unwanted terms, click the term you want to merge all the unwanted terms into. The term ID will appear in parentheses next to the term name. If the term ID is 7, for example, you can enter into the

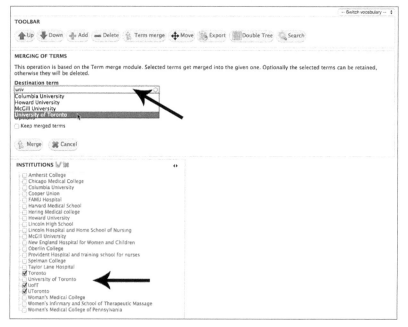

Figure 17.3. Merging terms.

autocomplete "term-id:7." In most cases, you don't want to check the "Keep merged terms" box; removing the duplicates is an important part of merging the terms. Once you click the "Merge" button, Drupal will go through every node that uses one of the unwanted terms, and will update it to use the preferred term, before deleting the unwanted terms.

17.5 Importing and exporting taxonomies

The taxonomy manager module, described in section 17.6, can also be used to export and import taxonomy terms. On the source site, where the terms already exist, go to the vocabulary you want to export using the taxonomy manager (*Structure > Taxonomy Manager > [Vocabulary to export]*) and click the "Export" button. You can choose between exporting the whole vocabulary, the child terms of a selected item, or root-level terms (only those terms that don't have a parent term).

If you select the form "Term names with hierarchy," you can copy and paste the resulting export into the "Add" window of the taxonomy manager on the site where you want to import the terms. The format of the CSV export isn't compatible with what Feeds expects from the CSV files it can import (it uses term IDs rather than term names to define parent-term relationships, for example), so it's better to use the "term names with hierarchy" format and taxonomy manager to do the import.

If you don't need the full power of the taxonomy manager module, you may want to use the stand-alone Taxonomy CSV import/export[5] module for importing and exporting taxonomies. You can also use Views Data Export, as described in section 15.2, to create a simple CSV of taxonomy data. If you want to draw on an externally maintained vocabulary for your site, the Web Taxonomy plug-in[6] is designed to support those use cases. An add-on, Web Taxonomy plug-in for Getty vocabularies,[7] supports the Getty Art and Architecture Thesaurus, Thesaurus of Geographical Names, and Union List of Artist Names. See the *Drupal for Humanists* site for information on how to use these modules.

---

5. https://www.drupal.org/project/taxonomy_csv
6. https://www.drupal.org/project/web_taxonomy
7. https://www.drupal.org/project/wt_getty

17.6 Summary

This chapter has covered the configuration of taxonomy term pages, alternative ways of displaying taxonomy terms, and ways to clean up vocabularies that have become cluttered.

Next, chapter 18 discusses themes, which determine the design, colors, and overall "look" of your site.

CHAPTER 18

Themes

18.1 Overview

This chapter discusses the role of a Drupal site theme, and provides some guidelines for choosing themes and for developing site designs that must be implemented as Drupal themes. It explains theme installation, configuration, and subtheming using the example of the AdaptiveTheme family, which exposes many configuration options through a Drupal user interface.

18.2 Drupal themes

A Drupal theme has two major sets of responsibilities: defining the *regions* where you can place blocks, and providing an overall "coat of paint" over the top of all the structures you've created using content types, views, blocks, and menus. The theme defines the colors and fonts, background images, and the exact display format for certain kinds of field data (e.g., whether a multivalued field appears as a list, as bullet points, etc.).

The selection of regions available in a given theme is arguably one of the more fundamental traits of the theme. While it's possible to add new regions to a theme, doing so involves writing PHP code, and implementing it carefully in order to not disrupt any responsive design or accessibility compatible features of the theme. It is much easier to change fonts, colors, or background images using CSS than to add a new region.

18.3 Approaches to site theming

There are, broadly speaking, three different ways of approaching the theming of your site. The choice for any given project depends on balancing the factors of skills available, money available, and specificity of the vision for the site's theme. The profiles of individual Drupal sites on the *Drupal for Humanists* website include information about the themes those sites use, as well as how much customization was done.

18.3.1   Using an existing theme

There are over 600 Drupal 7 themes posted on Drupal.org.[1] By default, the Drupal themes page sorts by "most installed," which means that base themes (which people build upon to develop a highly customized look and feel) appear at the top. Towards the middle of the first page of results, though, you begin to see themes that you can simply use out of the box. Some of them require that you install a base theme first; this works just like installing a module that has a dependency on another module—you just need to make sure that you've installed and enabled the base theme first, and everything should work. If none of the themes on Drupal.org are to your liking, there are other sites that offer "premium" paid Drupal themes, almost always for less than $100, with many under $50. If you want your site to be visibly affiliated with your institution through the use of the university's colors, fonts, and other graphic elements, there may be a group on campus (perhaps a web services group or the office of communications/public affairs) that offers a university-branded Drupal theme. Using an existing theme can potentially require a small amount of money, if you choose a paid theme from outside Drupal.org, but it involves little or no customization.

18.3.1.1   Identifying requirements for your theme

Before you set off to find a theme, you should decide on what your requirements are. What regions does the theme need to support? Do you want the option of a left and right sidebar? Do you need a footer? Is it

---

1. https://www.drupal.org/project/project_theme

important for your site to be easy to use on a mobile device? If so, look for a theme that uses *responsive design* or that indicates that it's *mobile optimized*.

Some themes have a menu region where you can put a standard menu block, or use a drop-down menu block (see section 11.3.6). Others have a specific way of displaying a main menu, and your only configuration choice is which menu to use as the main menu. You should consider whether you want your site to have drop-down menus or multicolumn "mega-menus," and make sure the theme supports it. All themes with a menu region should be compatible, perhaps with a small amount of tweaking; themes that control the menu configuration may or may not.

Universities are increasingly coming under scrutiny for their web accessibility practices. Are there university guidelines or requirements for accessibility that you need to follow? Looking for a theme that is WCAG (Web Content Accessibility Guidelines) compliant won't address all accessibility issues, but it will cover many of them.

18.3.1.2   Researching and testing existing themes

If you're looking for a theme that is ready to use, you should avoid themes that use the phrase "base theme" or "starter theme" in the description. These are themes that are intended to be used as scaffolding for designing a custom theme.

Some of the things you may be looking for (mobile optimized, WCAG compliance) are widely recognized as positive features, and require no small amount of work to implement. Themes that include these features will most likely mention it in the description. If you are exploring commercial (paid) themes, and you're unsure whether a theme meets your requirements (for instance, factors relating to accessibility), there is often a way to contact the developer to ask. Be as specific as possible when asking the question, using language from the university's accessibility requirements if you can. "Is this theme accessible?" is open to varying interpretations of "accessibility," but there should be a clearer answer to the question "Is this theme WCAG 2.0 AA compliant?" For free themes on Drupal.org, if there's no information about accessibility, mobile optimization, or another key trait, you can always download it, enable it on your site, and see if it behaves the way you want. For accessibility testing, you can enable the module on your site and run your site through one of many online accessibility testers, though take care not to confuse errors caused by your configuration (e.g., not providing alt-text for images) with shortcomings in the theme.

Browsing the issue queue for a theme can also be useful, if only as a way to ensure that there are no catastrophic problems that have not been addressed. There are no functional differences between the layout of theme pages and the layout of module pages on Drupal.org, so all the tips from section 4.3 about evaluating modules can apply equally to themes.

18.3.2 Modifying or configuring an existing theme

If you have a general sense for what you want your site to look like (e.g., particular colors, fonts, and styles) and you can't find a theme that's compatible out of the box, you can modify an existing theme, or choose a theme that provides a lot of configuration options. Choosing a highly configurable theme that meets common technical requirements (mobile optimization, WCAG compatibility, etc.) is also a good approach if you want to keep your theming fairly simple, and minimize the amount of CSS code that needs to be written, while still maintaining some control over the colors and fonts on the site.

Modifying an existing theme may require a small to moderate amount of skill with CSS, depending on the extent of the changes you need to make. Some themes minimize the amount of CSS you need to write by exposing many configuration options on the theme's settings page.

Follow the same guidelines as in section 18.3.1.1 and 18.3.1.2 when determining your requirements and researching different themes. Using this theming approach, you can be a little more flexible; if a theme otherwise meets all your major requirements, but you hate the colors the designer used, you can modify the theme's CSS to choose a different set of colors. Structural issues like number and position of regions and mobile optimization or accessibility are much harder to fix.

If you're looking for a simple, configurable theme for your site that provides numerous regions (including a menu region), mobile optimization, WCAG compliance, and many configuration options exposed through the theme settings page, consider using a subtheme of AdaptiveTheme,[2] such

---

2. https://www.drupal.org/project/adaptivetheme

as Corolla,[3] Sky,[4] AT Commerce,[5] or Pixture Reloaded.[6] The AdaptiveTheme developers also offer paid subthemes. Section 18.5 describes how to install, configure, and construct subthemes (or sub-subthemes) in the AdaptiveTheme family.

18.3.3 Developing a highly customized theme

Some project directors have a specific idea of what their site will look like when it's completed, before they even choose the technologies they will use to build it. In fact, compatibility with this final design vision may be a significant factor in deciding between technical platforms. For a project that is built using Drupal, it may be easier or harder to execute the vision depending on how well it maps onto Drupal concepts like blocks, regions, horizontal/vertical tab groups, etc. Single-page designs (where all content appears on one page, and the background color might shift between sections, which are marked using anchor tags), for example, are not as easily compatible with Drupal as designs that involve multiple pages, though there are modules and themes that attempt to enable single-page designs.[7]

If you have a very specific vision for your site design, it's worth looking around at existing themes and considering what would need to be modified about a particular theme to meet your expectations. If it becomes clear that you'll need to develop a theme from scratch, you should still start with one of the base, or starter, themes that are commonly used. Base themes provide little to no styling, but they provide useful scaffolding that would be time-consuming and frustrating to re-create, such as accessibility support, responsive design, and/or support for older versions of Internet Explorer.

Some of the base themes that are most widely used include Zen,[8] AdaptiveTheme, and Omega,[9] though Omega currently lacks some of the accessibility support of the other two. All three themes include links to

---

3. https://www.drupal.org/project/corolla
4. https://www.drupal.org/project/sky
5. https://www.drupal.org/project/at_commerce
6. https://www.drupal.org/project/pixture_reloaded
7. Such as https://www.drupal.org/project/single_page_website
8. https://www.drupal.org/project/zen
9. https://www.drupal.org/project/omega

documentation on their Drupal.org pages; this documentation provides theme-specific tips to developing a subtheme.

The Drupal.org site provides extensive documentation on theming in general,[10] though the theming handbook[11] in particular is not necessarily well curated, and you should double-check that a given tutorial applies to your version of Drupal before attempting to follow it, since the underpinnings of Drupal's theming layer have evolved with each version. In the right sidebar, you should look for a section towards the top called "About this page," and check for the Drupal version the page applies to (figure 18.1). Not all documentation pages have these metadata, but the information at the top of the page about the last time the page was updated may also provide a clue. As a reference point, Drupal 7 was released in January 2011, but widespread module support wasn't available until late 2011 or early 2012.

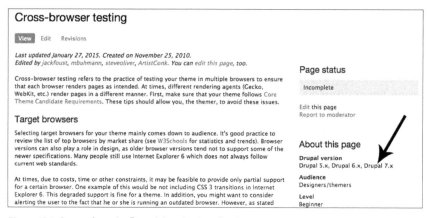

Figure 18.1. A page from the Drupal theming handbook.

It takes considerable skill and expertise to go from a set of wireframes or design proofs to a functional Drupal theme, even when building on a base theme. Even a person with strong HTML, CSS, and Javascript skills, and some familiarity with PHP, shouldn't be expected to simply make a Drupal theme without first spending time familiarizing themselves with the nuts and bolts of Drupal's theming system, studying the documentation for

---

10. https://www.drupal.org/theming
11. https://www.drupal.org/documentation/theme

the base theme they're using, and looking at how other subthemes are implemented. If you want to develop Drupal theming skills as part of your project team, it may be worth investing in some of the many paid video tutorials on theming that are available, but even these videos generally assume that the viewer is already comfortable with HTML, CSS, Javascript, and some PHP.

If it is not realistic for you to have a member of your project team dedicate a significant amount of time to learning how to do Drupal theming, and then to implementing the envisioned design, you could outsource this work to a freelance themer or a company that provides Drupal theming services. While costs can vary significantly, you can expect to pay anywhere from a few thousand dollars to more than $10,000 for a highly customized theming job.

18.4 Installing and enabling themes and subthemes

18.4.1 Installing themes

Installing themes through the Drupal user interface works just like installing modules; in fact, going to *Appearance > Install new theme* takes you to the same page as going to *Modules > Install new module.* You can upload a zip file, or provide a URL to a zipped file stored elsewhere, such as on a theme's page on Drupal.org. If you want to, or have to, install a theme by accessing the file system directly, you can place the theme in sites/all/themes. Themes that are uploaded via Drupal's user interface go into sites/all/themes.

If you have a multisite arrangement (see the *Drupal for Humanists* site for details on configuring multisites), themes in the sites/all/themes directory will be available to all sites. Because themes can be specific to an individual site (i.e., you may *not* want your theme to be available for any other site in a multi-site setup to use), you may wish to instead place your theme in the sites/default/themes directory, or sites/your-site-name/themes directory in a multi-site setup.

The question of where to put themes can become more complicated if you're not using a self-contained theme, but rather, a subtheme of an existing base theme (or even a subtheme of a subtheme of a base theme). If you're not concerned about other sites using your theme, either because your site is the only one using the Drupal code base, or because you're not bothered by the prospect of your site design appearing elsewhere, you can simply put all themes in sites/all/themes. If you are using a multisite setup and want to keep your theme exclusive to your own site, the *only* theme that should be in the sites/your-site/themes is the subtheme (or sub-subtheme) that is set as the default theme on your site; see section 18.4.2 for setting a default theme. Any themes that your subtheme is built on (base themes, and/or subthemes) should be placed in sites/all/themes. Themes, like modules, may be periodically updated (to address security flaws or other bugs, or to introduce new configuration features), and it will be easier to update a base theme for all the sites that build on it if it is located in the shared sites/all/themes directory.

18.4.2   Enabling themes and administration themes

Click on *Appearance* in the administration bar. By default, there are two enabled themes: Bartik and Seven. Bartik is the default Drupal 7 theme, and Seven is the default Drupal 7 administration theme (the theme used on all the administration pages, including the node creation pages).

Below the enabled themes are the disabled themes: Garland, which is similar to Bartik; and Stark, which has no styling beyond Drupal's default styles. Any themes you have installed but not yet enabled will also appear in this area.

At the bottom of the page is a section where you can select an administration theme. You can download other administration themes (like Adminimal[12] or Shiny[13]) from Drupal.org, and some themes— including AdaptiveTheme—include an administration theme. Unlike with regular site themes, you don't have to enable a theme before setting it to be the administration theme.

To make a theme visible on your site, you must enable it and *also* set it as default. Disabled themes have two options: "Enable" and "Enable and

---

12. https://www.drupal.org/project/adminimal_theme
13. https://www.drupal.org/project/shiny

set default." Enabled themes have options for "Settings," "Disable," and "Set Default."

Why would you have modules besides the default one enabled? The ThemeKey module, discussed on the *Drupal for Humanists* site, allows you to use enabled themes other than the default theme in certain contexts. An individual user could choose a different theme that is only visible to them; this is particularly helpful when developing a new theme for a live site. You can also choose a different theme for a particular set of pages, for instance, if the project is cosponsoring a conference, and wants to have a few conference-related pages with a different look and feel.

Keep in mind that any base themes or parent themes that a subtheme draws upon need to be installed, but do not need to be enabled.

18.4.3   Configuring global settings

By going to *Appearance > Settings*, you can configure the "global settings" that will be applied to all themes, unless they have been overridden in the theme's individual configuration settings. As part of the global settings, you can uncheck the box for "Use the default logo" and upload your site's own logo instead, and do the same for the site's favicon (the small image that appears next to a site's name as part of a tab label in a browser). You can also toggle on or off various theme elements, such as whether to display a logo at all, whether to show a user's picture along with their name as part of the post authoring information, whether to display the text of a site's name and/or slogan, etc. These settings correspond to information that you define on the "Site information" page, *Configuration > System > Site information.*

18.4.4   Configuring theme-specific settings

You can configure the settings for any enabled theme, but changes you make will only be visible for the default theme, unless you're using the ThemeKey module.

To configure a theme, click on "settings" on the theme page, or go to *Appearance > Settings > [Theme name]*. The scope and nature of the options available varies widely. At the bottom of each theme's settings page are a set of options identical to those on the global settings page. The configuration for these options is identical to the global settings by default, but you can change them on a theme-by-theme basis. Bartik, the Drupal 7 default theme, includes an area for selecting between five color scheme options, or defining your own using the color picker. It also includes a preview area that immediately reflects the changes you've made to the colors. If the color picker is not available when you configure Bartik, make sure that the core "Color" module is enabled.

Section 18.5 describes theme configuration for AdaptiveTheme subthemes, which expose many more options as part of the settings page.

18.5 AdaptiveTheme and its subthemes

For the example site, we will use Corolla, which is a subtheme of AdaptiveTheme. This approach makes the most sense if you will mostly be limiting your styling changes to options that are provided through the theme settings user interface (UI), with perhaps a small number of changes to the CSS itself (see section 18.5.1.1). If you need to make more extensive changes to the CSS, it would be better to create and use a subtheme of Corolla. The AdaptiveTheme developers provide a blank template subtheme—Footheme [14]—designed to work with all the AdaptiveTheme subthemes, though some additional configuration is needed if you choose a subtheme other than Corolla to base it on. This configuration is described in the README.txt file included with Footheme.[15]

Install AdaptiveTheme and Corolla. Click "Enable and set default" for Corolla, then click on "Settings" for Corolla. The theme settings available for AdaptiveTheme and its subthemes are divided into four parts, described below.

---

14. https://www.drupal.org/project/footheme

15. Using Footheme version 7.x-3.0-rc1 with any AdaptiveTheme subtheme will produce some variation on the following error message: "Notice: Undefined index: three_33_top in include() (line 52 of //sites/all/themes/corolla/templates/page.tpl.php)." This entry in the Footheme issue queue has instructions for how to resolve the problem: https://www.drupal.org/node/1976954.

18.5.1 Layout and general settings

The "standard layout" area of this section lets you define the width and position of the sidebars, as well as a maximum page width (figure 18.2). There are also subsections for customizing the layout for tablets (in portrait mode, and in landscape mode), and for "smalltouch" devices (smartphones and similar).

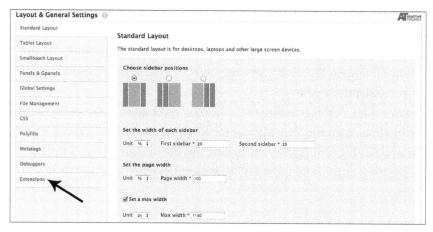

Figure 18.2. The Layout & General Settings configuration area for Corolla.

18.5.2 Extensions

The "Extensions" section gives you fairly fine-grained control over how fonts and text styles are used on the site, as well as other features like default image alignment, rounded corners, and drop-shadows, and the bullet style for bulleted lists. In the "Fonts" section, you can pick sets of standard, web-based fonts, or you can reference any of the fonts available through Google Fonts[16] by name. When you enable Google Fonts, users aren't required to have the font installed on their own machine. The font is dynamically pulled from Google's server as the page loads. For that reason, Google Fonts will not display if you are developing your site locally and do not have Internet connectivity.

---

16. https://www.google.com/fonts

18.5.2.1 Custom CSS

If there are theming changes you'd like to make that aren't configurable through the interface, you may wish to additionally enable the "Custom CSS" extension (figure 18.3). Click on the "Extensions" subsection of the Layout & General Settings configuration area. If you check the "custom CSS" checkbox and save your configuration changes, a box for custom CSS will appear below, in the "Extensions" section. Using the custom CSS extension provides an alternative to using or modifying Footheme as a sub-subtheme. Instead, you could set a subtheme like Corolla or Sky to be the default theme, and use the custom CSS extension to store any additional changes. These changes are stored in a file in your files directory by default (adaptivetheme /corolla_files/corolla.custom.css), but you can change the location of this file by clicking on the "File Management" subsection of the Layout & General Settings configuration. Storing this file outside the folder of the theme itself ensures that it won't be overwritten when you update the theme.

Figure 18.3. The Custom CSS area of the Extensions subsection, after it has been enabled.

If you only have a few small CSS changes to make, and you don't anticipate wanting to use your modified theme on another site, using this custom CSS extension will be quicker and easier than using a sub-subtheme. If you have more extensive changes, and/or you want those changes to be more portable, it's better to use Footheme and put those changes in footheme/css/footheme.css.

18.5.3 Color scheme

Like Bartik, this area of the AdaptiveTheme configuration page allows you to choose colors for different aspects of the site. You can either type in the hex value (e.g., #FF0000 for bright red), or click in one of the color boxes and drag the sliders on the color wheel around until you find a color you like (figure 18.4). Unfortunately, it does not have a preview option, so you'll need to save your configuration and close the administrative overlay to see the effects. The specific set of colorable options varies from subtheme to subtheme, and the labels do not always make it clear where or how the corresponding color will be applied. It may be useful as you familiarize yourself with the theme to change these colors one at a time. It can also be useful to pick a vivid, even garish color for settings where you don't understand what the label is referring to. Even if you have no intention of including neon green as part of your final color palette, you may want to use it temporarily to see where and how the "Fieldset border" appears on the site, before changing it to a more agreeable hue.

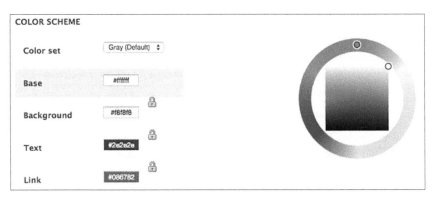

Figure 18.4. The color picker and some of the default color settings for Corolla.

18.5.4 Toggle display, logo image, shortcut image

At the bottom of the configuration page, you can toggle open these settings to upload a logo and shortcut icon, if you haven't already as part of the general settings, or toggle the display of other components on or off.

18.5.5   Example site configuration

For the example site, we will make the following configuration changes to Corolla:

> Under *Extensions* > Fonts, toggle down the "Titles" section. For the site name, set it to "Basic Google font," and enter the font name Montserrat. Check the box for "Styles" and choose "Bold 700." Set Page Title, Node Title, and Block Title to use the same Google Font, but without the bold setting.
>
> Under "Color scheme," choose the color set "Red."
>
> Under "Toggle display," uncheck Logo, User pictures in posts, User pictures in comments, User verification status in comments.

Save the configuration.

Now that you have applied a new theme to the example site, you should check the block settings for the new theme.

> Ensure that "View: Individual time line" and "View: Map" are enabled in the "Main content" region, underneath "Main page content."
>
> Move the "Search form" block from "Sidebar first" to the footer. You may want to disable it entirely if you have set up a view-based search as described in section 16.6.
>
> Disable the "Navigation" block.
>
> Disable the "User login" block. If this block is not available, users who should be able to log in will have to know the correct path to go to on your site (/user), but it will be much more unobtrusive for visitors to the site who should not have accounts.
>
> Disable the "Powered by Drupal" block in the footer.
>
> Enable the "Main menu" block in the "Menu bar" region.
>
> > You may also wish to rearrange the links in the main menu, so that "Home" appears first in the list. Go to *Structure* > *Menus* > *Main menu* and drag the "Home" link to the top of the list. Save.

18.6 Summary

This chapter has discussed pros and cons of different approaches to theme selection, and has walked through highlights from the extensive configuration options available in AdpativeTheme and its subthemes, which are recommended for their configurability, mobile optimization, and accessibility.

At this point, the example site is almost complete. Chapter 19 will address the final configuration steps for the example site, as well as provide a checklist of things to do before launching a Drupal site.

CHAPTER 19

Finishing and Launching the Example Site

19.1 Overview

If you've followed the steps laid out in previous chapters, the example site should be almost complete. A few small things remain to be done, including creating a welcoming front page and preparing the site for launch. This chapter covers those odds and ends.

19.2 Front page

The front page of the site can be used to provide a general introduction to the scope and goals of the project, as well as highlight some interesting content. In section 13.7 you used Views to create a slide show, and chapter 12 included a block that shows a random person from the database. Both of these have a place on the front page.

19.2.1 Adding a view of news posts

Let's also create a new view to show recent news on the front page. Routinely posting project news (conference presentations, major website updates, etc.) and displaying it on the front of your site provides an easy way for viewers to get a sense of how active the project is. At the same time, if the website you're creating is for a project that is about to go dormant (due to the end of grant funding, competing priorities, etc.), it may be better to not include a news section.

Before creating your first news item, go to *Configuration > Search and metadata > URL aliases > Patterns* and set the pattern for the default Article content type to news/[node:title]. Then, create a new node using the Article content type, and give it the title "Launch of new project website." Put whatever you'd like in the body field, and save.

Go to *Structure > Views > Add new view.*

View name "News," description: "News items on the site."

Show *Content* of type Article.

Create a page, title "News" and path news.

    Display format: *Unformatted list* of *full posts, without links, without comments.*

    Items to display: 10, use a pager.

    Create a menu link, in the Main Menu, link text "News."

    Include an RSS feed, use the default settings.

Create a block, title "News."

    Display format: *Unformatted list* of *titles (linked).*

    Items per page: 3.

Hit "Continue & edit." Click on the "Block" display. In the "Pager" section (center column at the bottom), click on "No" next to "More link." Check the "Create more link" box, and uncheck "Display 'more' link only if there is more content." This will add a link to the bottom of the block that will take users to the full News page. Also, under "Fields," add "Content: Post date." Uncheck "Create a label," and use the "Long format" for the date. Save the view.

19.2.2   Introducing Panels

We currently have three blocks to display on the front page (the slide show, the random person node, and the news block), along with a general welcome and overview statement. However, the site currently lacks any way to display them all in an elegant way. You could create a Basic Page node for the overview statement, set it to be the front page (by going to *Configuration > System > Site information* and putting in its URL as the default front page) and then enable the "View: Slideshow" block above the

"Main page content" on the front page, and enable the "View: News" and "View: People" blocks beneath it. However, this arrangement would put the slide show above the main page title, which should be at the very top of the page. The two blocks would look better next to one another, rather than stacked on top of each other, but the Blocks configuration page has no way for you to arrange blocks that way *within* the region of the main page content.

One way to get around this problem is with the Panels[1] module. Panels is a powerful module that can be used to create complex displays, particularly in combination with the Contexts module.[2] Panels, like Views, is the subject of more than one stand-alone book. In this case, we will limit ourselves to the simplest use of Panels: creating a Panel node and using it to arrange some blocks.

19.2.3   Creating a Panel node

Install Panels, and enable the Panels and Panel Nodes modules. Also be sure to enable the Views Content Panes module, which is a submodule of Views. It's been disabled on your site ever since you installed Views, but now you need it. Go to *Configuration > Search and metadata > URL aliases > Patterns* and set the pattern for the Panel content type to [node:title]. Then, go to *Structure > Content Types > Panel* and under "Comment settings," set it to "Hidden," under "Display settings," uncheck "Display author and date information." Save.

Next, go to *Content > Add content > Panel*. The first option you will see is "Choose layout." If you have a subtheme of AdaptiveTheme set as default (as described in section 18.5), select the category "AT Responsive Panels – 2 column," and the option "AT Two column brick". If you aren't using AdaptiveTheme, you can choose the "Columns: 2" category and the option "Two column bricks." The major difference is that the AdaptiveTheme variant may display better on mobile devices.

---

1. https://www.drupal.org/project/panels
2. There are some use cases where Panels could be used instead of Display Suite (which is discussed briefly in section 9.3.1). A comparison of Display Suite and Panels, written by one of the developers of the Display Suite module, is available on drupal.org: https://www.drupal.org/node/719244.

The next page is the standard node creation screen, albeit with very few fields. The title field will be the title of the Panel, and will appear at the top of the screen. Enter "Welcome to the Example Site." This is the only thing you have to configure on this page. After you save, Drupal will create the panel node, which will be empty. After working with other node types, you may be tempted to click on "Edit" to rectify the situation, but Panel nodes work a little differently. To edit a Panel node meaningfully (i.e., to edit anything besides the title), click on "Panel Content" (figure 19.1).

Figure 19.1. A newly created panel node.

19.2.4   Configuring a Panel node

The "Panel content" page is the heart of the Panel node interface (figure 19.2). Like the regions in the Block configuration interface, it shows the different areas where you can assign content.

Click on the cog in the upper left of the "Top" area, and select "Add content." If you have the Views Content Panes module enabled, you should see a "Views" category on the left (figure 19.3). Click on it, then click on "Slideshow."

You can select a display; choose Block and hit "Continue." No additional configuration is needed on the next page, so click "Finish." Now, if you hit the "Preview" button towards the bottom, at the top of the screen you'll see the title of your panel, along with the slide show. Save.

Next, let's add a couple sentences describing the site. Click on the cog in the upper left of the "Top" area again and "Add content." If we had an "About" page that already had the text we needed, we could pull it in using

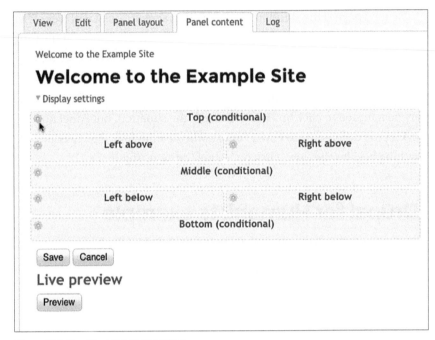

Figure 19.2. The Panel Content interface.

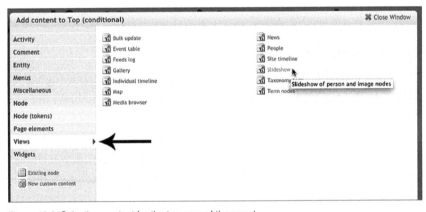

Figure 19.3. Selecting content for the top area of the panel.

the "Existing node" option in the bottom left corner. In this case, it'll be easier to add some custom text, so select "New custom content," also in the bottom left. For the administrative title, enter "Welcome text," but leave the title blank. This will make it easier to see what's happening on the Panel configuration page, without adding a new title. Enter a description of the site (for example, "Welcome to the example site for Drupal for Humanists. This site is based on CHAAMP Resources at the University of Virginia, a growing collection of digital media and teaching resources on the history of African Americans in the medical professions.") in the large text box, then click "Finish." Drag the "Custom: Welcome text" above the slide show so that it appears at the top of the page. When you hit "Preview," you should see the text appear above the slide show. Save.

Add content to the "Left above" area, choose "Views," and "People." Choose the "Block" display again, and "Finish." When you hit "Preview", a randomly selected person should appear in the bottom left of the preview area. Save.

Repeat for the "Right above" area, choosing "Views," and "News." Select "Block," and "Finish." Save.

Click on the View tab at the top of the Panels configuration interface to see the final result. It should resemble the preview.

19.2.5 Changing the front page of your site

Make note of the URL of your panel node when you view it by looking in your browser's URL bar. Copy the path for the page. Next, go to *Configuration > System > Site information*. Under "Default front page," replace the node with the path for the panel node you just created (e.g., "welcome-example-site").

19.3 Review of steps for creating the example site

You have now completed your configuration of the example site. If you followed all the steps, it should resemble the screenshots shown in figures 19.4 and 19.5 (taken while logged out of the site).

Figure 19.4. Front page of the finished example site.

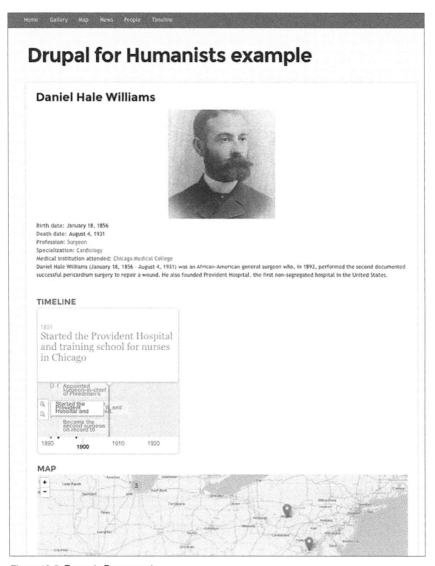

Figure 19.5. Example Person node.

The following list provides pointers to each of the steps involved in creating the public-facing components of the example site:

Section 3.4: Install Drupal.

Section 4.5: Install and enable essential modules (listed in 4.4).

Section 5.5: Preliminary data modeling.

Section 7.2: Create and configure Person content type.

Section 7.3: Create and configure Event content type.

Section 7.4: Create and configure Image content type.

Section 8.3: Configure WYSIWYG editor.

Section 8.4: Add content manually; additionally or alternatively, import example content using Feeds (Person nodes in section 14.4, Event nodes in section 14.5).

Section 9.2: Configure node display.

Chapter 12: Create Person page and block.

Section 13.3: Create Map page and block.

Section 13.4: Create site time line.

Section 13.5: Create individual time line.

Section 13.6: Create image gallery.

Section 13.7: Create slide show.

Section 18.5.5: Configure the Corolla theme.

Section 19.2: Create and configure the front page

19.4 Writing documentation

Writing documentation is a step that is often overlooked, but given the complexity of configuring a Drupal site, good documentation can mean the difference between success and failure in transferring webmaster responsibilities between the person who developed the site and the people responsible for maintaining it. If the people maintaining the site don't understand how to use it—much less how it was put together, which modules and views are responsible for what functionality, etc.—project staff may begin to insist that the site be rebuilt from scratch, which is always a costly endeavor in time if not money.

There are no standards as such for Drupal site documentation; for user-oriented documentation in particular, a great deal depends on the specific project, as well as the team composition and roles. Are the people involved in data entry also responsible for general site development or maintenance, or are there team members who only do data entry and don't need to understand much of Drupal besides the node-creation forms? The documentation for the site may also include many things that have nothing to do with Drupal itself, such as conventions for data normalization.

The *Drupal for Humanists* site contains multiple examples of Drupal site documentation, including documentation for the example site geared towards future maintainers of the site. When developing your own documentation, here are some things to include:

List the modules that are enabled, and briefly describe what you're using each one for. Going through this process may also allow you to disable and uninstall modules that you no longer need. You can use the checkboxes at the top of the Modules page, if you're using the Module Filter module, to only show enabled modules.

List the content types you have created, along with the fields in each one. Make a note of any special settings, like conditional fields (which fields trigger others, under what conditions). Include Automatic Nodetitle and Pathauto patterns used for each content type. If there are content types that are only meant to provide data for views and aren't intended to be viewed independently, indicate that.

List the views you have created, and describe how each one is used. If there is a block display, specify where it appears on the site. If you have a particularly complex view that involves significant use of field rewriting, relationships, and/or contextual filters, describe it in as much depth as necessary for someone to understand and be able to modify it. Indicate which views, if any, have their access restricted because they are designed for project internal use. This process may allow you to delete or disable test views, or other views that are no longer in use.

List the taxonomies you use, and whether they are controlled vocabularies (only project staff can create new terms) or uncontrolled vocabularies that need to be monitored and cleaned periodically.

List the menus you use, where they appear on the site (if somewhere other than the menu bar or somewhere obvious), and if they're visible to any user or just users with a particular role.

List the roles on the site, and the project conventions for determining what user should receive which role (e.g., only the project director and current webmaster should have the "admin" role; all undergraduate assistants should have at least the "undergrad" role).

If you are using Feeds to import data on an ongoing basis, indicate which feed it is, and how it's configured. What data are being created? How often does the feed run? How often should items created by the feed be automatically deleted, if applicable?

With any Drupal site, the settings described in the documentation are likely to change over time. Therefore, it is useful to revisit and update your site documentation at least once a year.

19.5 Preparing for site launch

Even after your site development process is complete, a few preparatory steps still remain before you should announce your site launch. These steps should be reviewed before launching any site. Because the hosting situation varies dramatically between projects, this section does not include instructions for migrating from one server to another, as some projects may need to do before launch. See the *Drupal for Humanists* site for further details on site migration.

19.5.1 Turning off and uninstalling unneeded modules

Disable, uninstall, and remove from your code base any modules that are not in use; see section 4.7 for details.

19.5.2 Updating and testing permissions

Particularly if you turned off public viewing access as you were developing the site (by unchecking the "View published content" permission for the anonymous role), it is essential that you thoroughly test the site as an anonymous user, and also as a typical nonadministrative user once you think you have permissions configured correctly for the site launch (e.g., by enabling "View published content" for all roles). It's convenient to stay logged in as an administrative user in another browser window as you do this so you can quickly fix permissions issues as they arise. You can do this by testing out the site in a different browser (such as Firefox, if you primarily use Chrome) where you aren't logged in, or by opening a new "incognito," "private browsing," or similar window in your existing browser (the exact language used varies between browsers). Click through the site as you expect users to do, including doing things like creating new accounts and content (if users are supposed to be able to do that), and editing a user profile. Create a dummy account, and send a password change request to make sure the system is successfully sending emails. If you run into access denied errors at any point, go back to the Permissions page (*People > Permissions*) and look for a setting that might have caused it.

Make sure that maps and time lines are appearing correctly, and the display of all your node types looks the way you want it. It's easy to configure the node display for a content type, go back later and add a field to the content type, and forget to adjust the node display for the new field, resulting in ugly arrangements of labels above field data, instead of being in line or hidden.

19.5.3   Creating 404 pages

Drupal has standard error messages when people arrive at a page that does not exist (404 not found), or at a page they don't have permission to view (403 access denied). If you want a friendlier, customized alternative, you can go to *Configuration > System > Site information* and put in the path for a node you have created (using the Basic Page content type, typically) with such a message. For instance, a custom access denied page might include a link directly to the login page, in case a user has forgotten to log in before trying to view a private page.

19.5.4   Performance tweaks

If you go to *Configuration > Development > Performance* you can look at Drupal's built-in settings for page caching and bandwidth optimization. By default, Drupal caches all pages for anonymous users (i.e., users that are not logged in). The default configuration on this page is generally fine, though you may want to set a minimum cache lifetime if you expect your site will receive high traffic. If you find your site runs slowly, there are modules that can speed up performance by providing more sophisticated caching. Of these, Boost[3] is comparatively easy to set up, and is compatible with inexpensive shared hosting. See the *Drupal for Humanists* site for an example of how to configure Boost.

19.5.5   Error messages

Best practices for launching a site suggest that you turn off the display of error messages before launch, by going to *Configuration > Development > Logging and errors* and selecting "None." Doing so certainly will reduce the risk of alarming users, but it will also require you to more actively monitor Drupal's log messages (*Reports > Recent log messages)*, particularly after you update Drupal core or modules (see section 20.3). If your site includes the use of CAPTCHAs (which can generate a high quantity of log messages), you may also want to set the number of retained log messages higher than the default 1,000, which you can also do on the "Logging and errors" configuration page.

When checking Drupal's log messages, it may be helpful to filter the messages by selecting php under "Type" (figure 19.6). This limits the errors to those that are more serious and problematic; errors that appear with a red circle would typically be displayed in a red error box on the screen. See section 20.9.3 for debugging error messages.

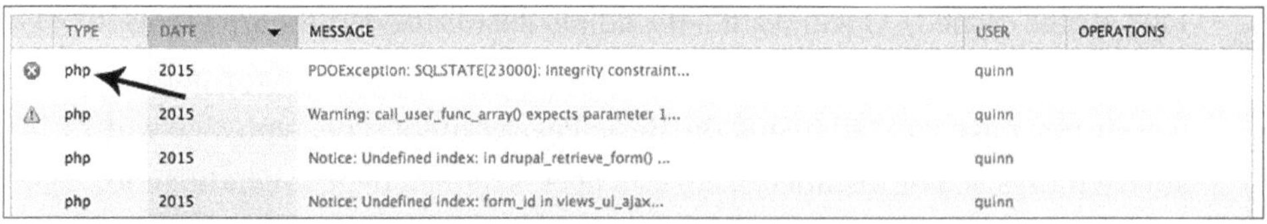

	TYPE	DATE	▼	MESSAGE	USER	OPERATIONS
⊗	php	2015		PDOException: SQLSTATE[23000]: Integrity constraint...	quinn	
⚠	php	2015		Warning: call_user_func_array() expects parameter 1...	quinn	
	php	2015		Notice: Undefined index: in drupal_retrieve_form() ...	quinn	
	php	2015		Notice: Undefined index: form_id in views_ui_ajax...	quinn	

Figure 19.6. Drupal's log messages, filtered to only show php messages.

---

3. https://www.drupal.org/project/boost

19.5.6 Status report

Go to *Reports > Status report* and look for any yellow or red messages. If you're developing your site locally on your own computer, it's not uncommon for cron to not be running routinely. Once your site is in the hosting environment where you plan to launch it, however, you should expect cron to be functioning normally (i.e., for that section of the status report to appear in green).

One common error is for the public files directory to not be fully secure. To fix this, follow the link included in the error message.[4] Look for some text in a gray box under the header "For Drupal 7:" that starts with "# Turn off all options we don't need." Select and copy all the text in this gray box, open a plain-text editor (like Notepad on Windows, or download TextWrangler for Mac) and paste the text into a blank new file. Save the file as *.htaccess* (starting with a period; overrule any objections your computer might have). Then, connect to the file system for your site and upload this .htaccess file to your site's files directory (generally sites/default/files, or sites/your-site-name/files on a multisite installation).

19.5.7 Link checking

You may want to install and run the Link Checker[5] module before launching your site, and check the broken links page periodically after launch. Install and enable the module, and configure it at *Configuration > Content authoring > Link checker*. Select all content types where you want to check for links (in most cases, you should choose all of them), and have it check both internal and external links. Under "error handling," you may want to set Drupal to update permanently moved links after one or more failed checks. After you save the configuration, Drupal will extract links from the database, and put them in a queue to be checked when cron runs. After you wait for some time (or manually run cron a number of times by going to *Reports > Status* report and clicking the "run cron" link), you can go to *Reports > Broken links* to see a list of broken links. There will be a link to edit the node where any broken link is located so you can easily fix it.

---

4. http://drupal.org/SA-CORE-2013–003
5. https://www.drupal.org/project/linkchecker

19.5.8   Setting up analytics

If you want to collect analytics about the use of your site, Drupal has a simple Statistics core module that you can enable which will provide simple tracking of the most-viewed pages. Using this module also makes that data available through Views; for instance, you can then sort nodes by most viewed. Once you enable Statistics, go to *Configuration > System > Statistics* to check the boxes for "Enable access log" and "Count content views." By default, access logs are deleted after 3 days, but you can set this to a longer period of time on the same page. The Statistics module makes a number of additional pages available under *Reports*: *Recent hits, Top referrers, Top search phrases, Top pages,* and *Top visitors.*

For more sophisticated analytics, the Google Analytics[6] module provides integration with the Google Analytics service.[7] Install and enable the module, and go to *Configuration > System > Google Analytics.* On this page, you can put in the unique tracking ID for your site, which begins with "UA-." This is generated by Google when you go to Google Analytics and add the site to your account. There are additional configuration options as well, such as turning off tracking for users with a given role (e.g., you may want to not track anyone with an administrative or any other project staff role, since their usage of the site may be unrepresentative of your audience).

19.6 Postlaunch monitoring

In the days after you publicly announce the launch of your site, you should routinely monitor Drupal's logs, by going to *Reports > Recent log messages* and keeping an eye out for PHP errors. Another useful page is *Reports > Top 'page not found' errors,* which extracts that set of errors from Drupal's log. If another site has linked to you, but has made some error in the URL they point people to, you can install and enable the Redirect[8] module, then go to *Configuration > Search and metadata > URL redirects > Add redirect*

---

6. https://www.drupal.org/project/google_analytics
7. http://www.google.com/analytics/
8. https://www.drupal.org/project/redirect

to create a redirect from the incorrect path to the correct one, so future visitors from that source find their way to the right place.

You may be surprised to see some unfamiliar pages showing up on the "page not found" list, including wp-admin (the path for a WordPress login page). These are usually cases of hackers testing out sites for security vulnerabilities they can leverage, and should serve as a reminder to keep your core and modules updated (see section 20.3).

You may also want to connect your site to a monitoring service running on a separate server that can alert you if the site goes down. See the *Drupal for Humanists* site for a discussion of some of the software and services available to accomplish this.

19.7 Summary

This chapter has covered the last steps for configuring the example site, as well as a pre-launch checklist that applies to any site. Launching a Drupal site is only the beginning of the maintenance work needed to ensure that the site remains functional and secure. Chapter 20 will address the care and maintenance of Drupal sites, as well as how to debug errors and contribute to the Drupal community.

CHAPTER 20

Running, Maintaining and Debugging a Drupal Site

20.1 Overview

Once you launch your Drupal site, you may feel like you've finished your project. Your Drupal-based project, however, will not be finished with you. This chapter covers the maintenance tasks that you need to routinely undertake to keep your Drupal site secure and functional. It also discusses debugging error messages. The chapter, and this book, conclude with some suggestions for how digital humanities projects can contribute to the larger Drupal community.

20.2 Maintenance activities

When you are actively developing a site, it's not difficult to notice and address maintenance needs as they arise. When an update is available for a module or Drupal core, a warning message will appear on administration screens, encouraging you to apply the update. Security updates will trigger a red warning. But once you have turned off error messages (section 19.5.5), it's easy to simply forget to check the module updates page. It's even easier to forget to update modules on a site where site development and data entry are largely complete, and you're just responsible for maintaining the site as is.

The activities detailed in Table 20.1 are an essential part of running a Drupal site. Each activity is listed along with a suggested frequency, a minimum frequency, and possible consequences if you don't do it.

Activity	Frequency	Consequences
Update Drupal modules, themes, and core	**Monthly** for regular updates, ASAP for security updates. You can configure the notification settings for updates here: /admin/reports/updates/settings	If you don't keep up with security updates, your site can get hacked. If you don't periodically do regular updates, the next time you have to install a security update, the module may have changed enough that it breaks some functionality on your site.
Back up your database	**Nightly** backups recommended; at a minimum, **before updating core, themes, or modules**	Your database contains all the non-media content on your site, and all the configuration. If you make a major configuration error, if a module update goes badly, or if your site gets hacked, you want to have a recent backup to restore from.
Back up your files	Depends on how important your files are, and how often they change. **Weekly** or **monthly** backups are usually fine. To be extra safe, back up files **before updating Drupal core as well**.	If your site gets hacked, or if you make a major mistake when updating Drupal core, you could lose files.
Back up your whole site	At critical points in the site's development, or in order to move the site to a new hosting environment.	If your site is undergoing a major change (such as a major version upgrade, installing a bunch of experimental modules, etc.), having a full-site backup gives you the peace of mind that you can easily restore it to a known, working state.

Table 20.1. Drupal site maintenance tasks.

20.3 Core, module, and theme updates

All content management systems need to be updated regularly, if only to ensure the ongoing security of your site. Sites that do not receive updates are at much higher risk of being hacked, and going a long time (months or more) between updates will make the updates more likely to break things on your site when you finally do them.

If you are responsible for maintaining multiple Drupal sites, you can reduce the time spent doing core, module, and theme updates by setting them up as a *multisite,* where each site has its own database but they share Drupal core and module code. See the *Drupal for Humanists* site for more on multisites.

20.3.1 Suggested frequency

There are two types of updates to Drupal code: regular updates (which improve module functionality through bug fixes and new features) and security updates. Security updates address security holes in the module's code, and should be applied as soon as possible. Not all security updates are equally serious; sometimes a particular security hole only applies if you allow untrusted users to create content, or to use certain text formats (like "Full HTML," see section 8.2). Occasionally, there have been security updates for Drupal core or widely used modules that impact every site that uses that code, such as the October 2014 "Drupageddon."[1]

There is a security team[2] for the Drupal open source project that works with module and core developers to ensure that they address identified security holes. Modules with maintainers who do not address security issues in a timely manner will be pulled from drupal.org. The convention for security releases is to make them available on a Wednesday; Drupal core security updates usually appear on the third Wednesday of the month, but module security updates can appear on any Wednesday. It's worth subscribing to the RSS feed for core[3] and module[4] security advisories, and/

---

1. https://www.drupal.org/node/2357241
2. https://www.drupal.org/security-team
3. https://www.drupal.org/security
4. https://www.drupal.org/security/contrib

or following the Drupal security Twitter account,[5] which tweets all security advisories on Wednesdays. If there is a security update for Drupal core or for one of your modules, update it as soon as possible.

Nonsecurity updates aren't as urgent, but it's best to not get too many versions behind. Updating these modules monthly is generally a good idea. Changes to module code tend to accumulate gradually, and in most cases you can update from one version of a module to the next with a smaller likelihood of encountering errors than if you jump multiple versions. Note that this may not be the case for "major" module updates, for instance, if the version numbering goes from 7.x-1.8 to 7.x-2.0. Changing the first number after "7.x" usually means that there has been some significant reworking of the module code, and you should read the release notes, README.txt, and check the module's page for any special instructions about upgrading the module.

Doing nonsecurity updates once a month is generally a good idea. If a module has been updated within a couple days of when you plan to do the update, you may want to push that particular module update back another month. Sometimes it takes a few days to a week for major intermodule conflicts or other problems to be identified, and there may be a fixed version available by the time you go to update the module the following month.

20.3.2   Method: Drupal UI (modules & themes)

Depending on your hosting setup, you may be able to update modules using the Drupal UI (user interface). (If you can install modules using the Drupal UI, you will be able to update them that way, too.) Go to *Modules > Update*, check the boxes for the modules you want to update, and click the "Download these updates" button (figure 20.1).

Figure 20.1. The Drupal UI for updating modules.

---

5. https://twitter.com/drupalsecurity

Next, Drupal will take you to a screen that reminds you to back up your database first (see section 20.2.2). There is also a checkbox for "Perform updates with site in maintenance mode (strongly recommended)"; this is checked by default, and you should leave it that way. Note that if you suddenly decide to stop the update after clicking "Continue" (for instance, if you reach the screen that requests FTP credentials, and you either don't have them or recall that your hosting provider doesn't support FTP), you'll have to take your site out of maintenance mode manually by going to *Configuration > Development > Maintenance mode*. This page also allows you to change the default text that Drupal displays for all users when the site is in maintenance mode.

Once you hit "Continue," if everything works correctly, you should see a progress bar and then a page that lists all the modules where updates were installed successfully. Next, click the "Run database updates" link at the bottom of that page.

This will take you to the page /update.php, which you can also run manually if you've manually installed Drupal module or core updates by directly uploading files to the file system (figure 20.2). This is required for Drupal core, and may be necessary for modules you can't update using the Drupal UI.

Click the "continue" button. Sometimes Drupal will show that no database updates are needed; not all updates require changes to the database. If database updates are needed, you can click on the "# pending

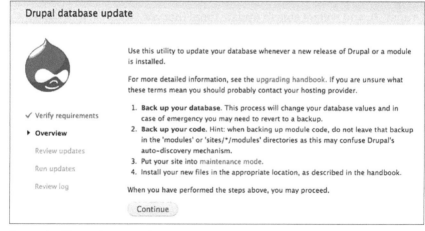

Figure 20.2. The starting screen for update.php.

update(s)" link to toggle down a list of which modules—including core modules, if you have done a core update—require database updates (figure 20.3). Click "Apply pending updates," and after a progress bar runs, you should see a final message indicating that if no errors are displayed, your database was updated successfully.

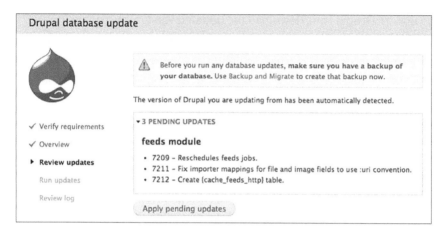

Figure 20.3. Reviewing pending updates.

20.3.3   Method: file system (core, and possibly modules & themes)

Drupal core code cannot be updated using the module updates interface, and you may need to use a similar method for updating modules if you don't have server permissions to install or update modules using Drupal's UI. If you need to install a development version of a module (see section 20.9.1.1), you will also need to do this by accessing the file system, rather than using the Drupal UI.

20.3.3.1   Updating modules

Updating modules by accessing the file system is much like installing modules through the file system, and is a bit less daunting than updating Drupal core. First, back up your database and put your site in maintenance mode by going to *Configuration > Development > Maintenance mode*. Download the updated module version from drupal.org, unzip the module, and place the folder with the module's code in the sites/all/

modules directory. Confirm that you want to overwrite the existing folder with the same name. Then, go to /updates.php and do any database updates as described in section 20.2.1.2. Remember to take the site out of maintenance mode when you're done.

20.3.3.2   Updating core

To update Drupal core, download the updated version, and unzip the folder. This next step is *essential*: open the folder with the updated Drupal core code and *delete* the "sites" subfolder. If you recall from section 4.5.2.1, the "sites" folder on your server contains all the non-database information that's specific to your site or sites, including the settings.php file that tells Drupal where to look for the database, all the files that have been uploaded, and all the modules and libraries you've added. Overwriting the "sites" folder would be catastrophic, so simply removing it from the newly downloaded Drupal core code is a sure way to avoid that. (You can also select everything in the Drupal core code folder *except* the "sites" folder if you choose to not delete it, but deleting it is an extra safeguard.)

Once you have deleted "sites" from the updated version of the Drupal core code, select everything else in that folder, and upload it all to the directory on your server that already contains the Drupal core code. Confirm that you want to overwrite the existing files.

After the upload is complete, follow the same instructions as earlier in this section—putting the site into maintenance mode, and running update.php.

20.3.4   Module and core updates on Drupal multisite setups

If you are running a multisite setup (multiple Drupal sites that use the same code base; see the *Drupal for Humanists* site for details on how to configure this) and want to use the Drupal UI to install module updates, you can do so from any of the sites on the multisite installation, and this will update the code for all the sites. However, you will need to go to /update.php on each site *individually* to accommodate any database updates. This also applies to doing core updates; remember to go to /update.php for each of the multi-sites. Unless all sites use all the same modules, you may also need to go to the module update page for each site, to ensure that any modules unique to that particular site get updated.

If you are comfortable using the command line, you can simplify this process as well as many other maintenance tasks by using Drush; see section 20.7.

20.4 Database backup

20.4.1 Suggested frequency

For greatest peace of mind, configure nightly backups. This ensures that if your configuration work goes awry, at most you will only lose a day's work. At a minimum, back up your database before doing any updates to core, modules, or themes.

20.4.2 Method: quick backup

If you're about to make a configuration change that you think might have negative consequence for your site, or you're about to do core, module, or theme updates, you can do a "quick backup" using the Backup and Migrate[6] module. Install and enable the module, and go to *Configuration > System > Backup and Migrate*. This will take you to a page with a "Backup now" button, which will allow you to download a compressed version of your database using the sensible default settings. If you are only backing up your site before doing updates, you may want to also save a copy off site by checking the corresponding checkbox. The NodeSquirrel off-site Drupal backup service is included by default, but additional modules like Backup and Migrate Dropbox[7] provide options for other services.

The first time you go to the Backup and Migrate page, you might see a warning "You must specify a private file system path in the file system settings to backup to the server." Click on the "file system settings" link and put a path in the "Private file system path" field. The simplest option is to append /private to the public file system path; if the public path is sites/default/files, enter sites/default/files/private. Drupal will create the folder you specify and apply the appropriate access controls.

---

6. https://www.drupal.org/project/backup_migrate
7. https://www.drupal.org/project/backup_migrate_dropbox

20.4.3   Method: nightly backups

The Backup and Migrate module also allows you to configure nightly backups. Go to *Configuration > System > Backup and Migrate > Schedules* and click "Add schedule." For schedule name, you can call it "Nightly database backup." The default backup source, "Default database," is correct. Using the default settings profile is fine, though the interface includes a link for where you can configure a new profile.

Run the backup using Drupal cron, as the default setting specifies. To avoid building up too large a backlog of old backups, you can check the box for "Automatically delete old backups." The "smart delete" option keeps daily backups for 30 days, or you can use the "simple delete" to specify how many backups you want to keep at once. When you're done, click "Save schedule."

20.4.4   Other methods

If you have access to phpMyAdmin as an interface for managing your database, you can use that to back up and restore your database. Some hosting providers, such as Pantheon, also provide their own backup options as part of the interface for their hosting environment. See the *Drupal for Humanists* website for more on these options. Drush, discussed briefly in section 20.7, supports backing up and restoring databases from the command line.

20.4.5   Restoring your database

If you do need to restore a backup you have done from Backup and Migrate, go to *Configuration > System > Backup and Migrate > Restore*. You can upload a backup you have downloaded from Backup and Migrate (for instance, using the "quick backup" option described in 20.4.2), or you can choose the "restore from a saved backup" if you want to select a nightly backup, or other backup saved to the server.

After you have uploaded the backup file, or selected the saved backup, make sure "Restore to" is set to "Default database," then click "Restore now." Note that this only works for restoring database backups that were created using Backup and Migrate; if you created a backup using phpMyAdmin or some other method, you'll need to restore it using the same method.

20.5 File backup

20.5.1 Suggested frequency

If media files (images, audio, video, documents, etc.) are a crucial part of your site, you should back up your file directory fairly often, particularly if content is being actively added to your site. This may be a temporary state when you're building the site, or if your site collects crowdsourced submissions, it may be the case on an ongoing basis. A weekly or monthly back up is generally fine. Also, you may want to back up your file directory before doing core updates, in case you accidentally overwrite the "sites" directory (see section 20.3.3.2). You can re-create most of your "sites" directory by redownloading modules and themes and re-creating settings. php files, but your files may only exist within the "sites" directory.

20.5.2 Method: Backup and Migrate

For doing a quick backup or setting a schedule for regular backups, you can largely follow the instructions in sections 20.4.2 and 20.4.3, but instead of "Default database" as the backup source, choose "Public files directory." For regular backups, in most cases you should use the "simple delete" automatic deletion option, and limit it to a small number (between 1 and 3, depending on how great you see the risk of a file being deleted, and this only being noticed weeks later). If you have a lot of files, and/or the files are large, keeping many backups can quickly fill up hundreds of gigabytes of space or more. This may also be a concern if you save backups to an external service such as Dropbox.

To restore one of these backups, follow the instructions in 20.4.5, but choose "Public files directory" instead of "Default database" under "Restore to."

20.5.3 Method: SFTP

Using SFTP to back up your file directory is less efficient than using Backup and Migrate, but it can be useful if for some reason your hosting environment doesn't allow you to use that module. Instead of dragging and dropping a folder from your own computer into the SFTP client (see appendix), you can reverse the process by dragging and dropping a folder from the SFTP client onto your desktop or another location on your computer. If you have a lot of files or your files are particularly large, downloading via SFTP can be a time-consuming endeavor, and an interruption to your Internet connection can cause it to stop before it's complete.

20.5.4   Other methods

If you are comfortable with the command line, you can set up backups of your files directory outside of Drupal itself, either by using Drush (section 20.7) or shell scripts. Some hosting providers, such as Pantheon, provide a way to back up and restore the files directory as part of their hosting platform.

20.6 Whole-site backup

A whole-site backup captures the code, files, and database for your site—everything you'd need to get it set up somewhere else, assuming a suitable hosting environment.

20.6.1   Frequency

You shouldn't need to do this often. If your site is going to undergo a major change in design or functionality, you may want to download a whole-site backup in order to have your own archive of the earlier form of the project. Also, if you are making some changes on the site where you aren't sure of the full scope and nature of the effects (for instance, installing and configuring some experimental modules), having a full-site backup will allow you to quickly return the site to its previous condition if you are unhappy with the results.

20.6.2   Method: Backup and Migrate

Follow the instructions in section 20.4.2, but instead of "Default database" as the backup source, choose "Entire site (code, files & DB)."

To restore one of these backups, follow the instructions in section 20.4.5, but choose "Entire site (code, files & DB)" instead of "Default database" under "Restore to."

20.6.3   Other methods

The Drush archive-dump command backs up the entire site; see section 20.7 for more on Drush. Some Drupal-specific hosting environments, such as Pantheon, may also offer full-site backup and restoring capabilities.

20.7 Drush

If you are at least moderately comfortable using the command line, Drush provides a way to quickly take care of maintenance and configuration tasks using a series of text-based commands. It also works well for multisite installs. It is somewhat complicated to set up, and requires configuration both on your computer and in the Drupal site's hosting environment. You can download Drush and read the full documentation at http:// www.drush.org/. The *Drupal for Humanists* site has additional links and tutorials for using Drush.

20.8 Major version upgrades

A major version upgrade (e.g., going from Drupal 7 to Drupal 8) is a significant task to undertake. When you download the Drupal 8 software, the "core" subdirectory includes an UPGRADE.txt file that describes the process in detail; you can also read more in the official Drupal documentation for upgrading Drupal 6 or Drupal 7 sites to Drupal 8.[8]

While it may be tempting to upgrade existing sites to Drupal 8 as soon as possible to take advantage of some of its new features (including many that improve the user experience for site builders), you need to ensure that there are Drupal 8 versions of all the modules that are important for your site's functionality, or if not, that there are new Drupal 8-only modules that can be used instead. Rather than starting with upgrading an existing site, it is generally better to assess the readiness of Drupal 8 each time you start a new project, and get some experience with Drupal 8 by building a new site from scratch. If you don't have any new projects, you can create a test

---

8. https://www.drupal.org/upgrade/migrate

Drupal 8 site to try it out and gain familiarity with the new interface. See the *Drupal for Humanists* site for additional resources on Drupal 8.

20.9 Debugging Drupal

Sometimes modules don't work the way you expect, or you make a configuration change that suddenly causes red error messages to fill up your screen. At some point, you may even encounter the Drupal "White Screen of Death" (WSOD): a completely blank page that offers no clue as to what has gone wrong. This section provides troubleshooting tips for these and other situations you will likely experience while building Drupal sites.

To fully take advantage of these suggestions, you should register an account on Drupal.org[9] and log into the site[10] when you go there for troubleshooting. In order to incentivize users of Drupal to create and use an account on the site, the administrators of Drupal.org have turned off the ability for anonymous users to search module issue queues.

20.9.1 When a module seems to not work correctly

It may happen that you install a module expecting it to do a particular thing, but you can't figure out where to go to configure it. There may not be a "Configure" option for it on the Modules page, or it may not show up where you expect it (for instance, as a Views display format). Or perhaps you have configured a module, but it doesn't seem to work the way you expect it to.

One place to go for help is the module's issue queue. Go to the module's page on Drupal.org (it may be fastest to find this using Google, just as you did when you first downloaded the module), and click on the "[#] total" link under "All issues" in the right sidebar. This allows you to browse all the issues that have been reported for the module, including those that the module maintainers have marked as fixed or otherwise resolved. For some modules, there are a lot of issues for Drupal 6 versions that may not pertain to you; in these cases, using the "Version" filter at the top of the issues list to limit it to "7.x issues" may be helpful. If you're logged into Drupal.org

---

9. https://www.drupal.org/user/register
10. https://www.drupal.org/user

(see section 20.9), you can also search for particular keywords. Browsing may be more effective than searching, however, since someone else might phrase the issue differently, in a way you would recognize if you saw it but a keyword search might not pick it up.

Sometimes Google is a faster way to debug module problems. Putting in the name of the module, "Drupal," then a key phrase or two describing the problem (e.g., Drupal views doesn't show up) can yield results from Drupal. org as well as other question and answer sites and blogs. Typing slowly enough to take advantage of Google's autocomplete suggestions can also be helpful.

20.9.1.1   Using a -dev version of a module

Discovering an issue in the issue queue that matches your own is the first step; next, you may have to decode a long thread of messages where people have attempted to solve the problem. (In some cases you may be lucky, and the answer can be as simple as a pointer to a particular path, or a straightforward set of instructions for configuration changes you can make in the UI.) The best resolution to this situation is a message indicating that a patch, or fix for the problem, has been "committed," or incorporated into the module code, or a status change that the problem has been fixed (figure 20.4).

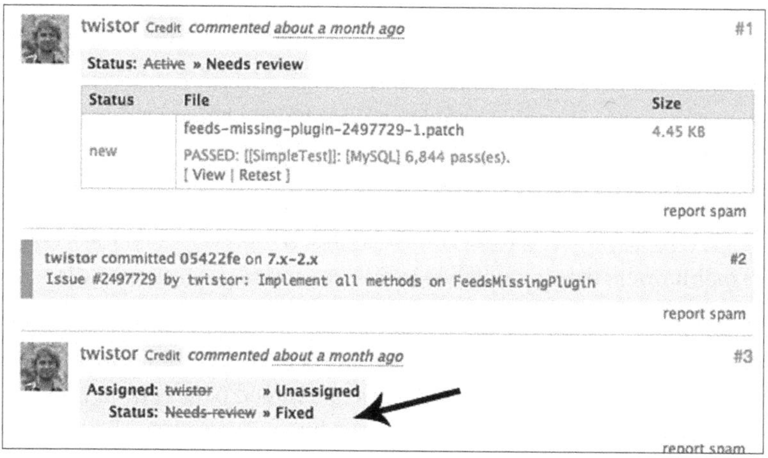

Figure 20.4. Comments in an issue queue.[11]

---

11. https://www.drupal.org/node/2497729

Make a note of the date on that message, and go back to the main page on Drupal.org for the module. In the "Downloads" section, check the release dates for the latest recommended and development releases for the module. If the date for the most recent recommended version is more recent than the message that stated the patch had been committed, you should go back to your site and update the module to that latest version where the problem is fixed. If it turns out that you're already running the latest version where the problem has allegedly been fixed, you should return to the forums and keep looking, at least for messages from other people indicating that they're still experiencing the same problem.

More often, particularly for noncatastrophic bugs, there won't be a new recommended release, but there will be a new development release since the code was committed. In these cases, it can be worth it to update your site to a development release, until a new recommended release comes out. Note that you need to use the SFTP or file system method to update a module to a development release—you can't do it through the Drupal UI. Also, for every module where you are running a development release, the Drupal update page will suggest that you "update" the module to the latest stable release, even if the stable release is older than your development release (and would therefore have the bug you're trying to avoid).

Development releases are more likely than stable releases to have bugs of their own, so be sure to back up at least your database before installing a development release, so you can return to a stable version of the module and restore your database if things go awry.

20.9.1.2   Patching modules

Modules that have a fairly active user base but less active maintainers may have one or more patches posted to the debugging thread, but no message from the maintainers that a patch has been committed. If you encounter this situation, and multiple people confirm in the comments that the patch has worked for them, you can apply the patch yourself. Drupal.org has a page on applying patches,[12] along with links to detailed pages about how to apply patches automatically in Windows, on Macs, and how to do it manually. There is also a beginner's guide to patching[13] that may be helpful.

---

12. https://www.drupal.org/patch/apply

Applying patches automatically requires installing tools that are more common for developers to have, and doing it manually involves changing lines of code yourself. If you aren't comfortable doing either of these things, find someone who is more comfortable with code and point them to the documentation on Drupal.org.

20.9.1.3   Filing a bug report

In some cases, you may be the first person to try something with a module that breaks it in ways that aren't reported elsewhere. Be sure to do your due diligence before filing a bug report, by searching Google and the module's issue queue, carefully checking the module's README.txt file, and making sure you're using the recommended version of a library, if the module requires one (sometimes a module that uses an external library only supports an older version of that library). If you've confirmed that you're following all the instructions in the README.txt file, and/or other documentation linked from the module's page, and you can't find a reference to your problem anywhere, you can file a bug report if you're logged into Drupal.org with your user account (see section 20.9). Drupal.org has a detailed page about how to file a good bug report;[14] be sure to follow those guidelines.

20.9.2   When the site suddenly looks strange or behaves oddly

Sometimes Drupal sites simply start looking strange (for instance, not reflecting theming changes you've made and uploaded to your code base, or drop-down menus failing to work properly) or behaving strangely (autocomplete fields not autocompleting, Views displays not updating as you expect, etc.). The quick and easy equivalent of the classic computer debugging trick of simply rebooting the computer is to clear Drupal's cache. "Keep calm and clear cache" is a Drupal aphorism, much like "There's a module for that."

Clearing the cache is easy with the administration menu. Go to the house icon in the upper left, and from the drop-down menu that appears there, choose "Flush all caches."

---

13. https://www.drupal.org/node/620014
14. https://www.drupal.org/contribute/testing

20.9.3   Error messages

A red error message may appear on your screen after you've installed or updated a module, after you've tried to configure it in certain ways, or after you've made other changes to your site. Anything from complex configuration changes to simply adding content might trigger an error message.

Sometimes you can tell what module is triggering an error message because its name appears in the message, or there's a pointer to code within an individual module's folder. Other times, the code referenced in the message is part of Drupal core, and there's no indicator about what might be causing it. In either case, Google is usually the best tool for trying to identify what is going on. Try putting in the initial text of the error message, the name of the module or theme referenced in the error (if there is one), the file mentioned (just the last part of the path—most of the path will be specific to your site, and won't give you any results), and possibly the line number. If including the line number doesn't give you good results, leave off the line number; doing so might yield useful results from a previous version of the module where the problematic code was in a slightly different place, with different line numbers.

How the problem is resolved can vary greatly between errors, though clearing the cache (section 20.9.2) can sometimes play a role, and in some cases you may need to use a development version of a module that resolves the problem (section 20.9.1).

20.9.4   White Screen of Death

If you load a page and it comes up completely blank—without even the administrative toolbar—you have encountered the White Screen of Death (WSOD). The WSOD means that something has gone wrong on your site at a level where Drupal can't even load a page. This can include a host of things like your server running out of memory (for instance, when trying to load an exceedingly large view, or a very complex page; content type editing pages where you have Automatic Nodetitles and Entity Tokens installed are common culprits here), or MySQL exhausting the allowed number of simultaneous connections (for instance, if you are suddenly getting a lot of heavy traffic on views that aren't cached).

Drupal.org has a long list of things that can cause the WSOD, along with suggestions for fixing them.[15] The first step in most cases is to find out what's causing it, by temporarily changing the index.php file in the Drupal core code to display the error. Then, follow the same guidelines as described in section 20.9.3 about Googling for errors. The *Drupal for Humanists* site also has tips for dealing with common WSOD issues.

20.10 Contributing to the Drupal community

There are many ways for scholars, librarians, archivists, and others who use Drupal as a platform for digital scholarship to contribute to the Drupal community. Funding the development of new modules, or improvements to existing modules—particularly those that support the unique needs of scholarly projects—is one way to turn the funding for your own project into something that many projects can benefit from. If your project team lacks staff with the right expertise to write Drupal modules, the *Drupal for Humanists* site includes a directory of developers who have done work on scholarly projects, or who are interested in relatively small-scale, academic development jobs. Many commercial Drupal firms only take on projects of a much larger scale and budget than digital humanities projects can afford, and lack experience dealing with the kind of bureaucratic overhead that can be required when working with public universities in particular.

Even if your project has no budget for module development, you can still contribute to the community of Drupal users in other ways. If you've figured out how to do something with Drupal that you think others might benefit from doing, write a brief tutorial on it. Post it to your project's website, and/ or submit it to the *Drupal for Humanists* site. The *Drupal for Humanists* site also allows users to create site profiles, to provide examples of the kinds of sites that can be built using Drupal, and the modules you used to build each site. Each tutorial and site description that you make available to the public adds to the base of materials that everyone can draw upon when developing their own projects, smoothing the path for those who will encounter the same issues later on. As you gain experience with Drupal and discover new approaches and solutions, consider taking a few minutes to give back to the Drupal community by sharing what you've learned.

---

15. https://www.drupal.org/node/158043

Using an SFTP Client

Drupal's interface allows you to upload certain kinds of files—modules, themes, and images/media/documents—to the correct place within the file system. For modules that have external dependencies (such as Javascript libraries), there is no way to put those dependencies in the correct place without accessing the file system directly. Similarly, while you can update modules and themes through the Drupal interface (section 20.3.2), you have to update Drupal core by accessing the file system.

A.1 Installing software

Unless your Drupal site is hosted on your own computer (see section 3.2.1), you will need to install and use an SFTP client to access the file system. There are a number of options for free and open-source options, including Filezilla[1] (Windows, Mac, and Linux) and WinSCP[2] (Windows); Cyberduck[3] (Mac and Windows) is an attractive modern option.

The Cyberduck website includes a download link for Windows and for Mac, as well as a link to download it through the Mac App Store if you prefer. Download and install the software as usual for your operating system.

---

1. https://filezilla-project.org/
2. http://winscp.net/eng/index.php
3. https://cyberduck.io/?1 =en

A.2 Connection information

Before you use Cyberduck to connect to the server, you need the following information:

Server name (may also be called "host" or "host name"): The name of the server that is hosting your site. If you're using inexpensive shared commercial hosting, you may be able to use your site URL for this (e.g., myproject.org). If you're using a university hosting service, Pantheon, or some other commercial hosting specifically for Drupal (e.g., Acquia hosting), this is likely to be something different than your site URL.

Username: The username you use to connect to the server; this will probably be different from the username you use to log into Drupal via the web-based interface. If you're using university hosting, odds are good that you'll use your university authentication credentials (username and password).

Password: The password that matches your username when connecting to the server; this will probably be different from the password you use to log into Drupal via the web-based interface.

Path (optional): The place on the server you should immediately be taken to once you log in.

Port (optional): Some hosting systems require that you use a port different than the default to make the connection.

Regardless of whether you have "Path" information (in many cases you won't), you should find out where the Drupal installation is on the server. If you're using university hosting, ask the IT or library staff who helped you get Drupal set up on the server for this information. See the *Drupal for Humanists* site for how to access the connection information if you are using Pantheon hosting.

A.3 Connecting

Open Cyberduck, and click on the "Open Connection" button in the upper left (figure A.1):

Figure A.1. Launching Cyberduck.

By default, the connection type is "FTP." While this may work in some cases (many commercial hosting providers will allow you to connect via FTP), most universities and Pantheon require you to connect via SFTP for increased security. Click and hold the small arrow to the right of "FTP" to see a list of other options, and select "SFTP (SSH File Transfer Protocol)" (figure A.2).

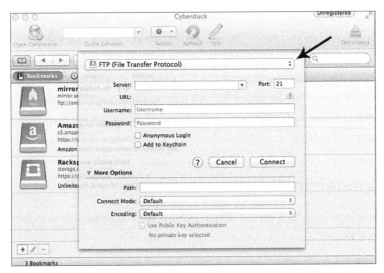

Figure A.2. Click and hold to see a list of other connection options.

Fill in the fields using the information that you've already gathered (figure A.3). In the server field, put in the server name (may also be called host name). Put in the username and password in those fields. By default, the port for SFTP is 22; only change this if your hosting provider requires it. In most cases, leave the fields under "More options" empty; these include the Path field, so if you do have that information from the server administrators, toggle down "More Options" and include it there.

Once you've filled in the fields, click "connect."

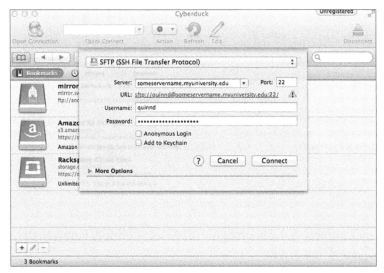

Figure A.3. Filling in the connection fields.

After you hit the "Connect" button, if this is your first time connecting to the server, an "Unknown fingerprint" dialog box may pop up (figure A.4).

Choose "Allow," and if you don't want to receive the same notification next time, check the "Always" box first.

Figure A.4. Unknown fingerprint box.

A.4 Troubleshooting connection problems

If you see the following error, you probably mistyped the username or password (figure A.5).

Login failed

Exhausted available authentication methods. Please contact your web hosting service provider for assistance.

Username: quinnd

Password: ••••••••••••••••••••••

☐ Anonymous Login
☐ Use Public Key Authentication
No private key selected

☐ Add to Keychain   (?)   Cancel   Login

Figure A.5. Login failed error.

This error indicates that you probably made some error in typing in the server/host name (figure A.6).

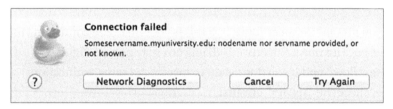

Connection failed

Someservername.myuniversity.edu: nodename nor servname provided, or not known.

(?)   Network Diagnostics   Cancel   Try Again

Figure A.6. Connection failed error.

A.5 Navigating to the correct place

Once you've successfully connected to the server, you need to find the directory with your Drupal installation. This will vary depending on your hosting arrangement. If you are using university hosting, ask the system administrator where the Drupal directory is. Their answer will probably take the form of a string of words (names of folders) separated by slashes; this indicates the nested relationship between the folders: each folder is contained within the folder before it in the sequence.

It's also important to note whether their answer starts with a slash or not. If they tell you Drupal is in "htdocs/drupal," you can expect to find an "htdocs" folder in the directory that immediately appears when you connect to the server. Double-click it to open it, and you should see a "drupal" folder. Double-click that, and you'll be in the folder with your Drupal installation. However, if they tell you Drupal is in /var/www/ localhost/htdocs/drupal, you'll first need to navigate to the "root" (top-level) directory of the server before you start looking for the "var" folder. Towards the top of the Cyberduck interface, there's a drop-down menu that shows your current location on the server. Activate the dropdown menu and select the option (at the bottom) that is labeled with "/" (figure A.7).

Figure A.7. Navigating to the root directory.

Once you're in the root directory, you should see a "var" folder, and be able to navigate to your Drupal installation from there.

A.5.1 Where to upload files

In most cases, modules should be uploaded in the sites/all/modules folder within your Drupal installation, not the modules folder. Themes, similarly, should be uploaded in sites/all/themes. See section 4.5.2 for more information on where to upload modules, section 4.5.22 for information on where to upload libraries, and section 18.4.1 for information on where to upload themes.

A.6 Uploading files

To upload files, drag and drop files or folders from your own computer into the folder where they belong in the SFTP window. Select the file(s)/folder(s) in Finder (on a Mac) or Windows Explorer, and drag and drop them into a blank space (figure A.8) or into an area that has individual files, rather than one that has folders (figure A.9). If you drag and drop files and

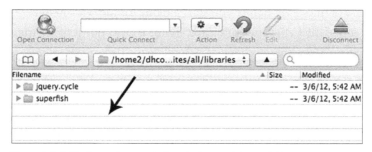

Figure A.8. A blank area is a good place to drag and drop a folder.

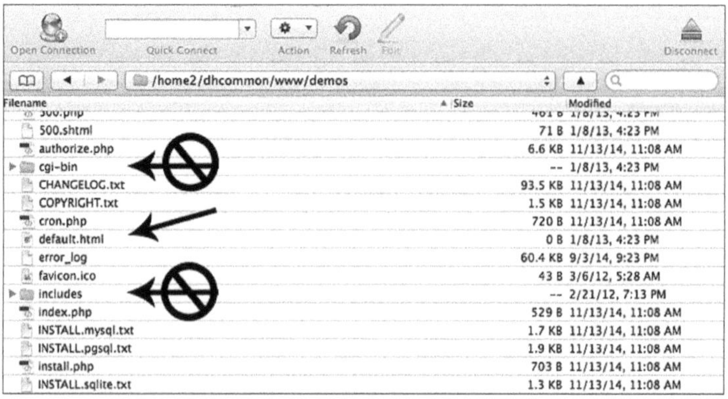

Figure A.9. It's safe to drag and drop files and folders in an area with individual files.

folders in an area with other folders, if you're not very careful, you may accidentally upload the data *into* one of the folders, rather than where you want it to be.

It can be a little tricky to upload new modules via SFTP, because the modules folder will probably be full of folders, without any individual files or blank space for dragging and dropping new modules. For that reason, it may be easier to navigate to the parent folder for the modules folder (in most cases, sites/all within your Drupal installation) and drag and drop new modules on top of the "modules" folder, so they upload into the "modules" folder (figure A.10).

Figure A.10. Drag and drop new modules on top of the "modules" folder to upload them within that folder.

A.6.3 Updating Drupal core, modules, themes, etc.

To update Drupal core, modules, and themes via SFTP, download the new version from Drupal.org (i.e., from the page for an individual module or theme, or from https://www. drupal.org/project/drupal for Drupal core) and unzip it. For modules and themes, take the resulting folder and drag and drop it into the sites/all/modules or sites/all/themes folder, as if you were uploading it for the first time. Cyberduck will pop up a window asking if you want to overwrite what's already there (figure A.11)

Figure A.11. Overwrite window.

Click the "Continue" button, and the new version will be uploaded.

To update Drupal core, *delete the "sites" folder from the new version of Drupal you have downloaded,* then select all files and folders and drag and drop them on top of the files in the folder with your Drupal installation. See section 20.3.3 for more information on updating Drupal and its modules and themes.

Glossary

Block: A small piece of content (e.g., a funding organization's logo, a map, a small amount of text) or functionality (e.g., a log-in window) that can be displayed somewhere on a page (within a *region*).

Content type: A template for storing data on your site. Content types contain *fields*, and may be as simple as a title and a body text field, or they may contain a complex combination of numerical, text, term reference, location, and/or date fields.

Contextual filter (Views): A filter whose value is automatically provided by the context in which the *view display* appears; often, views with contextual filters are *blocks* that appear on a *node* page. This makes it possible to show, for instance, all nodes that include a *node reference* to the current node.

Core: The fundamental infrastructure code shared by all Drupal sites. Provides basic functionality like being able to create users, define permissions, create content, etc.

Cron job: A set of maintenance tasks that Drupal carries out on a regular basis.

Display (Views): How the output of a *view* actually exists on the site; for instance, as a page, a *block*, an RSS feed, or a data export.

Exposed filter (Views): In Views, a filter limits the set of results to those that meet certain criteria. An exposed filter is visible to users, allowing them to select the parameters used for filtering the results.

Feature: A *module* that packages up Drupal configuration, which can be installed on a different Drupal site. The Features module is required to create or install a feature.

Feeds: A *module* that allows you to import data from various sources. It was primarily designed to import data from feeds (e.g., RSS feeds), but can also import from CSV files (a standard, text-based spreadsheet format), XML, JSON, and other sources, though some of these require additional modules.

Field: A way to store data granularly. Fields can be added to *content types,* user profiles, or files. Drupal *core* provides some basic field types for simple text and numerical data, but there are many *modules* available that provide additional field types, including links, dates, and locations.

Field collection: A *module* that is still somewhat experimental that allows you to create repeating groups of *fields,* and embed it as part of a *content type.* For simply grouping fields together for data entry or display, see *field group.*

Field group: A *module* that provides a way to group *fields* together for data entry or display. Does not allow users to create repeating groups of fields (e.g., name and role); see *field collection.*

File type: When using the *Media module,* a file type is similar to a content type, but it allows you to associate fields with files directly. By default, there are user-editable file types for images, audio, video, and documents, but you can create additional file types (e.g., differentiating screenshots from paintings.)

Media: A *module* that provides a more robust interface for managing files (including multimedia files) and their metadata.

Module: A piece of site functionality that has been packaged up and can be installed on a site. Drupal *core* includes modules, but the vast majority of modules are developed by the Drupal community.

Node: An instantiation of a *content type*. Every time you add data to your site using a content type, you create a node. Users most commonly interact with nodes as pages, but nodes can also exist just to store data for use with *Views*, and some may never be viewed on their own.

Node reference: A type of *field*, provided by the References *module*, that allows you to point to another *node*. Commonly used to specify relationships between *content types*.

Patch: A small bit of code that makes changes to one or more files within a *module* in order to fix a bug.

Pathauto: A *module* that allows you to define patterns for URL aliases (so that pages appear at URLs that look like "http://yoursite.org/about" rather than "http://yoursite.org/node/7"). Configuring Pathauto involves the use of *tokens*.

Region: A defined area within the site where *blocks* can be placed (e.g., left sidebar, right sidebar, footer, etc.). Regions are defined by your site's current *theme*.

Relationship (Views): Adding a relationship to a *view* allows you to pull in *fields* and other data from *nodes*, users, and *taxonomy terms* that are somehow related (e.g., via a *node reference field*, through being the author of a particular node, etc.).

Role: A set of permissions that can be assigned to a particular user account.

Taxonomy: Drupal's system for creating controlled and uncontrolled *vocabularies* of *terms*.

Teaser: A configurable, shortened display of *node* content. Usually includes fewer *fields*, and a shortened version of any body text.

Term: An individual tag, category, or similar metadata stored in a *vocabulary*.

Term reference field: A *field* that allows you to reference *terms* from a particular *vocabulary* as part of a *content type*, user profile, field, etc.

Theme: Code that defines the overall look and design of your site. Themes are also responsible for defining the *regions* on your site, which determine where *blocks* can be displayed.

Token: A snippet of data that is stored somewhere on your site; for instance, the value of a particular *field*, or the username of a user who created a particular *node*. Tokens are used to define things like *Pathauto* patterns.

Views: A *module* that provides an interface for querying your database, and displaying the results in a variety of ways (e.g., table, grid, list). Other modules provide additional formats for views, such as maps and timelines. The output of views is commonly displayed as a block or page.

Vocabulary: A structure within Drupal's *taxonomy* system that allows you to store a set of *terms*. Institution names, painting genres, and event categories are all possible examples of vocabularies. Vocabularies are associated with a *content type* using a *term reference field*.

Widget: How data is selected or entered into a *field*. Different kinds of fields are compatible with different widgets, and you may install additional *modules* to provide new widgets. For example, a date field might be configured to use a drop-down list widget, a calendar widget, or a plain text widget as the interface for how a user can put content into the date field.

Index

Module names are given in title case.

404 pages, 323

Access. *See* Microsoft Access
accessibility, 110, 299
account settings, 167–170
accounts, 167; maintenance, *see* user 1. *See also* users
Acquia. *See* hosting, cloud
AdaptiveTheme, 300–301, 306–310; colors, 309; custom CSS, 308; fonts, 307; layout, 307; subtheming, 306
add-ons. *See* modules
admin account. *See* user 1
Administration Menu, 44; finding configuration pages, 53–54
Advanced help, 45, 54
alt-text, 110
AMP stack, 26
Apache, 26
Apache Solr, 283
API. *See* Services
authentication, 21, 168
author, of nodes, 151
Autocomplete Widgets, 90, 123
Automatic Nodetitles, 71, 81, 114–117; configuration for Image content type, 139; configuration for Person content type, 130; conflict with Node Reference Create, 98, 115; issues when importing data, 269; updating, 116–117

automatic title generation. *See* Automatic Nodetitles

Backdrop, 11, 12
Backup and Migrate, 45, 335–336
backups, 13, 26, 329, 335–339; files, 337–338; nightly, 336; offsite, 335; using PHPMyAdmin, 336
bibliography, 6
blank screen. *See* White Screen of Death
blocks, 20; 179–183, 227; creating a block in Views, 192; exporting using Features Extra, 280; search block, 284; tag cloud block, 292–293. *See also* CCK Blocks
broken links, 325
bug reports, 343

caching, 324; conflict with Honeypot, 176; flushing caches, 343
CAPTCHA, 177–178
captions, 145
CCK Blocks, 165, 182
Chaos Tool Suite. *See* Ctools
Chosen, 91, 129
CKEditor, 91, 145–146; CKEditor Link module, 149–150; compared to WYSIWYG module, 146
cloud. *See* hosting, cloud
code, 13; displaying code, 145. *See also* core, modules, themes
color. *See* themes
Colorbox, 162–163, 164

comments, 69, 85–86; titles, 86

Conditional Fields, 66, 110–114

configuration, storage in database, 15

content, accessing, 153; entering, 150–152; editing, 152–153; previewing, 152; storage in database, 15. *See also* revisions, nodes

Content Access, 173–174

content types, 16–17; 59–60; adding fields, 87–90; Article, 60–61; author and date information, 85; Basic Page, 60–61; comment settings, 85–86; compared to file types, 67–68; creation, 83–36; description in documentation, 321; Event, 80–81, 131–137, 156–157; Image, 81, 137–139, 157, 163; menu settings, 86, 186; permissions, 173–174; Person, 77–80, 120–130, 156, 163; publishing options, 84–85; selection in Views filters, 189, 211. *See also* data modeling

core, 3, 13; updating, 333–335

Corolla. *See* AdaptiveTheme

costs, 1, 22; compared to custom code, 3; for module development, 233–234; for theming, 303; value for other projects, 10. *See also* hosting, module development

cron, 252, 284, 325

CSS, 14, 87, 300, 303, 306, 308

CSV: Feeds parser, 254; for archival storage of data, 273; importing, 251

Ctools, 45

customizability, 3, 5

database: backup, 335–336; Drupal's database, 12–13, 15; restoring, 336; syncing, 15

data entry. *See* content, entering.

data export. *See* exporting, data.

data import. *See* importing.

data modeling, 60–71; departmental website example, 17–18, 20, 23; differentiating data vs. metadata, 62–63; collaboration, 60; example site, 72–81; file types, 67–68; interview example, 62–63, 64–65; similar content types, 66–67; taxonomy field, *see* term reference field; title field, 70–71; Views implications, 75; user profiles, 68–69

Date, 88, 98–101; format configuration, 99. *See also* Partial Date

dates: module comparison, 98; token configuration, 116–117. *See also* Date; Partial Date

debugging, 340–345

design. *See* themes

developers: Drupal developer community, 6; experienced with academic projects, 345

development site, 15

Display Suite, 165, 166

distributions, 278

documentation, 320–322

drafts, 151–152

Drupal: as project infrastructure, 1; building a site with, 22–24; compared to other platforms, 3–5; contributing to the community, 345; "no code," 2, 6; versions, 10–11

Drupal 8, 10–11

Drupal for Humanists mailing list and website, 8

Drush, 335, 336, 339

Editview, 248

emails: security notices, 33; system emails, 170

embedding. *See* external multimedia.

Entity Reference, 96. *See also* References

Entity Tokens, 117, 139; *see also* Token

error messages, 324, 344

example site: background, 7, content types, 76–71; data, 72–75; goal, 75; steps to create, 320

exporting: configuration, 278–281, data, 16, 274–277; data using Node Export, 278, 280; data as RDF, 282; data via an API, 281; taxonomies, 295. *See also* Features

external multimedia, 94–95, 145

Features, 38, 278–281; building, 279–280; compared to distributions, 278; dissemination, 38–39; downloading, 280; field bases, 279–280; installing, 281; removing, 281; saving, 280

Feeds. *See* importing

Feeds Tamper, 259–263; Boolean filter, 263,

272; combining pieces of source data, 260–261; convert case, 262; debugging punctuation, 261–262; find and replace, 261; for multi-valued fields, 260, 268; keyword filter, 262; rewrite, 292–293, 268; strip tags, 262; trim, 260; temporary target, 261

Field Permissions, 174–175

fields, 16–17; adding to a content type, 87–90; arranging, 88; boolean, 135–136; conditional, *see* Conditional Fields; converting, 57; date field, 100–101, 132; date field display, 157–158; file field, 93–95; file field display, 163–164; geofield, 106; geospatial field display, 159–160; groups, 79, 107; image field, 95; image field in user profiles, 169–170; label, 87; list (text) field, 91–92, 123, 126; in vocabularies, 64; link, 105; long text field, 91; machine name, 71, 87; node reference field, 96–97; partial date and time field, 101–105, 132; partial date field display, 158–159; permissions, 174–175; provided by modules, 37; term reference field, 92–93, 124, 126–129; text field, 90, 123–124, 131; title field, 70–71; types, 88; user reference field, 96; widgets, 88. *See also* Field Collection; Views, fields

Field Collection, 79, 107

Field Group, 107

FileMaker Pro, 4

files: private, 108; public, 108; scheme selection, 109; security, 325; temporary, 108; uploading via Media module, 108; uploading via SFTP, 352. *See also* fields, file field

file types, 19; compared to content types, 67–68; configuration, 110

filters. *See* text formats

fonts. *See* themes; AdaptiveTheme, fonts

footnotes, 144

front page, 317

FTP. *See* SFTP

funding, 1. *See also* modules, development

Geocoder, 106

Geofield, 106–107

Gephi, 273

Getty Vocabularies, 295

Github, 38–39

Google Analytics, 326

Hierarchical Select, 128–129

Honeypot, 176

hosting, 6, 25–28; at your institution, 26–27; cloud, 28; generic, 27, 55–56; on your own computer, 26

HTML: allowed in Filtered HTML text format, 143; compared to Drupal for website development, 15–16; exporting, 275; exporting as part of XML export, 276–277; XPath parser for Feeds, 254

images. *See* fields, image field; Media; Views, image gallery

image styles, 160–162

Imagecache Actions, 162

importing, 250–272; attach to content type, 252; Boolean fields, 263; combining pieces of source data, 260–261; content type specification, 252; creating an importer, 251; dates, 259; description in documentation, 322; fetcher, 253; filtering, 262; find and replace, 261; identifying existing nodes, 257; images, 258; import page options, 263–264; manipulating source data, *see* Feeds Tamper; mapping, 256–257; modules, 250–251; multiple field values, 260; node reference fields, 258; parser, 253–254; partial date data, 259; Event nodes, 269–272; People nodes, 264–269; processor, 255–256; punctuation, 261–262; running an import, 263; taxonomies, 295; term reference fields, 257

installation, 28–30

launching a site, 322–326

Leaflet, 160, 220–225; troubleshooting, 223–225

libraries, 50

Libraries API, 53

lightbox. *See* Colorbox.

Link, 105

Link Checker, 325

maintenance, 328–329; maintenance mode, 332

MAMP, 26

maps, 106–107, 220–225; Google Maps, 221. *See also* Geofield, Leaflet

Media, 19, 67, 91; configuration, 93–95, 108–110; media browser configuration, 109–110. *See also* external multimedia

menus, 21, 183–187; adding a link in Views, 192; description in documentation, 322; drop-down, 187; enabling for content types, 86, 186

Microsoft Access, 4

mistakes, 5

modules, 2, 3, 6, 14; assessment, 37–44; bug reports, 43–44; configuration, 53–54; debugging, 55, 340–341; dependencies, 52–53; description in documentation, 321; dev versions, 341–342; development, 10, 22, 233–234; disabling, 56–57; downloading, 49; enabling, 51–53; essential, 44–46; installation, 46–51; installation via the file system, 49–50; installation using the Drupal interface, 47–49; location on the server, 49–50; maintenance, 42–43; necessity, 13, 54–55; on drupal.org, 36, 38; patching, 342–343; README file, 50, 53, 54; release notes, 44; removing, 57–58; searching for, 36; security, 330–331; uninstalling, 57; updates, 55, 331–333; user base, 41–42; versions, 39–40, 331; with libraries, 50–51. *See also* Features; updating

Module Filter, 45, 51–52, 172–173

monitoring, 326–327

multisite, 6, 50, 55–56, 216, 303, 330; applying updates, 334

MySQL, custom database, 4; Drupal's database, 12–13

Node Export, 278, 280

Node Reference Create, 97–98

node IDs, 117

nodes, 18; creating menu links, 185–186; display configuration, 155–166; previewing, 152; unpublished, 151–152, 175; unpublished nodes in Views, 210–211

notifications, 33

Omeka, 4, 6

open-source project: implications of using open-source, 1–2; contributing to the ecosystem, 10, 37, 101, 345; developers, 6, 9–10

overlay. *See* Colorbox

"page not found" errors, 326–327

paging, for nodes, 145

Panels, 313–317; custom content, 317; layout, 314; panel content, 315–317; panel nodes, 314–317

Pantheon. *See* hosting, cloud

Partial Date, 6, 101–105; compared to Date module, 98; format configuration, 101–102. *See also* Date

patches, 10, 342–343

Pathauto, 46, 70–71, 117–118; configuration for Event content type, 136–137; configuration for Image content type, 139; configuration for Person content type, 130; overriding with URL path settings, 151

PDF, previewing, 164

performance, 56, 323–324

permissions, 70, 172–175; for text formats, 142–143; of content types vs. taxonomies, 65; testing before launch, 322–323

phpMyAdmin, 13, 336

plugins. *See* modules

project status, 312

project teams, 60

quiz, 145

RDF, 282

Real Name, 171

Redirect, 327

References, 96–98. *See also* Node Reference Create

regex, 261

regions, 14, 180, 181, 182, 297

revisions, 85; 153–154

roles, 172, 182; description in documentation, 322

scalability, 6. *See also* performance
search, 283–288; block, 284; debugging, 285–286; indexing, 284–285, 286; permissions, 284; ranking, 285; result display, 286; types of content, 285
Search API, 283, 287
security, 21, 32, 330; advisories, 330–331; of modules, 38; security team, 330–331; security updates, 330–331; user accounts, 69
Services, 281
SFTP, 346–354; connecting, 347–348; connection information, 347; navigating, 351; software, 346; troubleshooting, 350; uploading files, 352–353
Simple Hierarchical Select, 129
site name, 31
spam, 145, 169, 176–178
speed. *See* performance
SQL queries. *See* Views
standards, 5
Statistics, 326
status report, 325
subthemes. *See* themes
sustainability, 2–3, 4, 5; 55. *See also* modules, assessment; documentation
sysadmin, 26–27
system administrator. *See* sysadmin

table of contents, 145
tag clouds, 292–293
tagging. *See* taxonomies
taxonomies, 18–19, 64–65, 127–128, 289–296; compared to list fields, 92; configuring term pages, 289–291; description in documentation, 321; displaying users and content with a given term, 291–292; exporting, 295; importing, 295; issues when used with Conditional Fields, 112; issues when using Views, 65. *See also* fields, term reference field; Taxonomy Manager
Taxonomy Display, 290–291
Taxonomy Manager, 293–295
Taxonomy Term Reference Tree, 128–129
technical components, 12–13
TEI, 4–5; use in Drupal workflows, 273
templates. *See* content types, file types

Term Merge, 293, 294–295
terms, 18. *See also* taxonomies, vocabularies
term ID, 112
text formats, 141–145; filters, 144; permissible HTML, 143; permissions, 143
themes, 14–15, 297–311; administration themes, 304–305; base themes, 301–302; enabling, 304–305; global settings, 305; installing, 303–304; location in filesystem, 303–304; menu display, 186–187; requirements, 298–299; testing, 299–300. *See also* regions, theming, AdaptiveTheme
theming: custom, 301–303; documentation, 302; modifying an existing theme, 300–301; using an existing theme, 298–300
time lines: using A Simple Timeline, 227–234; using Views Timeline JS, 234–237
time zones, 32
title, 70–71, automatic generation, 71
Token, 46, 115–118, 170, 171; display settings, 116
Toolbar, 46
troubleshooting. *See* debugging

updating, 329–335; core, 334; distributions, 278; frequency, 330–331; major version upgrades, 339; modules, 3, 7, 331–333; server, 26–17; using the file system, 333–334, 353–354; using the UI, 331–333
university website. *See* hosting, at your institution
user 1, 30
user profiles, 68–69, 170–171; user pictures, 169–170
user registration, 168–169
users, 21, 167–168; name, 171; unique email address, 32

View Unpublished, 175
Views, 19–20, 45, 188–249; access, 214; "add a new view" interface, 189–194; advanced search page, 286–287; blocks, 166; block settings, 215; caching, 216; constraints in content

Views (*cont.*)
display, 68; customizing taxonomy term pages, 289–291; description in documentation, 321; display name, 195; displays, 194–195; displays, cloning, 195; displays, overriding, 196-198, 212–213; displays, reverting overridden, 198; contextual filters, 225–226, 236–237, 291–292; exclude from display, 201–202; exposed filters, 239–241, 247; feed settings, 214–215; fields, 203–210; fields, adding, 203–204; fields, date, 204–205; fields, image, 205–206; fields, inline, 207–210; fields, inline labels, 207; fields, order, 206; fields, removing, 206; fields, replacement patterns, 208; fields, rewriting, 208–210; fields, style settings, 207; fields, user, 245–246; filters, 210–212; filters, and/or, 212; filters compared to contextual filters, 211–212; filters, exposed, 239–241; footer, 215; format, 199–202; grid, 199–200; grouping fields, 200–202; header, 215; image gallery, 238–242; impact on data modeling, 75; issues when displaying taxonomy content, 65; list of news posts, 312–313; map view, 220–227; menu, 214; page settings, 214; pager, 215; path, 214; preview, 199, 213; relationships, 230–234, 245–246; slideshow, 242–244; sort criteria, 193, 212–213; table, 245–247; time line using A Simple Timeline module, 227–234; time line using Views TimelineJS, 234–238; troubleshooting, 219–220; use with reference fields, 97; Views Content Panes, 314

Views Autocomplete Filters, 249

Views Conditional, 248

Views Content Cache, 216

Views Data Export, 274–277; access settings, 214; exporting HTML, 275

Views Datasource, 281

vocabularies, 18, 92. *See also* taxonomies

websites, using Drupal, 3

widgets, 88; autocomplete, 97; media browser, 93

WampServer, 26

Web Taxonomy, 295

White Screen of Death (WSOD), 344–345

WordPress, 3, 4, 5, 6, 16, 61, 76

WYSIWYG (What You See Is What You Get), 145–150; integration with Media module, 148–149; module compared to CKEditor module, 146; selecting CKEditor library, 147

XAMPP, 26

XML, exporting using Views Data Export, 276–277; importing using Feeds, 251, 254, 257

YouTube. *See* external multimedia

Lightning Source UK Ltd.
Milton Keynes UK
UKHW05f1202020518
321976UK00008B/155/P